The Presence of Persons

The Presence of Persons

Essays on Literature, Science and Philosophy in the
Nineteenth Century

WILLIAM MYERS

LONDON AND NEW YORK

First published 1998 by Ashgate Publishing

2 Park Square, Milton Park, Abingdon, Oxfordshire OX14 4RN
52 Vanderbilt Avenue, New York, NY 10017

Routledge is an imprint of the Taylor & Francis Group, an informa business

First issued in paperback 2019

British Library Cataloguing in Publication Data

Myers, William
    The Presence of Persons: Essays on Literature, Science and Philosophy
    in the Nineteenth Century.
    (Nineteenth Century series)
    1. English literature—19th century—History and criticism.
    2. Thought and thinking—History—19th century.
    I. Title.
    820.9'008

Library of Congress Cataloging-in-Publication Data

Myers, William, 1939–
    The presence of persons: essays on literature, science and philosophy in
    the nineteenth century/William Myers.
        p.   cm. (Nineteenth Century series)
    Includes bibliographical references and index.
    ISBN 978-1-84014-645-5
    1. English literature—19th century—History and criticism.
    2. American literature—19th century—History and criticism.
    3. United States—Intellectual life—19th century. 4. Great
    Britain—Intellectual life—19th century. I. Title. II. Series:
    Nineteenth Century (Aldershot, England).
    PR453.M94   1998
    820.9'008—dc21   98–23626
                                                                CIP

ISBN 978-1-84014-645-5 (hbk)
ISBN 978-0-367-88819-0 (pbk)

Typeset in Sabon by Manton Typesetters, 5–7 Eastfield Road, Louth, Lincolnshire, LN11 7AJ

Contents

The Nineteenth Century
General Editors' Preface

The aim of this series is to reflect, develop and extend the great burgeoning of interest in the nineteenth century that has been an inevitable feature of recent decades, as that former epoch has come more sharply into focus as a locus for our understanding not only of the past but of the contours of our modernity. Though it is dedicated principally to the publication of original monographs and symposia in literature, history, cultural analysis, and associated fields, there will be a salient role for reprints of significant texts from, or about, the period. Our overarching policy is to address the spectrum of nineteenth-century studies without exception, achieving the widest scope in chronology, approach and range of concern. This, we believe, distinguishes our project from comparable ones, and means, for example, that in the relevant areas of scholarship we both recognize and cut innovatively across such parameters as those suggested by the designations 'Romantic' and Victorian'. We welcome new ideas, while valuing tradition. It is hoped that the world which predates yet so forcibly predicts and engages our own will emerge in parts, as a whole, and in the lively currents of debate and change that are so manifest an aspect of its intellectual, artistic and social landscape.

Vincent Newey
Joanne Shattock

University of Leicester

Acknowledgements

These essays are based mainly on unpublished conference papers and teaching materials, amassed over a very long time. I am grateful to a now defunct university culture which encouraged me to work quietly on material of this kind without having to parade it in front of panels of assessors. Of the material that has already been published, the original version of 'Where are Nathaniel Hawthorne, Emily Dickinson and Daniel C. Dennett?' appeared under the title 'Where is Daniel C. Dennett?' in *Over Here: Reviews in American Studies*, vol. 10, no. 1 (summer 1990), pp. 96–111. I am grateful to the editorial board for permission to reprint it. 'Autobiography and the Illative Sense' was published in *Mortal Pages, Literary Lives: Studies in Nineteenth-Century Autobiography*, eds, Vincent Newey and Philip Shaw, Aldershot: Scolar Press, 1996, pp. 103–19, and 'The Radicalism of *Little Dorrit*' in *Literature and Politics in the Nineteenth Century*, ed. John Lucas, London: Methuen, 1970, pp. 77–104. Both have been slightly amended. I used portions of 'The Two Eternities: Race and Soul in *Daniel Deronda*' in *The Teaching of George Eliot*, Leicester: Leicester University Press, 1984, and most of the material in 'Justice and Freedom: *The Portrait of a Lady*' was dispersed through my book *Milton and Free Will: An Essay in Criticism and Philosophy*, Beckenham, Kent: Croom Helm, 1987.

For Bill, Pat, Danny, Meg and David

Introduction: Nothing New

I may venture to affirm of ... mankind, that they are nothing but a bundle or collection of different perceptions, which succeed each other with an inconceivable rapidity, and are in a perpetual flux or movement ... nor is there any single power of the soul, which remains unalterably the same, perhaps for one moment. The mind is a kind of theatre, where several perceptions successively make their appearance; pass, re-pass, glide away, and mingle in an infinite variety of postures and situations. There is properly no *simplicity* in it at one time, nor *identity* in different; whatever natural propension we may have to imagine that simplicity and identity. The comparison of the theatre must not mislead us. They are the successive perceptions only, that constitute the mind; nor have we the most distant notion of the place where these scenes are represented, or of the materials, of which it is compos'd.[1]

Beside this celebrated observation of David Hume's may be set the following:

No coward soul is mine
No trembler in the world's storm troubled sphere
I see Heaven's glories shine
And Faith shines equal arming me from Fear

O God within my breast
Almighty ever-present Deity
Life, that in me hast rest
As I, – Undying Life, have power in thee

Vain are the thousand creeds
That move men's hearts, unutterably vain,
Worthless as withered weeds
Or idlest froth amid the boundless main

To waken doubt in one
Holding so fast by thy infinity
So surely anchored on
The steadfast rock of Immortality

With wide-embracing love
Thy Spirit animates eternal years
Pervades and broods above,
Changes, sustains, dissolves, creates and rears

Though Earth and moon were gone
And suns and universes ceased to be
And thou wert left alone
Every Existence would exist in thee

There is not room for Death
Nor atom that his might could render void

Since Thou art Being and Breath
And what thou art may never be destroyed[2]

For Emily Brontë, too, the mind is a spectacle; but while Hume's is a randomly generated virtual reality experience, Emily Brontë's is grandly laid out to her own design. The site of Hume's spectacle is invisible; we are supposed not to know what exactly it is. Emily Brontë's, though equally mysterious, is simultaneously herself, the universe, and 'God', the first being apparently the *fons et origo* of the other two. Hume takes his seat and reviews the passing scene, a sensible, unobtrusive critic who judges what he observes but cannot control it, and disappears when the lights go out. Emily Brontë's consciousness is at once author, setting, action and audience, and even her putative extinction is a function of her own courageous will.

Hume's is the currently fashionable view; both his and Emily Brontë's accounts would be read by various writers to whom passing reference is made in these essays – Deconstructionists, Marxists, evolutionary biologists, cognitive philosophers and even postmodernist theologians – as 'fictions'. It is now an intellectual commonplace that the self is 'a subject-position', constituted in consciousness by factors external to the human being, or by a practical inner need to entertain the illusion of a centred individuality, or both; and that the sense of identity so generated is accidental and variable, personality not personhood. This is a conclusion Hume would embrace and Emily Brontë contemptuously dismiss.

There are two strategies for dealing with a Humean reduction of the self to an unexaminable nullity – foundational status must be given either to the world or to language and other systems of cultural interrelation. For empiricists, from Hume and John Stuart Mill to modern philosophers like Daniel C. Dennett and Galen Strawson, the ways of the (phenomenal) world provide criteria for the meaningful use of language. Relativists, on the other hand, in the tradition of Karl Marx, Walter Pater, Friedrich Nietzsche, Sigmund Freud, post-Saussurean Formalists and Deconstructionists, emphasise the importance of existing systems of understanding. Each tradition calls the other in aid, particularly by announcing an adherence to 'determinism' or 'materialism' or 'law'. Marxists and psychoanalysts claim to be 'scientific' – even though scientific findings may not always support their view of things. Empiricists appeal to laws of thought (Mill) or common sense (Dennett and Strawson), to give empiricism a push start, yet the outcomes of the empiricist endeavour may not be unproblematically consistent with such premises. There is an element of disagreement between the two traditions about language. Typical of relativist assertions is J. Hillis Miller's claim that language and other sign-systems are 'fundamentally constitutive'[3] in human life: we are unthinkable except in linguistic terms. An empiricist philosopher like Dennett attaches less importance to language and consciousness. For Dennett, as for Miller, the self is a fiction but it is invented to dissolve contradictions arising out of the ensemble of semi-autonomous computing subsystems of which our mental life is composed, and it is the non-self, the system on which the story floats, that is the real thing.[4]

The essays in this volume were all written out of a conviction, and have been arranged to suggest, that all such accounts of the self are unreal, that Emily Brontë is sounder on the subject than Hume, and that one of the splendid truths variously communicated by numerous writers of the nineteenth century is that selfhood is not illusory, and language not the exclusive determinant of understanding. I use the word 'unreal' in the sense that it has for John Henry Newman, whose account of thought, language, choice, belief and action encompasses both Hume's perspectives and Emily Brontë's, and is implicit in everything in this collection.

Newman was a serious student of Hume and Mill and learned a lot from them (especially Hume), not least the habit of inspecting his own mind. Newman's assertion that 'phenomena ... give us no exact measure or character of the unknown things beyond them'[5] derives from traditions which led Hume to insist that we can know nothing of 'the theatre' in which our perceptions are produced, and Mill to accept that we only know 'phænomena'. Hume's influence is also evident in Newman's attitude towards the argument for the existence of God from the order of nature. Hume was trenchantly dismissive of this argument,[6] but it was subsequently given wide currency in the writings of William Paley, and remained in high regard throughout the 1820s and 1830s. Mill thought 'the Design argument ... the best ... the most persuasive'[7] of the arguments for God's existence, an admiration shared in our own day by Richard Dawkins, who describes Paley's *Natural Theology* (1802) as the clearest and most articulate exposition of the argument from design.[8] He goes on, of course, to demolish Paley's thesis on the same grounds that both Newman and Hume do. The 'system of Nature by itself', Newman argues, does not force us 'to take it for *more* than a system';[9] in so far as it makes sense to speak of 'Divine Intelligence' as the author of the 'piece of machinery' which the physical creation appears to us to be, then that intelligence may be no more than 'the animating principle of a vast and complicated system ... subjected to laws, and ... connatural and co-extensive with matter' (*Discussions and Arguments*, p. 302). A personal creator-God is not disclosed in the order of nature: the highest theology Paley's argument yields is pantheism.

Newman's distrust of Paley derives from his sense of the limitations of empiricism. This he shares with the Scottish Common Sense School of Thomas Reid, as well as Reid's editor, Sir William Hamilton, and Thomas Carlyle. Hamilton is a key figure, Newman's philosophical precursor, and the victim of Mill's overwhelming polemic, but, as the first post-Enlightenment thinker to press relativism to its limits, an important influence on Victorian intellectual life. His escape-route from relativism – the thesis that, included in any set of premises, and yet outside them, is a substantive holder of those premises – was unacceptable to Mill, and he earned Mill's implacable intellectual enmity by elaborating this insight into a system. Carlyle chose the opposite method. While agreeing with 'modern Science' (that is, with Berkeley, Hume, Hamilton and Mill) that 'matter in general [is] *non-extant*' – a datum of consciousness only – he represents the body as 'rendering visible the divine mystery in us that calls itself "*Me*"'.[10] But he also recognises that in presupposing the '*Me*' that utters it, language cannot signify the self. The price he pays for the Silence thus imposed on him is that no one is quite sure what he means.

Newman's approach is different. He neither systematises like Hamilton, nor indulges in the vociferous refusals of Carlyle. If a foundational belief in the world leads to the obliteration of distinctions between the individual, the world and God, Carlyle's solipsistic alternative takes things no further. It is true that, like Hamilton and Carlyle, Newman holds consciousness of self to be 'prior to all questions of trust or assent. We act according to our nature, by means of ourselves, when we remember or reason [and] ... are as little able to accept or reject our mental constitution, as our being' (*Grammar of Assent*, p. 67). Newman also accepts Hamilton's argument that memory and reason imply a mental constitution which, as the condition of experience and language, cannot be contained in either. Hamilton goes on to argue that because the self cannot be conceptualised and so expressed in rational terms, we are justified in resorting to bare analogy when we speculate about free will, the absolute, the infinite, the origins of the universe, and so forth;[11] but this sounds like a weak last resort, and leaves him open to Mill's polemic. Newman is bolder. He perceives analogical and figurative language as powerful indicators of how human beings are mentally constituted in the first place. Analogy – literariness – does not have to wait for the logical resources of language to be exhausted before coming into play; on the contrary, without the mental powers disclosed in its use, logical and scientific discourse would lack authority.

Newman's humanism has, therefore, a double aspect – he affirms the personal wholeness of the individual human being but avoids identifying it with a reductively logical, transparent model of intelligence.

Wholeness is primary. At this level, his view of the self is the obverse of Hume's: 'every man', he writes, 'has a distinct soul ... as if there were no one else in the whole world but he';[12] 'every being ... is his own centre, and all things about him are but shades' (*Parochial and Plain*, IV, p. 82); 'as gathered from our experience of human agents', we are led 'to consider *personality* as equivalent, in its very idea, to the unity and independence of the immaterial substance of which it is predicated'.[13] This does not suppose a ghost in a machine; the words 'immaterial substance' imply no more than Hume's distinction between 'the mind' and 'the materials of which it is composed'. Newman's claim is simply that a person is not the outcome of events beyond scrutiny in (say) the body or the world. Personhood is not merely 'normative', as it is for Dennett[14] and so many modern philosophers: it is a state of being. So, even in his writings about the Trinity, where he recognises the inadequacy of the word 'person' to the doctrine under discussion, he insists that it denotes more than 'certain outward manifestations of the Supreme Being, relative to ourselves, which are of an accidental or variable nature' (*The Arians*, p. 366). Human personhood is certainly more than an accidental or variable matter of appearance. If a persona is adopted, it is adopted by a person; if personhood is attributed, it is attributed by persons to persons; if it is a story constructed by individual human beings or imposed on them by others, it remains a story told to and about persons. Dispersed as we may be, spatially and temporally, in body, mind, thought, action, sense and feeling, or even in narrative, substantial unity, something like George Berkeley's 'thinking active principle that perceives, knows, wills and operates'[15] may be, must be, attributed to each of us.

But this does not entail self-transparency. Only God is One in this full sense. Personal unity is not a 'homunculus', virtual or real, controlling the human organism from a command centre,[16] but the being in its entire sphere of thought and action taken as a whole, as it takes itself to be when it uses the words 'I' and 'me', without bothering whether such words include teeth, fingernails, air in the lungs, or thoughts in consciousness. It would make as much sense to seek a self within this whole as to locate the space–time continuum. The personal unity of human beings is foundational but indeterminate, self-experience 'inchoate'. For all 'our separation from things visible, our independence of them, our distinct existence in ourselves, our individuality, our power of acting for ourselves this way or that way, our accountableness for what we do' (*Parochial and Plain*, I, p. 19), 'it is very difficult to know ourselves even in part' (ibid., I, p. 41). A man is 'unable, as he well knows, to read his own heart in that clear unerring way in which God reads it' (ibid., III, p. 99). Selfhood is the site of a struggle in the 'inchoate and rudimental nature' (*Grammar of Assent*, p. 274) of every human being, a vast and far-reaching system, impenetrable to examination based on 'scientific rules and fixed standards for weighing testimony, and examining facts ... conclusions ... [that] can produce their reasons', for 'reasons ... [that] can be exhibited in simple propositions' are fundamentally insufficient to account for 'judgment and action'.[17] In this Newman stands with the empiricists rather than the relativists: 'the content of ... judgments doesn't have to be expressible in "propositional" form,' Dennett tells us, '– that's a mistake, a case of misprojecting the categories of human language back onto the activities of the brain too enthusiastically' (*Consciousness Explained*, p. 365).

Newman's view of language corresponds with his view of the unity and indeterminacy of human personhood. In the first place, just as substantial unity must be attributed to the individual subject, so the meaning of an intelligent utterance must be available to the honestly enquiring intellect. Newman writes of 'drawing ... their own doctrines' from the Church Fathers.[18] The Bible, in particular, has 'one meaning' and 'to make people think that it may have a hundred meanings, all equally good' is to suggest 'that it has no meaning at all' (*Discussions and Arguments*, p. 60). As 'a general rule ... every passage of Scripture has some one definite and sufficient sense, which was prominently before the mind of the writer, or in the intention of the Holy Spirit, and to which all other ideas, though they might arise, or be implied, still were subordinate'. This 'one main primary sense' might be 'literal or figurative' (*The Arians*, pp. 60–61), but even in the latter case, 'the use of figures in a composition is not enough to make it figurative as a whole. We constantly use figures of speech whenever we speak; yet who will say on that account that the main course of our conversation is not taken literally?'[19] Real communication is accordingly possible.

But Newman is also aware of the limitations of language, for which the elusiveness of personhood is in some measure responsible: 'the very same speech or sentiment [coming] from two persons ... has quite a different meaning, according to the speaker, and takes a different form in our minds. We always judge what meets us by what we know already. There is no such thing as a naked text, without note or comment' (*Essays Critical*, II, p. 252). Newman can also be radically historicist. Even the Moral Law, in his account, is historically contextualised: commandments, 'uttered in man's language and written upon tables', are inherently incommensurable 'with what is of an infinite and of a spiritual nature ... the Law of Moses represented the Law of God in its place and age; was the fullest revelation of it, and the nearest approximation to it, then vouchsafed, and was that Law' – but only 'as far as it went' (*Parochial and Plain*, V, p. 145). At best, language places us at the door of truth; we must 'bear to use words which we feel to be deficient, if they ... begin trains of reflection which they do not end' (*Sermons Bearing*, p. 356). Indeed it is because of the fragmentariness of linguistic representations of Truth that dogma uses simple, antithetical expressions to serve as 'faithful shadows of those truths, which unlearned piety admits and acts upon, without the medium of clear intellectual representation' (*University Sermons*, p. 65).

Newman's awareness of the limitations of language explains his commitment to the principle of reserve, which gave rise to Charles Kingsley's insinuations about his un-English and unmanly economies with the truth, and so to *Apologia Pro Vita Sua*. Newman's difficulty was not just that any doctrinal formulation can be misunderstood. Something more intimate was at stake, as Kingsley sensed and Newman admitted: the issue between them, in Newman's words, was nothing less than the 'living intelligence, by which I write, and argue, and act'.[20] Reserve is essential because, whatever it may explicitly signify, language also discloses deep uncertainties in those who use it, about themselves and the world, and their relations with one another.

Newman's thought has strongly deconstructionist tendencies. He anticipates deconstructionist notions of narrative as a makeshift version of a fuller, absent truth, forever, as far as its expression goes, deferred. 'Truth', he reminds us, 'is vast and far-stretching ... its advocate, unable to exhibit more than a fragment of the whole, must round off its rugged extremities, and unite its straggling lines, by much the same process by which an historical narrative is converted into a tale' (*University Sermons*, p. 90). The factual narratives of Scripture are 'plain and colourless ... we are continually perplexed what to think about them and about the parties concerned in them. They need a comment, they are evidently but a text *for* a comment, – they have no comment; and as they stand, may be turned this way or that way, according to the accidental tone of mind in the reader' (*Discussions and Arguments*, p. 178). We may compare this with Hume's account of reading as a copying process:[21]

> If one person sits down to read a book as a romance and the other as a true history, they plainly receive the same ideas, and in the same order; nor does the incredulity of the one, and the belief of the other, hinder them from putting the very same sense upon their author. His words produce the same ideas in both; though his testimony has not the same influence on them. (*A Treatise*, pp. 97–8)

Michel Foucault proved himself Newman's not Hume's disciple, therefore, when he wrote, 'Commentary averts the unpredictable in discourse by giving it its due: it allows us to say something other than the text itself, but on condition that it is the text itself that is spoken, and in a sense, fulfilled.'[22]

This explains why Newman scandalised liberals like Sir Leslie Stephen: his proto-deconstructionism threatened the unexaminable premises on which the empiricist world-view of Stephen's hero, Mill, was based, that is, Humean notions of the univocal, transparent text composed from impressions generated by a law-governed universe. It was necessary, therefore, to cast Newman, like Hamilton, in the role of reactionary; and this was done with such success that even writers strongly drawn to him, such as Matthew Arnold and Pater, represent him as 'chastened, high-strung, athletic'[23] in his resistance to the 'current of new life'. More bluntly, Stephen sees him as blocking 'improvement of the race'.[24] But in fact (as the subtle Pater discreetly acknowledged) empiricist doctrines of intellectual, social and biological development, of the *Zeitgeist* and Darwinism, have their own alarmingly relativist implications: 'the universality of natural law, even in the moral order ... that magnetic system of which modern science speaks, penetrating us with a network, subtler than our subtlest nerves, yet bearing in it the central forces of the world'[25] makes all cultural developments, itself included, contingent and temporary. So, however circumstantial Darwin's account of how the Humean theatre came to be built, the story of evolution implies that all such accounts are potentially unreliable. A scientist like Darwin constructing a narrative about the evolution of intelligence, or a thinker like Mill constructing a narrative of its operations, or a novelist like George Eliot and her positivist successors, Thomas Hardy, George Gissing and H. G. Wells, constructing stories about how people's thoughts and actions are typically determined, has to face the possibility that the same sort of determinants operate on them as they write, that they are all more like the Teacher of Languages in Conrad's *Under Western Eyes*, deterministically [mis]handling their sources, than they are like Charlotte Brontë's Lucy Snowe, the self-knowing mistress of her memories and her narrative.

Newman confronts these tensions in *An Essay on the Development of Christian Doctrine* and his later philosophical writings. He is not only prepared to 'go the whole hog with Darwin',[26] but anticipates more recent developments in Darwinian theory. The animating principle of evolution, as neo-Darwinists understand it, is the interaction of chance and necessity, by which bits of the universe with the capacity to create copies or replicas of themselves, gradually vary over time and thereby become more or less 'fit' in effecting further self-replication. The most celebrated exemplars of this competitive interaction are Dawkins's selfish genes; but he and Dennett are almost as enthusiastic about memes, that is, ideas, images, tunes, or any other units of cultural transmission, which propagate themselves by 'leaping from brain to brain via a process' which obeys the laws of natural selection exactly.[27] But this model of cultural evolution had been anticipated by Newman's suggestion that when 'an idea, whether real or not, is of a nature to arrest and possess the mind, it may be said to have life, that is to live in the mind which is its recipient'.[28] Newman moreover envisaged the development of ideas being carried on through 'communities of men and their leaders and guides; and ... [employing] their minds as its instruments' (*Development of Christian*, p. 38). Just as Dennett holds that 'there is a considerable competition among memes for entry into as many minds as possible' (*Consciousness Explained*, p. 206), so Newman writes of an idea 'invading' a community, and of 'the warfare of ideas', in effect their natural selection (*Development of Christian*, p. 39).

The natural selection of ideas, however, is self-evidently not a straightforward one between 'true' and 'real' memes against 'false' and 'unreal' ones. Far too many contradictory memes, and manifestly false ones, have flourished in the meme-pool for that to be the case. How do we manage to distinguish the wise from the foolish meme? Dennett and Dawkins argue that there is what Newman would call 'an antecedent probability'[29] that memes which accord with the facts of the world in which those who hold them live will flourish in the long term, that there are evolutionary advantages for memes which are 'real' and 'true' over those which are not; but even so the problem of how to distinguish the gold from the dross in the short and even the medium term remains, the short and the medium term being all we, as mere meme-carriers, can expect to enjoy. Evolutionary biology and cognitive philosophy ask the same question about truth, therefore, as the psalmist asks about justice and peace: How long?

This is a pressing question because, in Dennett's words, some memes 'tend to make their own replication more likely by disabling or preempting the environmental forces that would tend to extinguish them'. He gives the example, first proposed by Dawkins, of 'the meme for *faith*, which discourages the exercise of the sort of critical judgment that might decide that the idea of faith was all things considered a dangerous idea' (*Consciousness Explained*, p. 206). Hamilton and Carlyle would reply that such an idea needs to be distinguished from a related idea, that of faith in the self. This is a distinction Dennett accepts in practice. The self may only be a fiction in his book, but it is a fiction in which the average empiricist has to believe in practice, or at any rate to infer – a formulation preferred by Newman to that of faith in the self, which he thought nonsensical. In any case, if ordinary empiricists did not implicitly believe in or infer a self most of the time – it was only when he thought about his own identity that Hume started to have doubts about it – they could not function as intelligences, and empiricism would never have got going. The gap between Newman and Dennett is thus very narrow. Both accept that the operations of the human mind are 'inchoate', and that, while all sense of self and all accounts of self are provisional, we are none the less practically justified in having a workaday reliance on them. Both also agree that there is an anti-critical form of 'faith' which is destructive of intellectual honesty but which has a strong appeal to certain (Newman would have said Evangelical) temperaments. The only difference between them is about what conclusions we may draw from this curious self-developing weave of thought and action which makes up our 'histories'.

One way of approaching this problem is to examine the observable preconditions of story as such. Miller addresses this issue in *Versions of Pygmalion*. His thesis is wittily suggested by the following generalisation: 'It is an intrinsic feature of written pieces of language that they demand to be read':[30] the (entirely imaginary) assumption that texts can 'demand' anything is an exemplary instance of prosopopoeia, or personification, a figure, Miller asserts, lying at the heart of all story-telling. 'There is no story-telling without prosopopoeia, just as there is no access to the moral law without the intervention of some human figure' (*Versions of Pygmalion*, p. 212). But a person is only brought into existence for us in story. Narrative has therefore to presuppose what it alone can constitute. 'The initial prosopopoeia has always already happened, and there is no way to recall it, or to name it, since all our names belong to what is derived from it, including all the names of the material base presumed to underlie the first prosopopoeia and to be covered over by it' (ibid., p. 240). All thinking, and especially all thinking about being a person, therefore, rests on a prior apprehension of that idea, as on a foundation, in effect the 'metaphysical subject' of Ludwig Wittgenstein which, he declares, 'we must pass over in silence'.[31]

This is where Newman's thought parts from that of Wittgenstein, Miller and the rest. He insists on reaching back beyond the 'always already' which is their starting-point and their limit – in effect, on breaking the Humean and Wittgensteinian silence, and speaking figuratively but with certitude about the complex system of human experience which logically lies beyond language, but which casts faithful shadows on its use. The basis of our doing so he calls the illative sense – what Michael Polanyi was to identify as 'subsidiary awareness',[32] and Maurice Merleau-Ponty 'the hidden art of the imagination'.[33] The illative sense has to be recognised before it can be understood. It leads to real assents, which are private and incommunicable. It 'supplies no common measure between mind and mind' (*Grammar of Assent*, p. 287), and would descend into the kind of meaninglessness to which Wittgenstein assigns private languages were it not linked to, while remaining distinct from, logic, definition, language. The latter lead to notional assents, to the economies of theory, science and theology, to agreement and disagreement, but they always entail real assents, as a condition of their operation – it is through the illative sense, for example, that I know that the story of human evolution is not self-cancelling, even though formally it affirms the unreliability of all story without exception. However, it is only by virtue of other people's doing likewise in my presence, and constructing agreement, according to commonly understood rules, at the level of notions, that my illative sense is confirmed in its basic soundness. But even though we would be lost without that common ground of notions, those notions, precisely because we can put them into words, are inherently incommensurable with our being. That, always already, is presupposed; and in the end the individual 'may be justified in opposing himself to the judgment of the whole world; though he uses rules to his great advantage, as far as they go, and is in consequence bound to use them' (ibid., p. 277).

This suggests how 'close reading' may stand in relation to literary theory, or bare quotation without comment to any subsequent commentary. It rationalises criticism of the kind practised with such brilliance by F.R. Leavis, and, if great things may be linked with small, some of the judgements attempted in these essays. What is 'close reading', after all, but the skilled attention to the play of words by the illative sense? A related set of skills, both in reader and audience, is in operation when a text is read aloud. Spoken words, Dennett notes, 'come clothed in sensuous properties' (*Consciousness Explained*, p. 51).[34] They can gratify expectation or surprise it; they make the reader's illative sense present to the listener's as vividly as some of the text's possible meanings. But the knowledge thus known, as Dennett notes, is difficult to analyse, to communicate, or to relate to convictions anyone could put into words. And the same may be said of an author. A text can allow for the author's absence, can suggest a tonal range in choice of metre or diction, can invite attention to irony and ambiguity, or set up contrasts between first and later readings. These effects can be achieved with as little calculation and as much attention as inform a live reading, disclosing the skilled author to the skilled reader, and implying in the author an intimate if inchoate understanding of many possible readers. It is by such means that, in Newman's words, 'the inmost delicacies' of writers' lives and their 'intellectual and moral character' are made known to us in what they write.

In a comparable way the implied skills or lack of them in a fictional personage's interactions with others, or of a fictional narrator's relations with story and reader, can generate a virtual experience of 'characters' which is not limited to what can be, or has been, said or written about them. A person, Miller believes, disappears when the limits of words are reached. He gives the example of Maisie, in Henry James's *What Maisie Knew*, who, he alleges, 'vanishes from our circuit of knowledge' when she becomes unique, that is, 'not tied to the ordinary social round and scale of measurement', and so not susceptible to being 'spoken in words' (*Versions of Pygmalion*, p. 70). This sets intolerable limits on literary criticism; but if Newman, Polanyi, Merleau-Ponty and Dennett are right about the illative sense and the imagination, Maisie does not, after all, 'vanish from our circuit of knowledge' when she is no longer susceptible to being 'spoken in words' – she vanishes only from the circuit of our notions. It is for this reason that character analysis of the most unfashionable kind remains a central task of the critic – we need to understand William Dorrit, Lucy Snowe, Gwendolen Harleth and Isabel Archer precisely as the reasons and causes underlying their own words and actions – even though the effort to do so, like the effort to discuss literary texts through close reading, is bound to stop at mere quotation or degenerate into theory and *ism*.

The difficulties of the task are compounded by another aspect of Newman's thinking about the human person – his version of the doctrine of the fall, that 'every one of us is born into this world ... under the bondage of an inborn element of evil, which thwarts and stifles whatever principles remain of truth and goodness in us' (*Parochial and Plain*, VI, pp. 76–7). Nor is it just the individual who is thus radically disordered: 'the world, with all its ranks, and aims, and pursuits, and pleasures, and prizes, has ever from its birth been sinful', the site of 'manifold and complex corruption'; the best that can be said even of Christians 'is that we have two sides, a light side and a dark, and that the dark happens to be outermost. Thus we form part of the world to each other, though we are not of this world' (ibid., VII, pp. 31, 33, 36).

Here Newman is very much a man of his time. 'The world' as the concrete embodiment of untruth, of ideological complacency or, worse, the world as a community of more or less conscious and deliberate deceit and cruelty, is everywhere represented in the literature of the nineteenth century. It maddened Carlyle and Charles Dickens, not least, one suspects, because they knew how it had penetrated their own minds and hearts. It is repeatedly identified as the enemy of innocence. One of the interesting aspects of Victorian attitudes towards sex is the tendency of Victorian writers to represent worldliness (implicitly of course) in terms of sexual knowledge. Lust is not a major theme of their writing, as it is, say, of Dostoevsky's: the child, the virgin and the celibate are valued as witnesses against the world rather than against the flesh; but the limitations of innocence are recognised as well. The price of integrity is an acceptance, in one way or another, of less than adult status, with the limitations of view and of scope that this entails. The losses as well as the gains involved in maintaining personal integrity were well understood in the nineteenth century.

The issues raised by worldliness extend beyond fiction into theory. One of the curiosities of Newman's writing is his preoccupation with the prophet Balaam, who could not accommodate his will to the truth communicated to him about God's dealings with Israel. Summoned to prophesy against the Israelites, he found himself compelled to prophesy in their favour, but failed to separate himself from their enemies, and met his destruction in consequence. Newman is fascinated by the intellectual and moral inchoateness which this story implies, and refers to Balaam more frequently than to any other Old Testament figure. Here was a man to whom a revelation had been made and yet who struggled against yielding to its truth: 'he had light without love,' Newman concludes; 'his intellect was clear, his heart was cold' (*Grammar of Assent*, p. 155). What Newman denies here, as thoroughly as ever Karl Marx did, is that 'the theoretical is the only genuinely human attitude'.[35] Our relationship with our ideas has a moral component; we cannot speculate about ourselves or the world or literature, without having, more or less inchoately, more or less 'love'. As Carlyle might have put it, all speculation is conduct, and how we conduct ourselves – honestly, lovingly, anxiously, selfishly – in formulating thought and utterance cannot itself be put into words – it can only be shown.

No one can read the exchanges between Newman and Kingsley without recognising the extent to which the *truthfulness* of both men is on display and at stake. The same is true of ourselves. The relativism to which Hamilton drew Newman's attention was not, for Newman, an initial condition of thought at last disclosed to the enquiring modern spirit, but the outcome of a drama, in which philosophy with its thought experiments, and science with its real ones, have their parts to play. The 'always already' paradox, the radical and morally disordered contingency into which we are thrown simply by being what we are to each other, the linguistic Babel on which we are compelled to rely, all this is the consequence of 'some terrible aboriginal calamity', and not simply the ineluctable condition of our inclusion in the relativities of a signifying system or a Darwinian process.

Even recognition of this fallen condition, however, is 'an inchoate state', disclosing our need of 'Objective Truth', that is, of a system 'considered as existing in itself, external to this or that particular mind' (*Essays Critical*, I, p. 34). But the only way of engaging with the bare possibility of truth is a precipitation of the mind into whatever aspects of it are to hand. We need to 'throw ourselves forward upon that which we have but partially mastered ... to embrace, maintain, and use general propositions which are larger than our capacity, of which we cannot see the bottom'. This proto-existentialist action is at once private and moral: in numerous 'actions of the intellect,' Newman asserted, 'the individual is supreme and responsible to himself' (*Grammar of Assent*, p. 277). The 'always already' paradox is not, therefore, just a matter of understanding or signification; it involves judgement (*fronesis*). One can only be responsible for choices intelligently made, but intelligence, at the highest level, when it becomes certitude, is itself ultimately a matter of choice, 'an active recognition of propositions as true, such as it is the duty of each individual ... to exercise at the bidding of reason, and, when reason forbids, to withhold' (p. 271). Here is the fundamental difference between Newman and Dennett. Human beings, in Newman's judgement, not only tell stories about themselves; they are capable of intellectual and moral acts which result in certitude. This is an intensely individual event: real assents 'are of a personal character ... They depend on personal experience and the experience of one man is not the experience of another. Real assent ... is proper to the individual, and as such, thwarts rather than promotes the intercourse of man with man' (pp. 82–3). 'I believe' thus involves passivity before 'Objective Truth', yet an active choosing also, which presupposes (and does not just hypothesise) the truths about which it subsequently entertains certitude.

Nevertheless both Dennett and Miller do help us to clarify this structure. Let us suppose with Dennett that the 'I' in '*credo*' is a fiction, but let also us accept with Miller that all fictions, especially those involving ethical considerations, require an initial prosopopoeia. But the ethical can only arise if that initial prosopopoeia always already implies the possibility of responsible action. What would 'person', what would 'Maisie' mean, even in the inchoate condition of the initial prosopopoeia, if they did not imply that – if, in Miller's words, Maisie were not 'ethical'? The initial prosopopoeia involves us therefore not just in a mysterious seeing, but an inchoate doing. In this sense Newman is right when he describes the human person as 'emphatically self-made'.

Deconstructionism and cognitive philosophy also illuminate another of his claims, 'that [his] Maker and [he] were the two beings, luminously such, *in rerum natura*' (*Apologia*, p. 238). Newman puts this conviction down to conscience, which he regards as given in consciousness, impressing 'the imagination with the picture of a Supreme Governor, a Judge, holy, just, powerful, all-seeing, retributive' (*Grammar of Assent*, p. 101), 'the aboriginal Vicar of Christ, a prophet in its informations, a monarch in its peremptoriness, a priest in its blessings and anathemas'.[36] Slightly extravagant as this may strike modern readers, it is worth recalling that even Hume believed that the 'mind of man is so formed by nature that, upon the appearance of certain characters, dispositions, and actions, it immediately feels the sentiment of approbation or blame; nor are there any emotions more essential to its frame and constitution' (*Enquiries*, p. 102). Miller, moreover, takes this idea further. 'The personification of the moral law', he writes, '... is fundamental, original, and ineffaceable. It cannot be erased or suspended by a return to clear, philosophical, reasonable, nonfigurative first principles' (*Versions of Pygmalion*, p. 136). Newman's prosopopoeic intuition of conscience is thus at least thinkable in post-Christian terms; nor does it function for Newman as a *proof* of God's existence, though on occasion he loosely refers to it as such, first because it specifies a condition of thought and not a conclusion, and second because it depends 'on personal experience and the experience of one man is not the experience of another' (*Grammar of Assent*, p. 82). 'God', Newman argues,

> dwells intelligibly, prior to argument, in the heart and conscience. And though on the mind's first mastering this general principle, it seems to itself at the moment to have cut off all the ties which bind it to the universe, and to be floated off upon the ocean of intolerable scepticism

– 'solipsism' is the word that might occur to the post-Wittgensteinian reader; other readers might think of Emily Brontë's 'No coward soul is mine' –

> yet a true sense of its own weakness brings it back, the instructive persuasion that it must be intended to rely on something, and therefore that the information given, though philosophically inaccurate, must be practically certain. (*The Arians*, p. 76)

It seems, then, that Miller's initial prosopopoeia was what enabled Newman famously to 'rest in the thought of two and two only absolute and luminously self-evident beings' (*Apologia*, p. 89), himself and his Creator. Whether 'conscience' does or does not disclose the presence of 'God' to the individual consciousness, however, may be left to one side. What is clear from Miller, and implicit in the arguments of other deconstructionists and cognitive philosophers, is that making moral choices simultaneously involves an experience (however inchoate and rudimental) of the (potential) presence of another person. Prosopopoeia always already implies the *really* interpersonal.

The essays in this book are thus based on two assumptions. The first is that certitude about the real presence of other persons is the *sine qua non* of *all* thought. But another person is always already an agent, which brings me to my second assumption, that there 'is one, and only one, truly discerned but non-coercive value which the mind can cognize and respond to with unqualified freedom, and that is the freedom of another'.[37] All our free moral choices, no matter how internal and private, presuppose the presence of someone else, whose freedom to make moral choices independently of our own is always the ultimate object of our choosing. If freedom so understood belongs to the essence of personhood, *persons are in their very being mutually constitutive.*

Literature, I believe, presupposes, implies, represents and depicts this deep mutuality and its enemies. That is why studying literature is diffi-cult. The essays in the first section of this book, 'The Presence of Persons', set out the views expressed in this Introduction more explic-itly. The essays on Dickens in the second section, 'Manifold and Complex Corruption', take up an issue to which attention is drawn in the com-ments on Hawthorne's deceptively innocent New England in the first essay, namely the paradox that the mutuality in which we constitute ourselves as persons is inseparable from the shared depersonalisation of our lives by 'the world', which perversely can then become the medium for astonishingly rich if ambivalent personal interaction. It is no acci-dent, on the other hand, that two writers notably uncontaminated by the world, Charlotte and Emily Brontë, provide the material for the essays in the third section, 'Luminously Self-Evident Beings'. Selfhood was magisterially assumed in Emily Brontë's chosen isolation, and pain-fully claimed by Charlotte Brontë on behalf of her characters, her sisters and herself. Another paradox emerges in the essays in this section. Reserve, claimed for oneself and accorded to others, is a condition of personal wholeness, and so of interpersonal mutuality. This right to silence does not just inform the writing of the Brontës, however; it is fundamental to the self-understanding of Dickinson and to the drama acted out between Isabel Archer and Gilbert Osmond in *The Portrait of a Lady.*

The essays in 'The Management of our Hearts' develop in detail the claim that the intuition of heart speaking to heart, which prosopopoeia holds out to us, discloses the drama of human freedom as a coherent, and living principle of shared experience and mutual, unconditional respect. To revert to Hume's analogy with which this Introduction began – the theatre of the mind plays to a full house, not to Hume's lone spectator, and would be pretty sterile if it did not. The first essay in this section, on George Eliot, addresses at one level the antipathy between an evolution-conscious empirical tradition and the relativist tradition represented chiefly by Nietzsche and Yeats. This antagonism is essen-tially the same as that between Hamilton the relativist and Mill the empiricist, but with the roles reversed – the empiricist position is now perceived as the intellectually and morally regressive one. At another level, however, what emerges from George Eliot's writing is the presence of George Eliot herself, just as Mill's presence is the most striking precipitate of his attack on Hamilton. But whereas George Eliot can function as a bridge between the Positivist tradition and the drama of human freedom, Mill, iron-clad in his reasons and his laws, cannot. The free interaction between people which I find in *Daniel Deronda*, however, is implicit only, in a necessarily unstated relationship between the author and her readers. In Henry James's *The Portrait of a Lady*, on the other hand, the full implications of opening one's heart uncondi-tionally to the possibility of freedom in others is minutely and remorselessly depicted.

The abiding presence of other minds in our own informs all the essays in this book. They were written for various purposes over a very long period, as separate essays, reviews, conference papers, lectures and teaching materials. Hence their inconsistencies of tone. I have attempted to minimise repetition, though this has not always been possible. If, in spite of these shortcomings, the book has an overall sense, a direction, this may be due to the fact that everything it contains was written in the certitude that within and behind the systems of signification on which the mind plays and which play upon the mind, readers of literature can share, in the reticences of lyric, in the self-disclosures of fantasy, in the vulnerable earnestness of moralistic narrative and didactic discourse, as well as in the convolutions of theory, an awareness of intentions which can never be expressed, but which are shadowed within and are readily knowable to the illative sense, intentions which value our freedom as persons, and invite a comparable response from us. Even those for whom Newman's God is dead, therefore, may encounter the writers discussed in these essays, Charles Dickens, Charlotte Brontë, Emily Brontë, George Eliot, Henry James, Nathaniel Hawthorne, Emily Dickinson, Thomas Carlyle, Matthew Arnold, Walter Pater, Thomas Hardy and John Henry Newman as real and living presences, if only (for this is certainly a fallen world, whether or not it is a Godless one) through a glass darkly.

PART ONE

The Presence of Persons

CHAPTER ONE

Where are Nathaniel Hawthorne, Emily Dickinson and Daniel C. Dennett?

I

This paper began as a response to a provocation, an essay by Daniel C. Dennett in the *TLS* in 1988 entitled 'Why everyone is a novelist', which first appeared in *The Mind's I* (1981).[1] In both pieces Dennett declares that the self is the 'chief fictional character' each of us constructs to make the material of our lives 'into a single good story'. In the parlance of literary theory, we are 'subject-positions' like characters in books, or, in that of computer science, we are 'virtual' persons. In *Consciousness Explained* (1991) Dennett repeats this assertion: we spin stories about ourselves, 'weaving them like spiderwebs into self-protective strings of *narrative*' (until, that is, they begin to spin us) (*Consciousness Explained*, pp. 417–18). It follows that stories must in principle be writable by robots ('Why everyone', p. 1029): that is the only way a 'person-constituting' narrative could get going. 'I', therefore, am an autobiographical fiction a machine-like thing tells about itself. That I don't feel like a machine, and that my 'past' doesn't seem like the story a machine might assemble, are irrelevant, since logically my fictional self must be able to beguile me (that is, itself) into believing that today I am the ongoing subject I kid myself I was yesterday.

This argument depends on a particular view of literary texts. As early as 1978, Dennett was claiming that 'the introspective declarations, avowals, revisions, confessions of subjects or image-havers'[2] may be accorded the authority which the text has in New Criticism, a view he still defends – 'we can, and do', he insists, 'speak of what is true *in* [a] story ... the interpretation of fiction is undeniably doable, with certain uncontroversial results'. Both the autobiographies told by subjects of philosophical enquiry and the world textually 'determined by fiat' in a work of fiction are, he claims, 'stable' in the light of 'the best, most coherent, reading of the text we can find' (*Consciousness Explained*, pp. 79, 81). He evidently has not come to terms with the way texts as well as selves have been deconstructed in our time, that critics now assume that all narrators 'might be mistaken' – and not just if they are like Miles Coverdale in *The Blithedale Romance*, or Lockwood and Nelly Dean in *Wuthering Heights*. As a critic of literature, therefore, I feel justified in taking issue with Dennett, notwithstanding his formidable reputation as a philosopher.

I am encouraged in this by the fact that, while he takes science seriously, his tactics are 'those of an art'.[3] He likes thought experiments, of which his self-fictionalising robot is one example. Another, entitled 'Where am I?' (printed in both *Brainstorms* and *The Mind's I*), is about a brain in a vat but connected by radio to various bodies and finally sharing a body and its experiences concurrently with a computer duplicate of itself. This was rapturously received at a Chapel Hill colloquium. Dennett is a stylish writer. He and Douglas Hofstadter are also gifted anthologists: *The Mind's I* reprints some fine science fiction by Borges, Lem, Miedaner, Leiber, Ricker and Cherniak. In defence of his method, Dennett cites a section from *Philosophical Investigations* in which Ludwig Wittgenstein insists on replacing empirical *explanation* with description (*Elbow Room*, p. 18). (Wittgenstein goes on to warn against discerning deep pseudo-problems in confused language.) We may take Dennett's science on trust, therefore, and scrutinise his work as an arrangement, in Wittgenstein's words, of 'what we have always known' (*Philosophical Investigations*, p. 47c).

First something needs to be said about Dennett's philosophy. He believes that 'if we want to trace events to their ultimate causes, we are forced into reductionist views' (*Brainstorms*, p. 195); 'mental' states do not cause anything; 'the sole choreographer of the soul is physical law' (*The Mind's I*, p. 453), though this is not a verifiable claim, since 'causation is so hopelessly inscrutable as to be invisible' (*Elbow Room*, p. 77). Nevertheless, intentions, beliefs and desires keep their explanatory power at a certain level. This has nothing to do with consciousness. The moves of a chess-playing computer, for example, can be readily predicted in terms of 'beliefs' and 'strategies', even though it has none, but not in terms of the circuitry which it does have. In this sense all organic life is intentional – and therefore rational: it responds 'directly to meanings ... it [is] designed to be indefinitely self-redesigning' (ibid., p. 30). Its goal is reproduction (part of Richard Dawkins's *The Selfish Gene* [1976] is included in *The Mind's I*), and it arises by trial and error through natural selection (*Brainstorms*, p. 73). Brains, including the brains of rational beings, are thus rational in the first place by virtue of their design-relevance to the system in which they function rather than by virtue of the logic of their conscious thought-processes.

Computer programs are also like brains because they encode and decode information electronically and function heuristically. You cannot program a computer to analyse every possible response to a move early in a game of chess, but you can program it to make intelligent moves on a trial-and-error basis, and so to beat grand masters. Brains similarly cannot process all the data relevant to a particular situation, but can weigh enough of them to give their decisions a good chance of being good: like chess-playing computers we 'must relinquish control over the incomplete set of considerations on which we act, and hence we are always somewhat at the mercy of process' (*Elbow Room*, p. 87).

Another brain analogue developed by Hofstadter is an ant-hill, with its various classes of ants systematically responding to circumstances (attack, food supply, weather). An ant-hill is thus, in the technical sense, a 'representational system', that is, 'an active, self-updating collection of structures organized to "mirror" the world as it evolves' (*The Mind's I*, p. 192). Mirroring here does not imply copying, but a detailed correspondence between the structure of the world's action on the system and the structure of the system's reactions to it – ant-hills and minds *organise* themselves to fit the world. A 'representational' system of this sort can go on evolving, even when it is cut off from what it is 'reflecting'. It may 'sprout parallel branches for various possibilities that can reasonably be anticipated'; its representations can 'interact ... according to their own internal logic', and create 'a faithful model of the way the world works' (ibid., p. 193). This is achieved, in people and animals, through 'various semiautonomous subsystems' – scent-coded groups of ants, for example – and 'there is no "inner eye" that watches all the activity and "feels" the system' (p. 200).

But isn't consciousness the inner eye that perceives and processes the really important information in people if not in ant-hills? Dennett doubts it; he questions whether 'the concept of experience ... [differentiates] any one thing of [serious] theoretical interest' (*Brainstorms*, p. 148). If we do have an inner eye, Hofstadter suggests, it is at most 'a complex subsystem that is a model of the full system' and is incapable, in itself, of actively perceiving (*The Mind's I*, p. 200). That power, actively to '*represent*' the world, resides at the level of the whole system. As Stansilaw Lem puts it in a spoof review, 'There reigns ... around the conscious a never-ending crush, a pushing and shoving, and the conscious is ... a cork upon the fretful waves.'[4] In Lem's judgement, the brain is full of antinomies, incompatible languages, and bits of information that do not fit; the function of consciousness, he suggests, is to circumvent the paralysis this would induce in a simple digital machine by effecting a phoney closure. Paradoxes illustrate the point. Hofstadter cites the sentence 'Thiss sentence contains threee errors' (ibid., p. 276). First you think it has only two errors; then you see this very fact as its third error; but in that case the sentence does contain three errors, and is therefore true. This contradiction is the kind of thing that stymies a computer, but the human mind's spontaneous response to conundrums of this sort is to imagine it has glimpsed a real problem. 'There's something *in* that,' it tells itself. 'I'll come back to it later. Meanwhile ... ' But as Wittgenstein points out, it is an illusion to imagine that the 'problems arising through a misinterpretation of our forms of language have the character of depth' (*Philosophical Investigations*, p. 47e).

I find these arguments immensely attractive. I *think* I am persuaded that the mind operates like a computer system (*Brainstorms*, pp. 149ff.). I *like* the ant-hill analogy, particularly the notion that a system can operate 'representationally' without any of its bits – ants or groups of ants – 'knowing' more than they need to. Nevertheless I can't finally rid my mind of the thought that 'seeing' consciousness as Lem and Hofstadter do may be an instance of what they describe, a way of circumventing the problem of 'seeing' by making me think I have 'seen through' it. Does consciousness contribute in any way to the theory that consciousness only bobs about like a cork on the fretful waves? If consciousness is only an outcome, how can we trust what it tells us *about itself*? And how can a 'subject-position' *know* whether another 'person' is 'virtual' or 'real'?

I find myself in more familiar territory when I examine other grounds for finding Dennett's writing both engaging and problematical. Part of what I like about it is its Americanness. Dennett writes a kind of high-brow demotic. Half-way through 'Where am I?' his body is abandoned deep in the earth, its grave marked by an enormous derelict structure, 'with the word STUD emblazoned on its side' – STUD being the acronym for Supersonic Tunnelling Underground Device (ibid., p. 320). But his writing is also heavily ideological. Characteristically, he assumes that economic 'prediction ... succeeds to the extent ... that individual men are in general good approximations of the optimal operator in the market place' (*Brainstorms*, p. 16), and he has no difficulty in working with Rawls's supposition of 'a group of idealized persons, defined ... as rational, *self-interested* entities ... [with] individual and antagonistic interests' (ibid., p. 280, my italics). There is, in effect, a bias in his writing towards rugged individualism, symbolized in the metaphor of 'elbow room', which strikes the European reader as decidedly American.

This is particularly evident in his several accounts of how the kind of internal conversation with oneself which we call thinking might have evolved. Initially language would have functioned, he suggests, as a means of communication. Language users would have learned to warn each other of danger, to agree plans of action for hunting and fighting, to test each other's sexual availability and so forth. They would also have learned to ask for help and to give it. All these uses of language would have been 'out loud'. But an occasion might have arisen when a primitive human being asked for help and answered itself. 'Such an act of autostimulation', Dennett suggests, 'could blaze a valuable new trail between one's internal components'; what one says to oneself could be a crucial element in the 'self-stimulation' of which consiousness is at least a symptom (*Consciousness Explained*, pp. 195–7; 275). This new skill would be most beneficial, however, if exercised discreetly: 'for we must not suppose that the helpful commerce that was the seed for this process was an entirely altruistic and noncompetitive affair' (*Elbow Room*, p. 41). The ultimate form such discretion could take would be a conversation between one's internal components which did not involve vocalization at all: 'thinking', as we understand it, would have begun.

This seems to me to be a persuasive hypothesis, but also to be incomplete. Just as it never occurs to Dennett that most of the narrative of self may be written, not by the individual subject but by society for ends designed to *limit* the individual's operations in the marketplace and elsewhere, so the processes of self-interested secrecy and deceit may have socially based as well as individually based determinants, with disturbing implications for all our intellectual efforts, including literary crticism on the one hand and the thought experiments of cognitive philosophy on the other.

This becomes clear if we examine Dennett's ideas, as a literary critic may surely do, in the light of a different kind of American writing. Arthur Miller's *The Crucible* would suit my purposes, but I prefer a briefer, bolder text – Hawthorne's tale 'My Kinsman, Major Molineux'. This chilling story of atrocity and personal cowardice is also a story of social initiation. Robin is a Deterministic Deliberator in a new environment who asks for help. In doing so, he discovers that to get himself accepted by his kinsman's fellow-townsfolk he must join in their persecution of the Major, a ritualised scapegoating which serves apparently as a sinister but powerful social bond. Specifically when the 'tremendous ridicule' accompanying the Major's tarring and feathering affects Robin 'with a sort of mental inebriety', and the 'contagion' of the people's laughter (which is at Robin's expense as well as the Major's) seizes him, he stops asking questions *and answers himself*, 'with a shout of laughter'. Only then does it become possible for him, in the words of the 'kindly gentleman', to 'rise in the world without the help of [his] kinsman' – to become – for he is a shrewd young man – a successful Deterministic Deliberator in pre-revolutionary New England, to keep his counsel when others are in earshot, and behave like an optimal operator in the marketplace.[5]

'We laugh', Dennett tells us, '*because we are amused* ... because things are *funny* ... because of joy, and delight, and out of happiness' (*Consciousness Explained*, p. 63). If only we did! My point is that the antinomies which Dennett's theory discloses subvert the theory itself. Let us accept the model of semi-autonomous subsystems operating within 'representational' systems to generate a dynamic structural correspondence between the system as a whole and the world it operates in. But if ant-hills and human brains are such systems, so are corporations, universities, countries, and pre-revolutionary New England townships. Now, as Dennett points out, 'when larger goals can be achieved by cleverly organized armies of uncomprehending agents, such as ants, the "Need to Know" rule is ruthlessly invoked': soldier-ants are blind to the priorities of the ant-hill (*Elbow Room*, p. 28). But unlike soldier-ants, people do need to know some (but not all) of the goals built into other parts of the system, and perhaps also to have convincing reasons to explain their ignorance of others. States are particularly good at encouraging their citizens to take a pride in 'secret agencies', in MI5, the CIA and other *arcana imperii*. We cope also with perceptible conflicts of interest between 'selfishness' in the gene, the meme, the self, the corporation and 'society'. Language and self-consciousness help me to solve these problems by enabling me to invent stories about myself, and to endorse the stories my fellow-townsfolk tell about themselves. We engage in the mutually reinforcing, collusive and manipulative exchanges so shamefully exemplified in Hawthorne's story because they are biologically functional. The effects of this mendacity on rational adults are evident enough when countries or communities find scapegoats, whether they are local dignitaries or impoverished refugees. Of course, as Dennett points out, in much of what we do 'the presumption that we will be able to communicate with our fellow men is founded on the presumption of their rationality' (*Brainstorms*, p. 239) – and indeed their decency: both are a condition of much practical, cooperative enterprise. But rationality and decency are no less the precondition of our functional deceptions and self-deceptions.

That is how, to answer a question put by Hofstadter, the Nazis were 'able to convince themselves it was all right to kill Jews ... [and] Americans ... to "waste gooks" in the Viet Nam war' (*The Mind's I*, p. 114). Germans and Americans are by and large reasonable, decent people. The officer responsible for the atrocities at My Lai was in his time a shrewd youth, and went on to prosper as a jeweller in Georgia. For such deceptions to work, of course, they must also stand a good chance of escaping detection. They must be accorded the authority texts were deemed to have by New Critics. Admittedly, not all social intercourse is mendacious, but little is demonstrably uncontaminated by biological and ideological imperatives which we do not need, or would be advised not, to know. It is for this reason that philosophers should be cautious when their papers on these topics are accorded standing ovations at academic colloquia.

Dennett is too sensitive an analyst of his own ideas not to have recognised this danger. He has read 'Milgram's classic horror story about the obedient torturers' – students who were persuaded by their professors into (apparently) inflicting acute electrical shocks on the screaming human subjects of a psychology experiment: without realising it, of course, the 'torturers' were themselves the subject of the experiment (*Elbow Room*, p. 13). Dennett is conscious of the Nietzschean challenge to our 'moral conceptual world'. 'I have taken for granted my own rationality as well as yours,' he writes, '... and the suspicion may still be strong in some quarters that we have been averting our eyes from the deepest, most terrifying visions.' He meets this possibility by identifying it as nihilism, which he dismisses as 'a *negligible* position' because if nothing were true, nothing, not even nihilism, could be taken seriously. 'We may assume that something matters,' he continues, 'and that we are rational enough so that there can be some point to our attempts to understand the world' (ibid., pp. 155–6).

But does an account of human intelligence entirely based on the principles of Darwinism and computer science permit such an assumption? Dennett thinks it does. The 'rationality Nature has endowed us with is practical,' he admits, '... [but] we must not suppose ... that ... it is ... tied directly and rigidly to serving the biological ends that gave birth to it'. Language, for example, evolved for biological reasons, but, having done so, it 'makes room for all manner of biologically trivial or irrelevant or baroque (nonfunctional) endeavors: gossip, riddles, poetry, philosophy' (p. 48).[6] This is wishful thinking, the humane half of the story Dennett is telling about himself to set beside the sterner stuff of physicalism, randomly prompted heuristic decision making, and the autonomy of cerebral subsystems. But there is no point at which the relativisation of Dennett's text can be halted, no residuum which has authority. In any case all the items on his list have evident biological value, irrespective of content: each establishes, stabilises and modifies our relations with one another for 'unbaroque', and often reproductively useful ends. There are no grounds for supposing that meme-viruses (lies that speak like truth) don't have all sorts of biologically effective and morally sinister effects. Jokes, lies and even philosophy certainly do, as many academics who have dazzled a potential sexual partner on campus can attest.

All that Dennett's arguments allow us to conclude, therefore, is something we have always known – we are just rational enough to recognise that we cannot take our rationality for granted, and (briefly, before turning our attention to other matters) that we would be well advised to keep that particular insight under our hats; to proclaim it too loudly might be the philosophical equivalent of announcing our kinship with Major Molineux.

II

I have tried to show that Dennett's philosophy is ensnared in a paradox: Nature must have reasons which human reason is designed not to know. His own arguments may appeal to us, therefore, for no better reason than that we have been programmed to rationalise submission to signifiers of power such as the self-assurance of American scientific culture. (Doubtless, in his time, Trofim Denisovich Lysenko *convinced* intelligent and honourable Soviet scientists that his mad biology was rational.) It follows that the 'rationality' of natural intentional systems cannot be used to sustain a presumption in favour of our own rationality. Dennett thinks that we have no need to fear being 'zapped into ... "beliefs, desires and traits of character" by a process of conditioning' (*Elbow Room*, p. 34), but we do, we do.

To escape this danger we must reject his claim that selves are 'fictional objects' like centres of gravity, and treat them instead as 'inferred entities, such as atoms, molecules and neutrinos' ('Why everyone is', p. 1016). I shall call these 'inferred entities' – these selves anterior to biographical narratives of the ego, or even the mere experience of subjective ongoingness – 'substantial selves'.

I can begin to focus on the notion of a 'substantial self' by recalling a letter I wrote in reply to Dennett's *TLS* article. 'It is always fun to read Daniel C. Dennett,' it began, '– his style is unmistakable: *c'est l'homme même.*'[7] My point was that Dennett's 'substantial self' can be inferred from his prose, more or less independently of its persuasiveness. Thus while I approve of his insistence on the 'important difference between the person who is agonizing over whether to accept admission to Harvard, Stanford or Swarthmore, and the person who is *not* agonizing over whether or not to go to work today in the factory' (*Elbow Room*, p. 122), I find the argument which this illustration supports unsatisfactory. On the other hand, I am provoked when he attributes feelings to me which I do not think I have, as when he announces that *our* sole reason for caring 'about free will at all' is fear that certain 'dreadful things' would be *our* fate without it, that *we* 'don't want to let Hitler, or Nixon, or the kid who steals our hubcaps off the hook', yet I find the trait engaging, and I can't say why (ibid., pp. 6, 154). There is a *difference* between any verbal account I give of what Dennett says or even how he strikes me, and what Dennett would call my 'beliefs' about him.

'Belief', like 'representation', has a precise sense. Unlike 'opinion', it 'is best considered divorced from language' (p. 305). Beliefs 'have no syntax or structure' and they 'predict ... behaviour directly'. Here Dennett and I agree: 'beliefs' are fundamental to whatever it is we are, and they

cannot be linguistically constructed or deconstructed. It is my contention that Dennett's style enables me to 'believe' that he and I both have
'substantial selves', and that 'believing' as such is closely related to this
being so – which leaves me with the difficult task of putting that 'belief'
convincingly into words.

My difficulties are largely of Dennett's making. Thus what I regard as
evidence of 'substantial selfhood', he sees merely as evidence of 'personality', a topic on which he and Hofstadter write convincingly. At one
point, admittedly, Hofstadter implies that a radio ham infers the existence of a person simply by hearing the transmission of Morse (*The
Mind's I*, p. 76), but low-level machines can generate such messages
automatically; hams recognise persons by the *style* of their tapping.
Hofstadter would probably accept this because he identifies 'style' as 'a
whole constellation of subconscious biases ... a system of tendencies
and desires and beliefs and so on' (ibid., p. 85), and he and Dennett
define 'soul' as 'that opaque yet characteristic *style* of each individual'
(p. 385) – I would have chosen the word 'inchoate' rather than 'opaque'.
Each of us is thus characterised by an individual 'style' or 'soul', which
we recognise in each other in the way we move, speak, write, touch, or
tap Morse. But 'soul' in this sense – I shall continue to use quotation
marks for all these terms – is not 'substantial self' in mine; it does not
add up to any one thing.

Nor, for Dennett, does being a person. He grounds 'personhood' in
three interdependent 'themes' – 'being rational ... being intentional ...
[and] being the object of a certain stance' (*Brainstorms*, p. 271). Whether
'something counts as a person depends in some way on an attitude
taken toward it ... our treating it in this certain way is somehow
constitutive of its being a person' (ibid., p. 270). This seems odd – my
attitude towards a neutrino or a tomato does not determine what it is.
Wittgenstein might regard Dennett's 'in some way' and 'somehow' as
linguistic vacationing. However, we need also to remember that his
themes are interdependent, the third of them being reciprocity, by which,
following H.P. Grice, he means a capacity to form third-order intentions – '*U* must *intend* that *A recognize* that *U intends* that *A* produce *r*'
(p. 278). This does not need to be explicitly worked out; it is what
marks communication with a person as opposed to a computer. I never
intend my computer to *recognise* that I *intend* it to save some text – I
just expect it to do so on command. 'Personhood' so understood also
requires a capacity for moral accountability, and so for 'verbal communication and for awareness of one's actions' (p. 283). Finally, following
H. Frankfurt, Dennett holds that 'personhood' requires the ability to
frame 'second-order volitions', to have wants about one's wants (p.
284).

'Personhood' so understood is thus 'inescapably normative' (p. 285). Babies, lunatics and the mentally deficient are 'denied personhood' (p. 267). So, probably, are deliberate wrong-doers, since their actions must count against the assumption that they were aware they were doing wrong, and did wrong of their 'own free will ... When such problems arise we cannot even tell in our own cases if we are persons' (p. 285). Dennett saves his notion of responsible 'personhood', however, by explaining conscious wrong-doing as a conflict between 'opinion' – one's linguistically organised convictions – and 'beliefs' – 'one's deeper behaviour-disposing states' (p. 308): it is because we sometimes lapse from honestly held 'opinion' into ineluctably held 'belief' that the themes of 'personhood' can in principle operate in our lives. 'Personhood' is thus like 'soul' – a constellation of tendencies and capacities. If the facts of mind prohibit our making stronger claims about our personal unity, the concepts of 'soul' and 'personhood' at least allow us to make sense of our felt individuality and moral accountability.

To indicate why I hold these claims to be inadequate, I shall appeal to the evidence of a poem by Emily Dickinson:

> The last Night that She lived
> It was a Common Night
> Except the Dying – this to Us
> Made Nature different
>
> We noticed smallest things –
> Things overlooked before
> By this great light upon our Minds
> Italicized – as 'twere.
>
> As we went out and in
> Between Her final Room
> And Rooms where Those to be alive
> Tomorrow were, a Blame
>
> That Others could exist
> While She must finish quite
> A Jealousy for Her arose
> So nearly infinite –
>
> We waited while she passed –
> It was a narrow time –
> Too jostled were Our Souls to speak
> At length the notice came –
>
> She mentioned and forgot –
> Then lightly as a Reed
> Bent to the Water, struggled scarce –
> Consented, and was dead –
>
> And We – We placed the Hair –
> And drew the Head erect –

And then an awful leisure was
Belief to regulate – [8]

My claim is that only a 'substantial self' could read this poem adequately. To show this I shall attempt a thought experiment. I shall
imagine interrogating two hidden respondents about the poem in order
to find out which is a Dennett-system and which a 'substantial self'.
The design of this Turing test will justify my claim (see *The Mind's I*,
pp. 53–95).

I begin with a question. How could each of my respondents convince
me that it had read this poem as literature? Each would have to discuss
its metre and paraphrase it accurately enough to translate it into a
foreign language. Each would have to show that it could discuss second-
order issues, such as the indefinitely variable intonations and
stress-patterns with which the poem can be read aloud, or the syntactic
breakdown in stanza four – not just the form and possible content of
the missing clause ('that ... '), but what an inability or refusal to
complete such a sentence might mean to a speaker, and communicate to
a listener, and what letting it stand might mean for the poet and her
reader as experienced judges of poetry. Each, of course, would be alert
to the other's sensitivities in such matters (whether consciously or not),
while the almost limitless possibilities of nuanced interpretation disclosed in even a small number of readings must be regarded as an
allowed aspect of Dickinson's intentions. Each would thus have to
convince me that it could discuss how Dickinson intended her readers
to recognise that she intended them to respond to the poem in particular and yet not in fixed ways, even if neither she nor they could state
definitively what those ways were.

I shall accept the claim that a Dennett-system might have such capacities, that it might be capable of such an immensely sophisticated *dynamic*
'representation' of a linguistic world containing Dickinson's poem (and
the vast corpus of text the bare existence of that poem is predicated
upon). For this it would probably need the design feature Hofstadter
thinks may be required for the learning of a second language, and
which he describes as a reaching downward from the level of thought to
effect a reprogramming of 'some of the hardware underlying it', an
ability in the system 'to loop back and affect lower levels – its own
underpinnings' (*The Mind's I*, pp. 282, 380–81). Such a loop-back
capability is at present only a gleam in the computer designer's eye. If it
exists at all, it does so in us, an inferred design feature of our hardware.
It is what enables us to assimilate the personalised grammars of nuance
and intonation which every 'soul' brings to the public reading of a text.
But it probably isn't a design feature any of us shares with anyone else,
because just as 'soul' reveals itself in nuanced reading, so it operates in

the way we 'read' each other. In people, therefore, Hofstadter's loop-back capability would have a *characteristic* way of reprogamming itself, a 'style' to its 'representations' of other people's 'styles', in effect to its way of doing literary criticism.

Nevertheless I am granting the possibility of these almost unimaginably sophisticated interactions between machines, and between machines and poems and machines and people. I also accept that such interactions would not mean that consciousness, still less deliberate reasoning, had taken control. I do not think it would be irrational to imagine a machine making intelligible reports about its 'reception' of Emily Dickinson's syntax, or of how I read the poem aloud in different ways on different occasions, without its ever having to experience anything consciously. Most judgements about literature, after all, get articulated *before* their originator knows what they are. Indeed we can imagine a critic putting intensely personal and characteristic critical insights on paper and then suffering a fatal stroke without fully or even adequately realising what he or she had written.

But what if I were to interrogate my respondents, not about the nuances of intonation and silence in the poem, but the paradox in its last line? The problem of regulating Belief there sprung upon us applies as much to Dennett's notion of 'belief' as to religious faith. Faith after all is supposed to be a divinely bestowed regulator of thought and actions, an exact analogue, in effect, of Dennett's 'belief' which also regulates action, with or without the concurrence of 'opinion'. In both senses of the word, therefore, the claim to regulate belief seems odd. That of course is the point. A degree of top–down control is implied which is calculated to offend both predestinarians and physicalists. We need to bear in mind, however, the near-certainty that the line was not written to make a philosophical claim about self-controllers. The laconic perversity of its phrasing suggests that it was expected to evoke a complex of possibly incompatible mental states – a natural inability to take in the fact that a death has occurred, religious doubt, the quiet recognition that religious faith functions as an opiate for sorrow, a heroic determination to get the inner life truly, religiously, in order. How can we question our respondents about so complicated, allusive and subjective a communication?

Not by asking them about their own experiences. In setting up my experiment I have avoided using experience as a criterion. I have sought to distinguish between my respondents solely in terms of the way they use language. I shall not ask them, therefore, about what it is like to cope with doubt, or whether Emily Dickinson communicates what it was like for her to do so. Instead I shall ask them to compose, for their own consumption, an account of a similar introspective episode in their

own past, in a way that will involve an element of conscious or unconscious recall, a process of working out ('It must have been after her visit
in the spring ... '), and of composition for the sake of narrative clarity. I
shall next ask them if their respective accounts are not true but truthful.
If their replies give an intelligible report of what might be involved in
composing for private consumption a completely or partially or potentially (self-)deceptive report of the past, I shall then ask them what
would be involved in composing a further, truthful account, again for
personal consumption, of their own original performances as completely, or partially, or potentially untruthful narrators. This, after all, is
what Dickinson describes herself as doing – telling herself a story immediately after the death of her friend, a story which, at the time, may
have been more or less untruthful, and then putting on record in a
private poem the story of that private story-telling. If my respondents
produce convincing narratives, convincing reports on the truthfulness
of those narratives, and convincing reports on those reports, I shall
recognise them as having 'substantial selves', and of being capable of
Dickinson-like self-regulation.

My procedure derives from Wittgenstein's assertion that 'the importance of true confession ... resides ... in the special consequences which
can be drawn from a confession whose truth is guaranteed by the
special criteria of *truthfulness*' (*Philosophical Investigations*, p. 222).
As Dennett notes, this applies, in Wittgenstein's view, especially to
reports of dreams, to which 'a concept of "truth" as distinct from
"truthfulness"' cannot arise' (*Brainstorms*, p. 142). For one of my
respondents to be able to discuss truthfulness, and truthfulness about
truthfulness coherently, it would have to be able to discuss its own
capacity to lapse from such a state, to give telling 'a single good story',
for example, priority over irreducibly inconsistent elements in memory.
At least as Dennett has so far described it, a Dennett-system could not
engage with truthfulness as a problem of behaviour in this fashion, and
could not therefore learn the language in which discussion of the problem in self-referential terms is possible.

It is in her sensitive registering of the paradoxes of self-regulation, in
her linguistic enactment of the uncertainties of self-control, that Dickinson
demonstrates the control she is uncertain about, her own substantial
integrity within the 'gappy and sparse' confusions of consciousness
(*Consciousness Explained*, p. 366). Such truthfulness presupposes 'substantial selfhood', which may take its 'character' from her 'soul' and her
capacity for 'personhood', but which binds them into a unity the Dennett-
system cannot have. This unity derives from the presence within her,
not of a centring consciousness, but of a supreme *active* principle. The
latter is only, and can only be, an inferred entity, without syntax or

structure, just like Dennett's 'beliefs'. It is not open, therefore, to direct
introspective scrutiny. Truthfulness does require us, however, to speak
of a capacity of the whole system to subordinate, however briefly, the
action of all its subsystems, its heuristic practices, and the body of its
'beliefs' to a goal discovered by, and freely accepted at, the highest level,
that is, to honour 'the special criteria of *truthfulness*'. Whether this is
compatible with physicalism I cannot say; nor is the question an interesting one. What matters is that, governed by such a supreme active
principle, consciousness could have other functions besides dreaming
up illusory insights into, or telling stories about, antinomies.

In Dickinson's case, for example, it implies a strongly individuated
integrity. We can hardly doubt how *she* would have felt about the
scapegoating of Major Molineux. I can discover a comparable integrity
in many other human beings besides poets – in lovers, in family, and in
other thinkers. Such true understandings of other people, and not a self-
defeating, Darwinian claim about the 'naturalness' of rationality and
sincerity, are, I maintain, a necessary, though by no means a sufficient,
condition of our sharing true understandings of the world. Without the
ability to believe in each other's truthfulness, we would be incapable of
distinguishing the authentic exhilaration of a successful academic colloquium from the specious and collusive excitements of a political rally.
Nor do you have to be capable of reading Dickinson or going to
Harvard, Stanford or Swarthmore to be truthful in this way. Anyone
with the *capacity* to be shocked or ashamed by untruthfulness – and
that includes many who would not qualify by Dennett's criteria 'foren-
sically' or 'metaphysically' as 'persons' – has the capacity to *add up* to
one incontrovertibly valuable thing, not a fiction but a fact, a 'substantial self'.

There is a long-established philosophical tradition of thinking about
the self as a process of self-definition – Dennett cites Charles Taylor's
essay, 'Responsibility for Self'.[9] Taylor, he writes, holds that 'we define
ourselves ... by making "articulate" and more definite that which had
been inchoate and ill-formed' (*Elbow Room*, p. 90). In *An Essay in Aid
of a Grammar of Assent* (a work which anticipates Dennett's distinction
between 'opinion' and 'belief' in its distinction between 'notional' and
'real' assents), John Henry Newman said something very similar. It is a
position which Dennett thinks vulnerable: 'if', he argues, 'I happen to
have defined myself so as to be able to listen to the voice of reason (on
occasion) that is just my good luck' – effectively one consequence of
what I was the day I was born: but we cannot be 'responsible for
anything we subsequently do, so long as our characters today are
deterministic outgrowths, however constructive or creative, of our characters yesterday, and the day before' (ibid., pp. 91–2).[10] This suggests

that the kind of 'substantial selfhood' on which, I claim, not only truthfulness but our capacity for making scientific truth a crucial component of our shared life depends, is only possible if the supreme active principle we infer of ourselves and others is not subject to deterministic law. Unless, like Dickinson, we are capable of *choosing* truthfulness when we recall a dream, or construct the past, or judge the evidence in favour of a scientific hypothesis, in short, of regulating belief, we are lost 'souls', style without substance. For myself, and not least because I enjoy the work of Dennett and Hofstadter so much, I am convinced that we can so choose, and that in consequence, in the words Newman chose for his coat of arms, heart does speak to heart, *cor ad cor loquitur*.

CHAPTER TWO

Evolution and Progress:
Herbert Spencer, Thomas Hardy
and Amartya Sen

Amartya Sen's 1992 Darwin Lecture[1] asks how evolutionary success should be evaluated – in terms of the reproductive success of the species (or genotype) or quality of life. Sen draws attention to the difficulties in both sets of criteria: measuring progress in terms of reproductive success is arbitrary and crass, but measuring it in terms of quality of life risks being anthropocentric. I hope to broaden and clarify still further some of the implications of the problem he addressed by examining a selection of other writers who have considered it since it was first discussed in the nineteenth century by Herbert Spencer. Spencer was a far from satifactory thinker on evolution, but in his early work, *The Principles of Psychology* (1855), he identified a set of criteria which seem to be genuinely objective.

The degree of life in any organism, he maintains, depends on the degree to which it can actively 'correspond' with the complexities of its environment.[2] The single cell exhibits simple reactions limited in space and duration to the world in which it survives and reproduces. The mammal engages with relatively large areas of space, has a longer individual life, and reacts with greater complexity to the minutiae of sight, sound, smell and touch. Human intelligence does not introduce any radically new criteria by which progress defined as correspondence may be measured. It simply extends that correspondence still further in space, time, detail and 'generality'. (The latter criterion is not exclusive to human beings. As Daniel Dennett puts it: 'mammals and birds, reptiles, amphibians, fish, and even many invertebrates exhibit the capacity to use general information they obtain from their environments to presort their behavioral options before striking out'.)[3] Thus Spencer's criteria for quality of life apparently allow us to take account of the evolution of culture, technology and even morality without appealing to values which are themselves specific to any particular culture, or even to humanity as a whole – except, possibly, the value of objectivity itself.

Evolution, for Spencer, is centrally psychological. Just as the organs of the body show a mutual dependence in their interaction with the environment, so, he maintains, there is a mutual dependence and ever-advancing 'consensus' in the operations of mind. Animal life is initially instinctive, but evolving organic forms gradually add to their stock of inherited behaviours by improvising and learning new reactions through memory. Rationality is the same phenomenon as memory under another aspect, since the organism can only use memories to regulate activity by making comparative judgements between them, or (to use a modern idiom) by developing rational procedures for implementing one subset of instructions rather than another. Instinct, memory, intelligence, choice are thus all aspects of 'consensus' – the increasingly unified, extended, prolonged, complex and discriminating correspondence of the organism with its environment.

Spencer's concept of correspondence thus offers a model of 'improvement', of quality enhancement, that can only take place in time, while providing specifiable grounds for distinguishing between 'better' earlier and 'worse' later developments. Sen offers the example of a variant species of human slaves which is 'kept in inhuman conditions ... [and] adapts and evolves into being not only very useful slaves but also dogged survivors and super-rapid reproducers', and asks whether we must 'accept that development as a sign of progress' ('On the Darwinian View', p. 18). Spencer's answer would be yes, if it were associated with enhancements of correspondence, no if it were not. Were the capacities of the slave species for working together enhanced? Did their increased rate of reproduction result in more sophisticated or cruder interpersonal systems of communication between members of family groups? Were these developments passed from one generation to the next?

Evolution so understood is not genetic in Mendelian terms. As the criterion of evolutionary progress, correspondence takes account of the evolution of the environment as well as of the genotype, that is, of the biosphere, and of human technology and culture. Evolution complicates the environment and so generates the conditions not only for further evolution at the same level, but also for more complex interactions between species, for predatory and parasitic relationships, for symbiosis and the elaborate ensembles of coexistence represented by an ant-hill or the digestive tracts of animals. Thus while not all evolutionary developments are progressive, natural selection has an in-built progressive tendency.

In his essay 'Progress: Its Law and Cause' (1857), Spencer explained the inherently progressive character of evolution in terms of what may be called his law of multiple effect. '*Every active force produces more than one change – every cause produces more than one effect.*'[4] In showing how this principle applies to the spread of flora and fauna over the earth, he came very near to anticipating Darwinian natural selection; and he applied it no less confidently to human history: 'Whether it be in the development of the Earth,' he wrote, 'in the development of Life upon its surface, in the development of Society, of Government, of Manufactures, of Commerce, of Language, Literature, Science, Art, this same evolution of the simple into the complex, through successive differentiations, holds throughout' ('Progress', p. 154). Thus for Spencer there was a single, demonstrably 'progressive' process connecting the amoeba's efficient but limited exploitation of its environment to (say) Stephen Hawking's 'correspondence' with the Big Bang, and Sen's elucidation of the moral and conceptual complexities of our awareness of natural selection itself.

This last example, however, helps us to identify a difficulty with the Spencerian model. Among the difficulties Sen identifies in the way of a reasoned evaluation of criteria of evolutionary progress is the likelihood that our reasoning is only properly employed in doing what it has evolved to do, that is, helping us to survive and reproduce; in which case it may be irrational to look to reason to provide us with answers to any other kinds of question. 'A proposition', Gottlob Frege noted, 'may be thought, and again may be true',[5] and he warned against our confusing the two things. But how can we know that this very distinction impresses us, not because it is itself true, but only because it is the kind of thinking that has survival value, and therefore may be thought? In other words, a purely evolutionary understanding of reason prevents us from applying Frege's injunction to itself or to evolution. Sen attempts to get round this difficulty through Spencer's law of multiple effect – the fact that our sense of colour has survival value does not stop us seeing 'the beauty of Cezanne's or Picasso's colours' ('On the Darwinian View', p. 18). In principle, therefore, reason may begin by facilitating practical thinking, but have the additional effect of enabling us to 'see' truth in the way that we 'see' beauty. It is unclear, however, how far this takes us. Frege, for one, would not have been satisfied with the implication that, like beauty, truth may only be in the eye of the beholder. Nor would neo-Darwinists in their just war with fundamentalist Creationism.

Sen offers a way through this dilemma by looking at values. *Prima facie*, reason might be expected to endorse the conditions of its own evolution, but in spite of its evident evolutionary usefulness we do not, Sen points out, adopt an uncritical attitude towards pain. It would seem, then, that reason can take its own view of things – perhaps even of itself. Sen tellingly cites Buddha's 'dismay at ... the sufferings of disease, old age and death', and his 'judgment that killing animals and eating their flesh is a terrible way to live even though nature has tended to favour the devouring of one species by another'. The question

Buddha thus puts to us is whether human values are merely an evolutionary accident, or, worse, an evolutionary mistake. Tennyson believed that a resolution of this dilemma could only lie 'behind the veil'.[6] He and Buddha were effectively committed to the bare possibility of transcendent experience. But supposing such an experience is for most human beings an impossibility: values in such a case would simply persist as a problem. Would they merely be something that may be thought – more's the pity! – or would they be, after all, in some absolute, 'Fregan' sense, true?

On this Thomas Hardy at least knew what he thought. He seems wholly convinced that human values are irrelevant to evolution, precisely because he shares Buddha's compassion for people and animals. Biologically, he suggests, life is structurally committed to ends which we cannot identify, never mind identify with, yet not even this tragic insight frees us from our sense of self and of moral allegiances; *nor should it*. The power of Hardy's writing derives largely from his willingness to side with individual consciousnesses and with values in their unequal contest with the logic of evolution. He assumes that once values have supervened upon the project of survival and reproduction, they cannot be argued away. Mercy, Pity, Peace and Love are precious even if they are irrelevant to evolutionary criteria of progress, even if they actually diminish our capacity to 'correspond'.

Such, certainly, is the implication of the dairy-maids' passion for Angel Clare in *Tess of the D'Urbervilles*. They know 'their infatuation' is futile, 'purposeless', 'self-founded', and socially stupid; but they also know that it is natural, and that it fills them with 'killing joy'. This knowledge and this emotion impart to them a 'resignation' and a 'dignity' which would have been lost if they had had any chance of success with Clare.[7] Instinctively they resort to a group solidarity which enables them to endure frustration, but supervening on this adaptive response ('resignation') is an apparently non-functional value ('dignity') which more successful adaptation, more exact correspondence, would surely have aborted. What is the point of valorising a failure to mate? Not surprisingly, the two noblest, most intensely valued of Hardy's characters, Sue Bridehead and Jude Fawley in *Jude the Obscure* – Jude shares his author's compassion for animals – are heroic precisely because they are defeated by evolution, because they do not 'correspond', and their efforts to reproduce are appallingly stultified. The same is true of the novel's other, apparently more robust heroine, Arabella.

The one writer on evolution in the last thirty years to confront this problem honestly (making the optimism of his most prominent disciples, Richard Dawkins and Daniel Dennett, seem reductive) was Jacques Monod. In *Chance and Necessity* (1970), Monod emphasises 'the *totally* blind' character of biological processes;[8] they are 'chemically *arbitrary*', 'intensely conservative ... utterly impervious to any "hints" from the outside world' and consequently resistant to further pressures to correspond (*Chance and Necessity*, pp. 106, 108). Spencerian 'development' only takes place, therefore, through chance mutations in the way genetic 'information' is locked into the molecular structure of DNA, through accidental failures in the reproductive system. It follows that '*evolution is not a property of living beings*, since it stems from the ... *imperfections* of the conserving mechanism' (ibid., p. 112). 'The universe was not pregnant with life nor the biosphere with man' (p. 137).

In the long run, of course, the logic of natural selection ensures that only changes leading to greater reproductive efficiency in the resulting genotypes – their 'correspondence' – are preserved: hence Dawkins's celebrated selfish gene. Dawkins's almost equally celebrated 'selfish memes' – patterns of mind-activity which are successfully replicated in the soup of human culture, like primitive life-forms in the primeval ocean – also derive from Monod, but Monod is less optimistic than Dawkins (or Spencer) about evolutionary processes determining human culture. Ideas are passed from brain to brain not because they are 'true', nor even because they are 'beautiful' or 'good' – all three words are themselves memes – but only because, like organisms in the gut, they suit the hosts in which they lodge, or because, like viruses, their hosts suit them.

Ideas with particularly high 'invading potential' of this kind, Monod suggests, 'are those that *explain* man by assigning him his place in an immanent destiny, a safe harbour where his anxiety dissolves' (p. 155). The need for such explanations arose in prehistoric times, when survival depended more on the 'cohesiveness' of the human group than on truth, and was sufficiently protracted to have 'influenced the genetic evolution of the innate categories of the human brain'. Almost from the beginning, Monod argues, human beings were genetically predisposed to animist beliefs. They still are – hence the ongoing power of 'animist' theories of human existence. Monod cites the examples of Islam and Marxism, but he would also have included Buddhism among the animist myths, as well as what he calls the 'disgusting farrago of Judeo-Christian religiosity, scientistic progressism, belief in the "natural" rights of man and utilitarian pragmatism' (p. 159). Twenty-five years later, this farrago seems to have survived better in the meme-pool than the Marxist alternative.

But even if Monod's theory 'that the fear of solitude and the need for a complete and binding explanation are inborn' (p. 164) is ill founded, the combination of genetic and cultural factors in human life still leaves us with problems. In line with Spencer's dictum that '*Every active force produces more than one change – every cause produces more than one* effect', language, for example, has other, genetically grounded functions beside that of saying things; speech individuates us – every voice pattern is distinct – and unites us to a particular group; it facilitates sexual interaction, play, aggression, and various kinds of bonding, conscious and unconscious. In other words, it functions like an animist belief, while of course serving other purposes, including that of conveying information. Moreover when we observe the interactions of human groups from which we are relatively detached, we can recognize the difficulty they have in distinguishing the 'affective' and 'rational' components of their linguistic interactions. We may even recognize that this is why they feel strange to us and familiar to each other, that a shared taste for unspecifiable, a-rational ingredients in a particular meme-soup, irrespective of the merits or demerits of those memes on other grounds, is a condition of human society and so of human speech.

But this involves us in immense difficulties. How can we tell whether a judgement that reproductive efficiency is a better measure of evolutionary progress than quality of life (or vice versa) is at heart animist or rational? Monod believed he had identified the one escape route from this dilemma. We can transcend the genetically grounded, irrational meme-maze, which is the condition of our ability to 'correspond' as social beings, only if we recognize and act on what he calls 'the postulate of objectivity' (p. 31), which states: 'in the realm of ideas ... those presenting objective knowledge [are] the only source of real truth' (p. 158). It was this postulate which I invoked in my claim that in principle 'correspondence' and 'heterogeneity' are measurable.

Adopting it, Monod argues, is a matter of choice not insight: 'the positing of the principle of objectivity as the condition of true knowledge *constitutes an ethical choice and not a judgment reached from knowledge, since according to the postulate's own terms, there cannot be any "true" knowledge prior to this arbitral choice*' (p. 163). Moreover, it is not compatible with our genetically grounded predisposition to opt for the comforts of animist thought. 'Cold and austere, proposing no explanation but imposing an ascetic renunciation of all other spiritual fare', the postulate is unable to 'allay anxiety' as animist theories do, but rather it brings to an end 'the ancient covenant between man and nature, leaving nothing in place of that precious bond but an anxious quest in a world of icy solitude' (p. 158). Traditional systems present humankind with values given from above, or at best, as in the case of Marxism, in the dialectics of nature. By adopting the postulate of objectivity, modern man 'knows that [values] are his and his alone, but now he is master of them they seem to be dissolving in the uncaring emptiness of the universe' (p. 161). The Hardyean note is unmistakable: what the postulate has to offer us is dignity.

And the Hardyean note also exposes the weakness of the claim. Monod's argument that the postulate is alien to genetically organized predispositions, and so is in some sense 'free', does not stop its being consistent with others and so (almost certainly) determined. The argument is trapped by Spencer's law of multiple effects. The discomfort which the postulate generates in minds constitutionally predisposed to animist views could appeal, after all, to a functional instinct for asceticism: membership of an austere, select band of savants devoted to a high ideal might meet emotional needs in intellectuals struggling to survive in a world dominated by competitive, animist go-getters. The appeal of asceticism is evident in Islam, Christianity and Buddhism – why not in science? As Monod's own rhetoric shows, the power of 'the objectivity meme' may owe a lot to puritan self-valorisation.

The quest for a value system by which to judge evolution seems therefore to be self-defeating because we have no reason to believe that the 'fittest' idea, the successful meme, will either be the 'truest', if like Dawkins and Dennett we are empiricists, or the 'best', if like Hardy we hunger and thirst after justice and such like chimeras. It only needs to be an idea that lodges comfortably in our intellectual gut, and that will depend, among other things, on our previous intellectual diet. As such it may perform an important function unrelated to its meaning as an idea. The irony of Hardy's position is that even our sympathy with Sue and Jude may be a product of social bonding, a way of being 'modern', or 'tough-minded', or (for some readers) 'English'.

The problem is particularly acute when we apply the model of biological evolution to history and thought. Both Spencer and Monod make this move, Spencer in applying the principle of heterogeneity to the range of biological and cultural phenomena, and Monod in applying a model developed by geneticists to the realm of ideas. The example of Spencer makes clear the dangers of the latter.

Spencer made three serious mistakes. He assumed that evolution could only take place if the organism was *not* 'impervious to any "hints" from the outside world', but responsive to them; in other words he believed in the heritability of acquired characters. Cultural differences were therefore genetically transmitted, and so some races were inferior to others. He also believed that the logic of evolution ought to operate unhindered in society: he was the only begetter of 'Social Darwinism'. He regarded it as 'proved' that 'savages' had smaller brains than Europeans, and that Sandwich Islanders, Hindoos and Australians lacked cognitive complexity. In 1858 he wrote: 'As the child's features – flat nose, forward-opening nostrils, large lips, wide-apart eyes, absent frontal sinus, etc ... resemble ... those of the savage – so, too, do his instincts. Hence the tendencies to cruelty, to thieving, to lying, so general among children.'[9] He opposed all forms of state support for education as 'unnatural'. Yet if anyone in the nineteenth century believed that he believed in the postulate of objectivity, Spencer was that person.

Recent exponents of Darwinian theory and cognitive philosopy have made assumptions about consciousness not unlike Spencer's assumptions about inheritance. In *Consciousness Explained*, for example, Dennett makes great play of avoiding any explanation of consciousness which would involve the implied, move, 'And then a miracle occurs' (p.38). As a cognitive philosopher he believes that the computer provides the best available model of how the mind works – he likens 'animist' memes, for example, to computer viruses. The main thrust of his account of the mind, moreover, is against the presumption of its unity. The systems of the brain, including those associated with consciousness, are programmed to cooperate. Consequently, though consciousness in general and a sense of selfhood in particular may contribute to, or at least arise from, the functioning of the organism, neither operates as a coordinating centre of the whole system, which has no need of a centre. 'Consciousness' does not 'direct' behaviour – this might indeed require a 'miracle'. It possibly just happens alongside behaviour and its determinants in the system.

But even if we accept this model, problems remain. As Galen Strawson, no opponent of empiricism, has pointed out, experience 'is as real as rock'.[10] To downgrade it does not account for it, but only makes doing so less urgent. Second, as long as explanations of consciousness remain guesses, guesses with a lot going for them perhaps (just as Spencer's about the transmissibility of acquired characters had a lot going for them a century ago), the role of consciousness in human life remains unassessable. Either it is practically functionless, an accidental outcome of the functioning of real mental powers – the psychological equivalent of the human chin, which is not an organ in its own right, but a feature of the human face arising out of the arrangement of the bones of the lower part of the skull – or it has a job to do. Such a job may have arisen as a side-effect of the emergence of an originally non-functional effect, rather as in some cultures the chin has acquired significance as a pseudo-secondary sexual characteristic. Such a chance outcome would, of course, be consistent with models of evolutionary process which embrace Spencer's law of multiple effects, and there is an antecedent probability that so prominent and universal a feature of the human species gives advantages to those who have it. Nevertheless, consciousness, on Dennett's own showing, has not been explained at all, either in terms of how it operates, or in terms of what it does. But Dennett is right in this, that as things stand it does not have much evidential value in a discussion of how we operate in the world.

Sen may be convicted of overconfidence, therefore, when he argues that 'no matter how or why our ability to reason may have developed, we may use it as we like' ('On the Darwinian View', p. 18). So too Monod when he asserts that the 'ethic of knowledge does not impose itself on man; *on the contrary it is he who imposes it on himself* (*Chance and Necessity*, p. 164). Both claim for the consciously rational human being powers which cannot be explained in theory or tested in practice. Monod actually uses the word 'transcendence' of his postulate (ibid., p. 165). Nevertheless, he and Sen must be right after all. Otherwise it is hard to see how Dennett, Dawkins and Strawson can hold their ground since their own theories point to the possibility of there being short- and medium-term biological advantages in many intellectual self-deceptions. Strawson is aware of the dilemma, and honestly begins his book by declaring the unproved assumptions on which it is based, but this can only win interim acceptance. In the end, Monod is right to insist that it 'is obvious that the positing of the principle of objectivity as the condition of true knowledge *constitutes an ethical choice and not a judgment reached from knowledge*'. But it follows from this that no theory of human life and thought is scientifically adequate if it denies us the capacity to make just this choice. What has to be decided, therefore, is whether transcendence of the kind proposed by Monod and Sen is compatible in principle with the Darwinian account of the emergence of humanity, so fiercely defended by Dennett, Dawkins and Strawson.

Let us try a thought experiment. We will assume that a group of beings has evolved who spontaneously perform more or less separate innate or learned routines, often without being conscious of doing so, and in any case never being fully conscious of all that such processes must involve. Among these innate or acquired routines is a capacity from time to time to try something out, to select alternative possible courses of action, to 'choose' between them, and to learn from the results. There is no reason, if there are no innate or learned promptings towards one option rather than the other, why such 'choosing' should not be random, that is, a sub-routine independent of the sub-routine involved in the initial (also random or at least arbitrarily limited) deliberation. When alternative choices have been surveyed and perhaps categorised, an entirely separate and unconscious routine plumps for one out of those that seem appropriate, and it is duly subjected to the test of implementation.

Let us now suppose these creatures develop language skills. These include the ability to speak, but verbal language is supplemented by culturally developed signing – frowns, shrugs, smiles and so forth. Language so understood and practised would have definable reproductive advantages for the individual: in extending cooperative activity between members of a group, in facilitating access to suitable mates, and as a way of competing with rivals. The skilled use of language, for example, might involve deceiving competitors in appropriate circumstances, but such deceptions would always be dependent on most uses of language facilitating cooperation between group members. As Dennett puts it, there 'is much to be gained from communication if it is craftily doled out – enough truth to keep one's credibility high but enough falsehood to keep one's options open'. Either way, there is evidence that 'developing and testing hypotheses about what [is] going on in the minds of *others*' stimulates 'the development of *self*-consciousness', and that 'an ability to make one's behavior sensitive to, and manipulative of, the thinking of another agent' also enhances one's 'ability to make one's behavior sensitive to one's own thinking' (*Kinds of Minds*, pp. 126, 120).

How would language skills operate when one of these creatures was engaged in the routine for trying something out? It might, for instance, ask for help. For this to be a wise course of action, it would have to have strong grounds for expecting help to be forthcoming, even though, from time to time, a rival might give the wrong advice, or disingenuously profess ignorance, or aggressively humiliate the asker. Another possibility might be for the creature who asked for help to answer itself, out loud in the first instance, but then in secret, to keep the advantages of its course of action, or the vulnerability inherent in taking a risk, from the minds of competitors. Dennett thinks such a development would be immensely significant in the evolution of consciousness, of a fully human inner life.[11] Next, language might be useful in easing the tensions of choosing by articulating 'good reasons' for the choice *after* it has been made. Our creatures might make up a more or less fictional story about their choosing and believe it. Again this is a theory favoured by Dennett (*Consciousness Explained*, pp. 416-18). Finally, language might enable these creatures to communicate the results of their experiments to each other – to warn one another 'altruistically' against a possible course of action, the pay-off for such 'altruism' being indirect but substantial in survival and/or reproductive terms. There is nothing in this scenario incompatible with complete determinism, provided we assume that, notwithstanding our current ignorance on the topic, there is nothing 'miraculous' in consciousness, and that in any case no state of consciousness *as such* is the determining factor in any of these creatures' actions.

Let us now imagine one of these creatures being born with a new, randomly developed adaptive mechanism which enabled it to *believe*, at the deepest, wordless level,[12] that creatures like itself could act freely, that when one of them tried something out, it did so in a state of real self-command and radical autonomy. This, it needs to be emphasised, would not be the outcome of a narrative composed to explain behaviour, but of a prior belief, operating independently of verbal articulation. As a determinant of action, of course, such a belief would have to take its chance. Other organically constituted behaviours and beliefs might also come into play, spontaneous or deliberate. On occasion, for example, our newly evolved creature, acting on different beliefs, might try to coerce a companion, or allow a companion to try something out because it wanted to check the result without taking any risks itself, or because it wished to gain credit for not interfering, or because it was afraid. In none of these cases would it be primarily motivated by its companion's perceived freedom as an end in itself, and in all of them it would be determined by foreseeable consequences. But there *might* be occasions when it could 'see', 'theorise', 'intuit' a companion as genuinely free; of course consciousness, or (again following Dennett) consciousnesses in various drafts,[13] would be involved in this vision, this 'theoria', but only as part of the system as a whole. It might also be possible for all the subsystems and decision-making routines which make our creature an 'agent', 'the host of competences that [its] body has developed'[14] and that it 'automatically' knows about, to *combine* in wanting its companion, then and there, to act freely. It might proceed through speech and gesture to make these wishes clear; it might, on the other hand, do and say nothing, abstain from interference, keep its will a secret, and thereby 'permit' its companion to act as it chose. Either way such a creature would be in a state of genuine freedom, because its behaviour would be rational but not determined by any foreseeable outcome. Moreover, if its companion were similarly motivated, they might both be able to see and give expression to a sense of the mutual freedom uniting them.

Fragile and intermittent as its operation might be, there are good reasons for believing that a capacity of this kind would be useful in evolutionary terms. A shared predisposition towards non-coercive relationships might enhance the cohesiveness and adaptability of members of a group; it might stimulate cognitive activity, and make the individual's behaviour even more responsive to its thinking. It would admittedly generate a new kind of vulnerability – a freedom-bestower could never outmanoeuvre a calculating advantage-seeker, though it might set an example for the advantage-seeker to follow. Nevertheless the freedom-bestower's condition would be the ultimate adaptive mechanism, the point at which, in pursuit of genetic survival, the evolutionary process ceased to rely on supremely sophisticated but essentially prudential calculations of the kind developed among Dennett's crafty competitors,

ceased, in effect, to 'correspond' with the universe, and launched itself
into authentically innovative exchanges between agents. Individual identity and responsibility would thus have supervened, however tentatively,
upon a universe which until that moment had been rigorously determined.

Whatever the chances of such a scenario having actually occurred –
and we are only exploring possibilities – some such development is a
necessary, though not a sufficient, condition for the transcendence on
which Monod's postulate and the entire empiricist enterprise depends.
Empiricism requires 'transcendently' truthful as well as rigorously intelligent agents, and it is truthfulness, along with a whole set of other
norms or values, which comes into play when one intelligent agent
consents to the freedom of another. Lying, deceiving oneself or others,
sharing in collective, animist self-deceptions, withholding the truth, are
self-evidently forms of unfreedom, giving rise to actions which are
rationally *determined* by needs and desires, by programmed bits of the
self, over which, *ex hypothesi*, control cannot be exercised. When two
persons are mutually committed to truthfulness, on the other hand,
when they choose to avoid, even implicitly, deceit or competitiveness in
their relationship, they acquire not only the ability to make and keep
promises, to love, honour and even obey each other, but also to engage
in intellectual exchanges grounded in allegiance to Monod's postulate.
There is no other way of doing it.

Values of a related kind operate in the lives of Tess's companions in
the milking-shed, of Sue Bridehead at least until her children die, of
Jude when he is not drunk, and of Buddha. Jude and Sue have their
fragile freedom and personal identities virtually crushed out of them;
Buddha apparently moved towards an unqualified personal wholeness
in which all his desires, the entire array of routines, sub-routines, instincts, habits, hopes and attachments out of which the 'fiction' of
Siddhartha the Brahmin had emerged, were obliterated in a consent to
'freedom' so unqualified that even his centred, freedom-bestowing identity was given up. If this is so, then the answer to Sen's question is
frankly anthropocentric: progress in a Darwinian universe is movement
into humanity; but full humanity is an act of unqualified humility
before all that we are not, even if that involves abandoning the intentionality written into evolution itself.

A final question remains, however. The contrast between Buddha and
Jude Fawley is a disturbing one. Can Hardy have been right after all,
that the evolution of consciousness, and so of the freedom and personal
perspectives which it can generate, even the perspectives or sublime
non-perspectives of Buddha, is a cruel accident? The model of personal
freedom I have proposed is fragile. Even if it corresponds with the facts,

in Darwinian terms it has not had great success, either in fiction –
witness *Jude the Obscure* – or in fact – witness human atrocities over
ten millennia and five continents. Perhaps Buddha is no more than an
animist myth, a comfort serves in a whirlwind, and even then only for
those whose material and personal circumstances enable them to enter
into its logic. Compassion, however transcendental, however rational
and free, may leave things much as they are:

> Pity would be no more,
> If we did not make somebody poor
> And Mercy no more would be
> If all were as happy as we.
>
> William Blake, 'The Human Abstract'

CHAPTER THREE

Why John Stuart Mill chose to go to the Devil

In a celebrated passage in *An Examination of the Philosophy of Sir William Hamilton*, John Stuart Mill argues that while we 'cannot know God as he is in himself', we can judge actions attributed to him by his followers. After all, we judge human actions without knowing human beings as they are in themselves, and why should God be different? He grants that attributes such as 'goodness, knowledge, power, are relative', and that God is supposed to be Absolute, but, he contends, to argue that 'the Relative attributes of an Absolute Being are unknowable', and that divine goodness 'is not the goodness which we know and love in our fellow-creatures' is an abuse of language. There can only be one set of moral standards, and one kind of moral language, for God and for us, even if God is all-knowing, all-powerful, 'infinite' and 'absolute', and his creatures not so. It follows that if God's actions are incompatible with 'the best human attributes', Mill will not worship him. 'I will call no being good,' he declares, 'who is not what I mean when I apply that epithet to my fellow-creatures; and if such a being can sentence me to hell for not so calling him, to hell will I go' (*An Examination*, pp. 119–24).

This grand *non serviam* is joined to an angry denial of Hamilton's claim that only 'a free agent ... has ... responsibility' (ibid., p. 550), and that 'the legitimacy of retribution, or punishment' depends on free will (p. 575). The necessitarian, Mill replies, can defend the utility of punishment that benefits the offender or protects others. When a reviewer pointed out that punishing people for their own good was inconsistent with views Mill advances in *On Liberty*, he replied that children may 'be punished for their own good', and he had expressly left open the possibility of adopting the same principle with 'adult communities which are still in the infantine stage of development' (p. 577[n]). The 'infantine' peoples of India, in other words, must submit blindly to Mill's 'adult' values, but Mill himself may question God's exercise of, for example, the virtues of prudence and distributive justice, even though God doesn't have to make educated guesses about the future and Mill does.

An Examination contains many such contradictions. It misreads Hamilton, and its reliance on Euclid, Newton and 'psychological truths ... proved by experience' has worn badly (p. 219). But the polemic is so assured, the hauteur so stylish, the argument so detailed and apparently exhaustive, that its own confusions are overlooked. Moreover the basic charge against Hamilton is apparently damning. Hamilton's claim that free will in human beings requires 'a Creator who is a free intelligence' (p. 550) allegedly exposes his 'over-anxiety to make safe a foregone conclusion' (p. 621). His 'obviously' untenable notion of personal freedom functions as an illicit premise for 'the doctrines of natural religion'. But why 633 pages to make this point?

The answer lies in two essays by Hamilton, on Cousin (1829), and on Reid and Brown (1830), endorsing the relativist premise (long antedating Saussurean linguistics and its deconstructionist offspring) that the 'condition of intelligence ... *is difference*; and an act of knowledge ... only possible where there exists a *plurality of terms*'.[1] Now, as de Saussure emphasises and Hamilton insists, systems of understanding or signification based exclusively on difference have no external foundation. Cousin tried to get round this problem by identifying the unconditioned (God) as 'the generative principle' of mind, and so 'conceivable by consciousness and reflection, under relation, difference, and plurality'. Hamilton rejects this easy fix. He specifically denies that God can be 'positively construed to the mind'. He allows no exception to the principle that all knowledge is of 'the different ... the modified' ('M. Cousin's *Course*', pp. 202–3). The self, for example, is known only through 'a conception of not-self'.[2] But God, as Absolute and Infinite, cannot be known even in this way. The 'Infinite' and the 'Absolute' are *ex hypothesi* 'out of all relation', and so provide nothing positive for finite consciousness to hang on to. They cannot be related to anything that can be imagined, nor to anything that can be conceptualised. Both imagination and understanding are therefore precluded from engagement with them.

Mill found these relativist arguments deeply disturbing, and they remain a problem, though modern empiricists like Richard Dawkins and Daniel C. Dennett do not always see them that way. Dawkins writes of ideas or 'memes' reproducing themselves like genes, and identifies some memes – 'the meme for, say, belief in life after death' – as parasitical, like viruses (*The Selfish Gene*, p. 192); but he never explains how (without a vicious regress) 'a good idea' can be distinguished from a 'virus'. Dennett holds that as a 'tactic of self-protection [and] self-control' we construct 'selves' in the form of fictional narratives (*Consciousness Explained*, p. 418), and was gratified to find this commonplace of literary theory in David Lodge's *Nice Work*; but Lodge's Robyn (like Hamilton) argues that stories about the self are stories about the world, and vice versa, leaving nothing outside the text. What about 'all the bookcases, buildings, bodies, bacteria ... ?', Dennett asks (ibid., p. 411), like Samuel Johnson kicking a stone to refute Berkeley; yet by not staying for an answer he leaves the boundary between fiction and science to be defined *ad hoc* by such fictional entities as miracle-despising scientists. Among the suggestions I make in this paper is that distinguished thinkers can thus shrug off the relativist challenge because Mill has convinced nearly everybody that Hamilton was a fool and his followers religious fanatics, that there was nothing in relativism for empiricists to worry about anyway, and that Mill himself is as constant as the northern star.

In the 1860s, however, relativism presented serious problems to empiricists and traditional theists alike. The problem for Mill was that Hamilton's resolution of their shared dilemma compromised empiricism. Hamilton gets a fix on relativism by challenging the Humean claim (subsequently endorsed, as we have seen, by Dennett, 'Robyn' and others) 'that *self* is only an *illusive phænomenon* ... and our present unity merely that of a system of co-ordinate activities' ('Philosophy of Perception', p. 206). As a premise or a conclusion, Hamilton argues, this deconstruction of the self is self-defeating, since it requires 'an organ to tell the lie of our personality; and to quote as authority for the lie itself, the perfidy of consciousness'. But 'Intelligence cannot gratuitously annihilate itself', nor endorse a theory by which intelligence is itself effectively fictionalised (ibid., p. 196). But if at the same time 'personality' is closed to immediate scrutiny – and Hamilton insists that it can only be understood as an inference from the experience of difference – it follows that *both reason and a reasoner* must be given, independently of empirical evidence, as 'primary convictions', and irrefutable because an argument inconsistent with them would 'be inconsistent with its [own] premises' (p. 200).

But, like free will, primary convictions or generative beliefs make the observer an active contributor to experience, which is precisely what Mill cannot allow. In his Humean model, therefore, a law-governed world generates consistent impressions on a receptive mind. (This is a very traditional idea – in effect Mill is reviving the *intellectus passivus* of Thomist philosophy.) Mill accordingly endorses Hume's 'bundle' theory of consciousness: 'every part of the [experiential] series [is] linked with the other parts by something in common', but nothing else is affirmed except 'the states of consciousness themselves' (*An Examination*, p. 257). Like Hume, Mill hypothesises a foundation for consciousness, but insists that it is no more than a neutral medium, in which 'spiritual' effects are the outcome of 'spiritual antecedents' (ibid., p. 552). Mind is consciousness and its workings are transparent. Specifically they generate 'the conception of Possible sensations', and are subject to the Laws of the Association of Ideas.

The Laws of Association are:

> 1st. Similar phænomena tend to be thought together. 2nd. Phænomena which have either been experienced or conceived in close contiguity ... tend to be thought of together ... 3rd. Associations produced by contiguity become more certain and rapid by repetition ... 4th. When ... the bond between ... two ideas has been ... firmly riveted ... the facts or phænomena answering those ideas come at last to seem inseparable in existence. (pp. 219–20)

Granted these premises, Mill contends, 'associations naturally and even necessarily generated by the order of our sensations and reminiscences of sensation' will effect belief in an external world, and even 'cause it to be regarded as an intuition' (p. 221), but this belief is demonstrably only an acquired product which does not require a prior intuition of self. To these Laws of Association must be added the Law of Oblivescence, the detailed working of which Mill does not specify, but which is crucial to his system.

In important respects this is a thoroughly modern theory, having structural affinities with Alan Turing's Universal Turing machine, precursor of the digital computer. A Turing Machine, in Dennett's summary, has five components:

> (1) a *serial* process (events happening one at a time), in
> (2) a severely restricted *workspace*, to which
> (3) both *data* and *instructions* are brought
> (4) from an inert but super-reliable *memory*,
> (5) there to be operated on by a finite set of primitive *operations*.
> (*Consciousness Explained*, p. 212)

Dennett holds that 'Conscious human minds are ... serial ... machines' of this type (ibid., p. 218). So does Mill. The senses, he insists, 'are only open to let pass single attributes at a time' (*An Examination*, p. 316). Consciousness is thus a *serial* process operating in a restricted *workspace*. Descartes proposed a similar model by making the pineal gland 'the turnstile of consciousness' (*Consciousness Explained*, pp. 105–6). Descartes and Mill therefore have to cope with something like 'the notorious von Neumann bottleneck' in Turing-style computers, 'a single register for results and a single register for instructions' (ibid., p. 264), a problem Mill cleverly overcomes by attributing lightning rapidity to the operations of consciousness and the operation of the Laws of Oblivescence. He holds, for example, that a skilled pianist's every finger-movement is a momentarily conscious act which is promptly forgotten. So is the scrutinising of every word, and the turning of every page in the reading of a book (see *An Examination*, p. 337). He also denies Hamilton's claim that we see wholes first (say the human face) which we subsequently break down into component elements. On the contrary, he argues, we scan the details of a complex object one at a time in rapid succession and subsequently construct the larger whole by combining them together. The majority of these distinct moments of consciousness are promptly erased under the Law of Oblivescence, but *memory* of *instructions* (the Laws of Association) is reliable, and those past experiences that are recalled (more or less accurately), 'inasmuch as they are believed, are as much objects of immediate knowledge as things ... present' (ibid., p. 145). When not in use, however, all memories are *inert*; they are not even 'latent', though 'the power of reproducing [that is, 'accessing'] them' is (p. 330). The Laws of Association and Oblivescence thus operate as a set of *primitive operations*.

The similarity between Mill's and Dennett's thinking, however, ends here. For Dennett 'consciousness' is only 'more or less' a 'virtual' machine. It is not really what it seems, but is 'implemented – inefficiently – on the parallel hardware that evolution has provided for us' (*Consciousness Explained*, p. 218); and that hardware is also part of mind: 'all varieties of thought or mental activity ... are accomplished in the brain by parallel, multitrack processes of interpretation and elaboration of sensory inputs. Information entering the nervous system is under continuous "editorial revision" (ibid., p. 111). This would be anathema to Mill. He insisted that consciousness is mind pure and simple: no event outside consciousness is a mental event, and its operations are in principle perfectly efficient. He would have been appalled by Dennett's suggestion that the 'order of representing' in consciousness does not always represent the ordering in real time of the content of experience (pp. 151–3). Mill knew that if the content of consciousness were determined by *mental* factors outside it – say by unconscious 'editorial processes' – the Laws of Association would lose their explanatory power. The question that modern empiricists have to answer, therefore, is whether, in reaching conclusions wholly incompatible with Mill's Associationism, they have effectively denied their own premises.

Hamilton, on the other hand, is much more Dennett-like than Mill. His model of mind resembles a slimmed-down version of the 'architecture of the brain' which Dennett hypothesises, that is, a 'massively parallel' system, 'with millions of simultaneously active channels of operation'. As 'the complement of our intellectual energies', consciousness admittedly remains central for Hamilton ('Philosophy of Perception', p. 163), but it provides only coded knowledge of the world and of the past, and many of its other 'energies ... and ... modifications' are unconscious. It is 'constructed out of what we are not conscious of' and is only 'a small circle in the centre of a far wider sphere of action and passion'. We can also carry on 'several distinct states of consciousness' at once (*An Examination*, pp. 327, 331, 339). Hamilton would have

had no difficulty, therefore, with Stanislaw Lem's claim that consciousness is not the 'sovereign helmsman of all mental phenomena' ('Non
Serviam', p. 305). However he would have denied that 'personality' is
therefore *only* an illusion. The specifics of my sense of myself at any one
time may be more or less accidental, but if the 'sphere of action and
passion' is to be redeemed from self-annihilation, Hamilton argues,
something like the Thomist agent intellect, or George Berkeley's 'thinking active principle that perceives, knows, wills and operates'
(*Philosophical Commentaries*, p. 198), is a necessary inference.

The significance of these different models of mind can be usefully
examined in relation to Concepts, Deconstruction, Representation, Real
Presentation and Language. In each case the position taken by Hamilton will appear consistent with modern philosophy of mind, and that
taken by Mill will not.

First, Hamilton's theory of concepts. According to Mill, we 'think by
means of ideas [that is, impressions] of concrete phænomena ... presented in experience, or represented [that is, copied or reproduced] in
imagination, and by means of names ... associated with certain elements of the concrete images' (*An Examination*, p. 386). Hamilton,
however, denies that impressions alone (direct or copied) can generate
thinking properly so called. Thought, he maintains, also requires general notions or Concepts, a concept being a 'form of thought' (ibid.,
p. 438) which discloses 'a quality, property, power ... relation ... under
which we recognise a plurality of objects as a unity' (p. 366). Thought,
therefore, is distinct from sensation, and is founded upon concepts. But
concepts are 'cognizable ... only in ... relation ... to one or more ...
objects' (p. 370), and only by the understanding: the imagination cannot 'figure to itself anything general or universal' (p. 374). *Potentially
universal relations* are thus, for Hamilton, fundamental components of
thinking. Mill, however, refuses to distinguish between imagination and
understanding and denies that 'any line between the Matter of Thought
and its Form' can be drawn (p. 441).

But Gottlob Frege's identification of concepts with arithmetical functions draws just such a line, and effectively confirms Hamilton's definition
of a concept as 'a term of relation, to one or more objects' (p. 370).[3]
Mill is particularly scornful of Hamilton's admission that a concept,
'formed by an abstraction ... would again fall back into ... confusion ...
were it not ... fixed and ratified by a verbal sign' (p .378), but, as Frege
acknowledges, a set of arithmetical relations without an argument (as in
an expression in which a number is not substituted for 'x') is also
practically unthinkable. Nevertheless he rightly insists that a function's
specificity and independence of any 'argument', its universality, are not
in doubt. We may speak, therefore, of a function without an 'argument'

which would make it thinkable (for example, 'x + 1'), and we may speak of a concept without an object which would make it thinkable (for example, ' ———— conquered Gaul'). Frege calls functions without 'arguments', and concepts without objects, 'unsaturated'. They become saturated when numbers replace algebraic terms in a mathematical expression, or when the names of objects replace the blanks in a conceptual expression. Saturated expressions in arithmetic have 'values' depending on the numbers replacing the letters: 'x + 1', for example, acquires the value '8' when '7' replaces 'x'. Saturated concepts (and mathematical equations) either have the value 'The True' or the value 'The False': 'Pompey conquered Gaul' has the value 'The False'; 'Caesar conquered Gaul' has the value 'The True'.

All of this is in explicit opposition to Mill. In particular Frege rejects Mill's argument that arithmetic is empirically based. Nevertheless both Frege and Mill believed that in principle language could be accurately aligned with the world. For Frege this meant that *every* coherent sentence, that is, every grammatically correct sentence-form in which all the concepts are 'saturated', either has the value 'The True' or the value 'The False'. So, when the grammatically correct sentence-form 'All horses are ————' is completed with the words 'grey' or 'fish' or 'moons of Saturn', it has the value 'The False'; when it is completed with the words 'animals' or 'warm-blooded' or 'the offspring of one stallion and one mare' it has the value 'The True'. Bertrand Russell, however, famously put a paradox to Frege. He pointed out that the class of classes which do not include themselves cannot be included in itself, nor excluded either, so there are logically complete sentences which do not fall under either 'The True' or 'The False'.[4] This compelled Frege to acknowledge the limits of his conceptualism. His conflation of concepts with functions, however, was not invalidated.

Hamilton's relativism, I suggest, was to Mill what Russell's paradox was to Frege, an apparently trivial but in fact a potentially disastrous piece of news. However, unlike the chastened Frege, Mill stuck to the Enlightenment ideal of a systematic correspondence between the world, experience and language. For him phenomena are signified unambiguously in proper names and class names, and their relations expressed in correctly constructed sentences. Hence his inability to grasp Hamilton's proto-Deconstructionism. Again concepts are relevant. Hamilton maintains that 'the mind furnishes itself with concepts ... before it begins to judge', but 'that every Concept is built up by a succession of judgments'. For Mill this is 'the very crown' of self-contradiction (*An Examination*, pp. 406, 408). How, he asks, can 'a thing ... be prior, or posterior, or prior and posterior to itself'? (ibid., p. 450[n]). But all he is objecting to here is the 'always already' inherent in relativism, of which his own empiricism is an example. What are 'psychological truths ... proved by experience' (that is, psychological truths proved psychologically) if not always already? By comparison, Hamilton's always already is remarkably modest: his ur-concept is an intuition of existence linked to an ur-experience of difference. In the words of his editor, John Veitch: 'If we are only conscious as we apprehend an object, and only apprehend it as we affirm it to exist, existence must be attributed to the object by the mind; and this could not be done unless existence as a notion virtually pre-existed in the mind.' But the mind does not know that it has the 'concept' of being until it also has the experience of difference which enables it to compare and judge. 'The first act of experience awoke it, and the first act of consciousness ... was an affirmation of the existence of something. The first ... act of comparison is thus the discrimination of existence from non-existence; and the first ... judgment ... is the affirmation of existence ... the denial of non-existence.'[5] What is wrong with this from Mill's point of view is that it requires a primitive understanding to judge a primitive imagination; it predicates a generative processing of experience by mind, not a constitution of mind by experience. He accordingly insists that the given is, must be, in the world not the mind.

Unfortunately, this ideal of unqualified mental passivity before experience creates a problem in relation to memory. Hamilton only needs memories to be representations in the technical sense, that is, *structurally conformable* to the experiences recalled rather than copies of them. In Hamilton's system, for example, remembering 'the rapid sweep of [a] river' may not even be 'a form of motion at all' (*Hamilton*, p. 158). Dennett argues similarly that 'the products of visual perception are not, literally, pictures in the head even though *what they represent* is what pictures represent well: the layout in space of various visible properties' (*Consciousness Explained*, p. 131). Mill prefers the model of memory copying past experience, its contents being 'as much objects of immediate knowledge as things ... present'. He is stuck in effect with the primitive Humean theatre,[6] in which memories are 'equivalent to impressions', only weaker. 'When I shut my eyes,' Hume writes, 'and think of my chamber, the ideas I form are exact representations [that is, *copies*] of the impressions I felt' (*A Treatise*, pp. 82, 3). But, as Mill admits, this cannot explain how impressions which literally cease to exist when they leave consciousness are reconstituted within it, how 'something which has ceased ... can be gathered up, as it were, into a single present conception, accompanied by a belief of reality' (*An Examination*, p. 242). He declares this problem to be philosophically unsolvable.

Hamilton's much more sophisticated reliance on memory as representation not reproduction of past experience accounts for his Real

Presentationism. Hamilton and Mill agree that we are conscious only of 'phænomenal attributes', and do not have direct access to things 'in themselves'. Yet in what looks like the most flagrant violation of this principle, Hamilton asserts that we do have 'immediate knowledge of [an] extended object *as extended*' (ibid., p. 18). His claim, however, is not that 'notions of the primary qualities *resemble* ... [but only] that they *truly represent* these objects', and he distinguishes between '*similarity in existence* and *similarity in representation*' (*Hamilton*, p. 159). He holds that spatial relations between the parts of an object, or between different objects, can be both *conceptualised* and accurately *represented*. This corresponds neatly with Dennett's account of the brain learning to represent the world 'by a process of generation-and-selection of patterns of neural activity in the cerebral cortex' (*Consciousness Explained*, p. 193). Thus the movement of passing traffic is *represented* to consciousness in the action of the Doppler effect on the hearing, but the same effect operating in light waves to produce changes of colour never becomes immediately information-specific, at least in the human brain. But the Doppler effect on light *can* be conceptualised, represented mathematically and empirically tested. Indeed, as Turing demonstrated, *all* relations, *all* concepts, '*all* "rational thought" and perhaps all "irrational thought" as well' can be expressed and preserved digitally or in any other representational system (ibid., p. 214). The entire communication system of the modern world indeed depends on Real Presentationism as defended by Hamilton. Dennett can have his 'bookcases, buildings, bodies, bacteria ... ', but as representations, not as realities or impressions of realities. As manifestations of variously representable relations they are 'real' without being 'outside the text'. The potential universality of concepts has thus been theoretically justified and experimentally confirmed. Hamilton was right and Mill wrong.

The final topic on which Mill is at odds with later philosophers is Language. Cousin, it will be recalled, seeks to avoid the contradictions of relativism by asserting that 'the unconditioned, the absolute, the infinite, is immediately known in consciousness by difference, plurality and relation', that 'God' is a generative belief. Hamilton's reply is remarkably Wittgensteinian. He argues that Cousin in effect creates an illusion of metaphysical depth by sending the word 'Unconditioned' 'on holiday' (*Philosophical Investigations*, p. 19). The terms absolute and infinite require thinking away 'those very conditions under which thought itself is realized' ('M. Cousin's *Course*', pp. 202–3). Thus the absolute is not a part, nor composed of parts; it is unqualified wholeness and unity, 'the unconditionally limited' (or *de*limited). Similarly the infinite is the unconditionally *un*limited. Neither is a concept, because neither can be conceptualised 'within or under something else', *but that does not mean they may be united in a single term*. They are, in fact, mutually exclusive. Cousin's 'Unconditioned', therefore, is 'not a notion, either simple or positive, but only a fasciculus of negations; – negations of the conditioned in its opposite extremes, and bound together merely by their common character of incomprehensibility' (ibid., p. 206). Mill, however, reports Hamilton as arguing 'that our *ideas* [impressions] of the Infinite and the Absolute are "only a fasciculus of negations"' (*An Examination*, p. 51 – my italics). This mistake was only partially corrected in the fourth edition; Mill continued to argue that an Absolute Being must possess '*all* predicates ... [and be] absolutely good, and absolutely bad; absolutely wise and absolutely stupid; and so forth' (ibid., p. 57), as if Hamilton included 'the absolute' in 'the infinite' after all.

He gets into this muddle by ignoring the argument that negations of the conditioned are united only in a word. An argument of this type, however, is potentially very dangerous to his basic stance, which is why he tries to get round it. His quarrel is not, of course, with Hamilton's conclusion. They are agreed that the 'Unconditioned' or 'God' is *not* given in thought. For Mill, however, experience is all – anything not known in or through experience is a nullity. Language must therefore receive its structure and validation from the same set of laws as govern experience. Words like 'Unconditioned', 'Infinite' and 'God' cannot be subject to different rules from words like 'happiness', 'horse' and 'James Mill': the settled and determined order of the world by which impressions organise themselves in experience and are copied in memory determines the only word-game the thinker is permitted to play. Incompatible qualities can, of course, be attributed to the same object; 'every simple idea', Hume argues, 'has a simple impression, which resembles it', but 'our *complex* impressions and ideas' may not be 'exact copies of each other' (*A Treatise*, p. 3). Further opportunities for error arise when complex impressions, especially in their weak remembered form, are attached to words. Even experience can be misleading: Mill conducts thought experiments about possible worlds in which the data of experience suggest that two and two make five, and that parallel straight lines do meet. What he cannot do, however, is approve of an argument that discovers incompatible meanings in words at the *conceptual* level, since he denies that such a level exists. Our use of the words 'inconceivable', 'infinite', 'absolute' and 'God' must arise through the operation of the laws of mind operating on experience, and their misuse can only be in demonstrable violation of those laws.

Mill thus finds himself laboriously explaining how these terms arose and the limits of their legitimate use. If God exists, for example, he is a

God of Phenomena, 'Absolute' in qualities known phenomenally, 'in goodness, or ... in knowledge ... in ignorance, or ... in wickedness'. 'Infinite', too, must refer 'to some particular predicate' (*An Examination*, pp. 55–6, 58). God's mind, like ours, is only thinkable as a 'bundle', as the 'series of the Divine thoughts and feelings prolonged through eternity'; and the 'relation between his works ... and [his] thoughts and feelings' is also like ours (ibid., pp. 239–40): as all our volitions are 'determined by spiritual antecedents (*e.g.* desires, associations of ideas &c.)', so 'there is nothing absurd ... in ... believing that [God] is necessitated to will what is good, by the love of good and detestation of evil which are in his own nature' (pp. 552–3).

This, of course, is to refuse to meet Hamilton on his own ground, just as it fails to meet Dennett on his. Hamilton argues that one way or another the inconceivable must be the case. His use of the word 'inconceivable', of course, assumes it to be a category of the understanding ('that which cannot be conceptualised'), not a category of the imagination ('that which cannot be imagined'). So either we are free or we are not, but neither condition can be *thought*, however close we may come to *imagining* either or both. There are two reasons for concluding that freedom is unthinkable. In the first place, we 'cannot conceive absolute commencement' which free will requires, however vividly we may imagine it. In the second, a 'determination by motives cannot, to our understanding [that is, conceptually] escape from necessitation ... and [besides] the free acts of an indifferent, [would be] morally and rationally, as worthless as the pre-ordered passions of a determined will' (*An Examination*, pp. 555–6). In other words, if reason is decisive in motivating my actions I am not free, but if my choice is contrary to reason, I am plainly mad and therefore not free either.[7] So freedom is in principle not susceptible to conceptualisation. But the same is true of 'the doctrine of necessity' which supposes 'an *infinite* non-commencement'. Similarly, either the universe had a beginning, or it did not, but again neither absolute commencement nor infinite duration is conceivable. We have thus reached the limits of conceptualisation, without having reached the limits of our knowledge, since we know that in each case one or other of these contradictions must be true; either we are free or we are not; either the world had no beginning, or it, and possibly events within it, in some radical way did not happen as part of a predetermined sequence. (How easily Hamilton would have accepted quantum theory – how horrible it would have seemed to Mill!) We are thus required to accept 'the existence of principles ... as true in practice, though they cannot be explained in theory'.[8] In this extreme circumstance, having no other way of thinking coherently, we may fall back on analogy based on antecedent probability. We *know*, logically, that *some* metaphysical truth obtains that cannot in principle be conceptualised. But if the human mind is unified in its intellectual activity, as a condition of its having any coherent thoughts at all, then it would be unwise not to predicate a comparably intelligent unity at the otherwise unthinkable origin of things; and similarly to the extent that human beings are deemed to act freely, so by analogy the origin of all that is the case may act freely also.

It is clear that Mill would much rather admit the existence of God on empirical grounds (hence his professed respect for the argument from design) than concede the validity of this *way* of arguing. For if the mind and the world are a bad fit, if 'the capacity of thought is not to be constituted into the measure of existence' ('M. Cousin's *Course*', p. 204), or if consciousness is not determined by its own contents, but is subject from time to time to freedom of choice, then the empiricist programme, as a self-sufficient account of human understanding, must fail. *An Examination* is a massive, anxious attempt to resist this conclusion.

The problem for Mill is not the existence of God – this is a sideshow – but Hamilton's claim that, as 'the conditions under which all else is comprehended', the 'primary data of consciousness' are not *in relation* to what they enable us to perceive (*An Examination*, p. 89). This is yet another proto-Fregan argument. In his late essay, 'Thoughts', Frege calls the contents of experience 'ideas', but, he insists (as ever resisting the 'psychological' traditions of the school of Mill), 'Not everything is an idea.'[9] 'Ideas' have to have an owner, and that owner cannot, without a vicious regress, be an 'idea'. 'I', therefore, is what Frege calls a 'thought', specifically of that which 'has "ideas"' and which 'grasps "thoughts"'. 'I exist' is a thought. It can be grasped, and it is either true or not true. But it is not an experience, like the smell of lilac, of which the words true and false are meaningless.

Hamilton's position is no less proto-Wittgensteinian, in this case an anticipation of Wittgenstein's claim that 'the description of a sensation does not contain a reference to either a person or a sense organ'.[10] Consciousness, in other words, cannot point to itself as it can point to particular sensations and inferences. But it cannot be dismissed as a nullity, like the concept of something which is not identical with itself. In Hamilton's words, we have access only to 'the relative manifestations of an existence which in itself it is our highest wisdom to recognise as beyond the reach of philosophy' ('M. Cousin's *Course*', p. 204). Or in Wittgenstein's, 'What we cannot speak about we must pass over in silence' (*Tractatus*, p. 74). Frege makes exactly the same claim from a different direction by refusing to say what the word 'true' signifies. As a 'thought', 'I exist' is true exactly as Pythagoras' Theorem is true, but neither 'thought' is verified empirically, and what you mean in claiming either or both to be true is not among those things about which it is possible to speak. This entire complex of argument, so fundamental to modern philosophy, Mill 'decline[s] to recognise' as 'a complete perversion' of 'established meanings' (*An Examination*, p. 89).

Recent philosophers might question the price he has to pay for this and his other refusals of Hamilton's claims, especially those about concepts and representation. The collaborative work of Dennett and Douglas Hofstadter, for example, is founded on the notion of the '"representational system" ... [as] an active, self-updating collection of structures organized to "mirror" the world as it evolves'. Such mirroring involves the reproduction, not of Humean impressions, but of Hamiltonian structural patterns in different media. Hofstadter argues convincingly that a 'representational system should be able to keep on going even if cut off from contact with the reality it is "reflecting" ... [and] should ... continue to evolve in a way that reflects, if not the true way the world will evolve, at least a probable way' (*The Mind's I*, pp. 192–3). This is possible because, when structures – relations – are translated from one system to another, the logic of their possible development can be translated also. A false note in recorded music is in principle correctable in digitally expressed rules; a computer can generate its own variations on a musical theme; it can even generate a pastiche of a symphony by Mozart, without a note being played, or heard in any mind's ear. And like computers, we too can reproduce, translate and restructure the *patterns* in our experience, even if the exact copying of particular experiences, their flawless reproduction, is not so much impossible as meaningless. Hofstadter's assertion, that the 'general thesis ... "Mind is a pattern perceived by mind" ... is perhaps circular, but it is neither vicious nor paradoxical' (ibid., p. 200), is perfectly sound. Hamilton would have found it quite unexceptionable, but it would have been deeply shocking to Mill.

And he would have been right to find it so, because Hoftstadter implicitly confirms Hamilton's claims rather than Mill's, and thereby *demonstrates* the need for generative beliefs or 'thoughts' or certitudes about the self, which are prior to and independent of the empiricist programme. He writes of representational systems mirroring the world, but all they in fact mirror, by his own account, are relations, precisely other systems of *difference*, of which the concepts 'out there', 'the world', and 'not me' are instances. This, for Cousin and Hamilton, is proof of the limitations of empiricism, but empiricists have created the illusion that the move from Hume's impressions and Mill's phenomena to the representations of Dennett and Hofstadter is an unproblematical development of the empiricist idea. Mill knew better: that is why he made such a fuss about the Hamiltonian paradox, and stuck stubbornly to his four principles – the identification of mind with the theatre of consciousness, of the mind's contents with phenomena or impressions, of the mind's activity with the Laws of Association and Obliviscence, and of 'spiritual antecedents' as the sole determinants of volitions. He would have no truck with Real Presentationism, even in the form of representations of relations which his professed successors, Dennett and Hofstadter, find so persuasive.

This very stubbornness, however, explains why he was so successful. *An Examination* is the supreme expression of empiricist intransigence. It is not surprising, for example, that when Dennett detects signs of 'extravagant metaphysical theses' in a passage of *An Examination*, he assumes that Mill is incapable of such egregious error (*Elbow Room*, pp. 90–91). He is wrong, but empiricist ideology can never acknowledge *fundamental* differences between its supporters, and usually succeeds in exacting unearned deference from its opponents. As a result Bertrand Russell was able to dismiss Hamilton as having 'had little influence';[11] but in fact, directly or indirectly, he did influence both Carlyle (who was reluctant to admit it) and the later Arnold; his defence of representation enriched Newman's principle of economy; the relativist tradition haunts the writing of James, Conrad and Kipling; and through his other editor, Henry Longueville Mansel, Hamilton demonstrably influenced Pater and so Wilde. But Mill is rarely challenged directly. Even Newman avoids direct confrontation with empiricism in *A Grammar of Assent*, while the material in his 'Philosophical Notebook' was never published. All the other writers I have mentioned make appeasing gestures towards empiricism in general and determinism in particular. Mill may have lost the intellectual battle, but his opponents left him in possession of the field.

And they did so partly because, for all his protestations that we are just a series of thoughts, feelings and necessitated volitions, Mill himself is truly present in his book as an active principle of formidable substance, freedom and power. In Frege's words, 'What would this whole play be without a spectator?' ('Thoughts', p. 366). Frege is right: when Mill says he will not bend the knee to a God who does not meet his own exacting moral standards, he is speaking nothing but the truth.

CHAPTER FOUR

Walter Pater
and the Higher Decadence

In the Preface to his most celebrated work, Walter Pater writes:

> The Renaissance, in truth, put forth in France an aftermath, a wonderful later growth, the products of which have to the full that subtle and delicate sweetness which belongs to a refined and comely decadence, just as its earliest phases have the freshness ... the charm of *ascesis*, of the austere and serious girding of the loins in youth. (*The Renaissance*, p. 30)

This paper is concerned with both the early and late phases of nineteenth-century decadence. It is my contention that the thought of Pater, and of his disciples, especially Oscar Wilde, derives from a carefully articulated body of conservative and ultimately religious philosophising reaching back to the 1820s, that Pater's exhibitionist indulgence in textual play, and the witty deconstructionist anarchy of Wilde's prose, have an elaborately theorised intellectual basis which links him to Sir William Hamilton and John Henry Newman, and separates all three from the entrenched empiricism of John Stuart Mill.

In that extraordinary exercise in intertextuality, *Marius the Epicurean*, Pater's hero turns to the teachings of Heraclitus of Ionia to discover the earliest articulation of his own instinctive Epicureanism, according to which the 'impression of permanence or fixity in things' is condemned as 'false'.[1] Heracliteanism of this order is still very much with us. In a recent review of Hillel Schwartz's *The Culture of the Copy* in the *London Review of Books*, Terence Hawkes takes exactly Pater's line on the permanence and fixity of things when he condemns the 'culture of the copy'. We need, he argues, to

> 'think difference' ... Since there can be no immaculate 'sameness', there can be no absolute repetition. Whatever returns affirms, by returning, its difference. However carefully crafted, copies only gesture towards an 'identity' they cannot possibly realise ... If there is no absolute repetition, there exist only degrees of difference, and, seen thus, difference becomes central to experience.[2]

No experience, no thought, no word can be an exact copy of another. The world, consciousness and language are Heraclitean fire. But, according to Pater, the rejection of fixity is only a 'first, merely sceptical, merely negative step': it may seem 'to make all fixed knowledge impossible ... to be almost identical with the ... doctrine ... that the momentary, sensible apprehension of the individual [is] the only stand-ard of what is or is not, and each one the measure of all things to himself', but this is an illusion. Mischievously appropriating positivist terminology, Pater argues for 'a large positive system of almost religious philosophy' (*Marius*, I, pp. 130–32). In the '"perpetual flux" of things and of souls', he tells us, there is, after all, a return, a return not of particular sensations, not of copies, but of form itself,

> a continuance, if not of their material or spiritual elements, yet of orderly relationships, like the harmony of musical notes, wrought out in and through the series of their mutations – ordinances of the divine reason, maintained through the changes of the phenomenal world; and this harmony in their mutation and opposition, [is], after all, a principle of sanity, of reality, there. (*Marius*, I, p. 131)

This use of the word 'harmony' might cause alarm. Pater is notorious for trying 'to bring literature ... under those conditions, by conformity to which music takes rank as the typically perfect art'.[3] But this is by no means the trivial formalism it is taken to be. On the contrary, Pater insists that 'over and above ... colour and mystic perfume and ... reasonable structure' – the merely aesthetic – truly great literature 'finds its logical, its architectural place, in the great structure of human life'. The key words linking the two halves of this claim are 'harmony', 'reasonable structure', 'logical', 'architectural' and 'structure of human life' – all implying determinate systems of relation, coherent and recur-ring patterns of difference, which persist 'in and through the series of their mutations'. This is a much tougher idea than the deference to human values signalled in the phrase 'the great structure of human life'. The principle of sanity in art, in logic, in language, and in mind is not, Pater argues, the permanence of things, or meanings, or possibilities of sensation, or even values, but the permanence and the return of 'rela-tionships ... wrought out in and through the series of their mutations'. This is a conception which takes us to the heart of what may be called the literary theory of the Decadents.

In his essay on 'Style', Pater noted that 'the late Dean Mansel ... wrote a book of fascinating precision ... to show that all the technical laws of logic are but means of securing, in each and all of its apprehen-sions, the unity, the strict identity with itself, of the apprehending mind' (*Essays*, p. 21). Actually Mansel is a rather trite philosopher. What Pater is claiming, however, is not trite at all. There are, he suggests, in sensation, reason, passion, desire, language and the arts, systems of difference and systems of systems of difference, by which the unity of the world, of the work, and of persons is constituted. Hawkes argues that a 'strategy dedicated to establishing that this is the same as that ruthlessly subordinates difference to identity ... presupposes unity and coherence in the perceiver and ... [so] serves to validate the prejudices that finally crystalise in the cogito' ('Making = Taking', p. 16). But if Marius *is*, Pater suggests, it is not because he *thinks*, but because he *sees*; and what he sees are not things to be copied, but systems of difference in systematic relation.

Citing Mansel was an interesting tactic. Henry Longueville Mansel was editor with John Veitch of the posthumous works of Sir William Hamilton, and was the subject of some of John Stuart Mill's most strenuous and dismissive polemic in *An Examination of Sir William Hamilton's Philosophy*. To praise him was therefore to oppose Mill, as Pater consistently did. In his first essay, on Coleridge, which appeared in the same issue of the *Westminster Review* as George Grote's laudatory review of Mill's book,[4] Pater announced his preference for the relativist doctrines that *An Examination* treats with such scorn. Mill's definition of 'Matter ... [as] a Permanent Possibility of Sensation' (*An Examination*, p. 227) is no less in Pater's sights in *Marius the Epicurean*, when he declares that only those 'heavy with wine' attribute to 'the phenomena of experience a durability which does not really belong to them' (I, p. 129). Pater is thus from first to last in radical opposition to the school of Mill, and the culture of the copy to which Mill gives his allegiance.

The mind, according to Mill, is constantly engaged in the production of copies of accumulated experiences through the law-governed association of ideas. Hamilton, on the other hand, is committed to a much more sophisticated model of mind based precisely on difference in Hawkes's sense: his entire career as a philosopher is based on the claim, discussed in detail in two important essays in 1829 and 1830, that the 'condition of intelligence ... *is difference*; and an act of knowledge ... only possible where there exists a *plurality of terms*' ('M. Cousin's Course', p. 215). From first to last, Pater gives his allegiance to this principle. 'Modern thought', he declares in the essay on Coleridge, 'is distinguished from the ancient by its cultivation of the "relative" spirit in place of the absolute ... To the modern spirit nothing is or can be rightly known except relatively under conditions' ('Coleridge's Writings', p. 1).

But even in this first essay, he moves beyond a merely negative relativism. Coleridge, he notes, believed that perception engages with 'form or mould' as well as with matter, and that in forms 'such as space, unity, causation ... we arrest and frame the many attributes of sense' (ibid., p. 15). But for Pater this makes artistic production too passive, 'almost mechanical ... the associative act looks like some organic process of assimilation' (p. 16). He wants to give proper emphasis to agency and deliberation in the mind of the artist.

By exquisite analysis the artist attains clearness of idea, then by many stages of refining clearness of expression. He moves over his work, calculating the tenderest tone, and restraining the subtlest curve ... Culture, at least, values even in transcendent works of art the power of the understanding in them, their logical process of construction, the spectacle of supreme intellectual dexterity which they afford.

Coleridge's criticism ... recalls us from the work of art to the mind of the artist; and after all, this is what is infinitely precious, and the work of art only as the index of it. (p. 17)

Here, in phrasing as well as idea, is the kernel of Wilde's 'Preface' to *The Picture of Dorian Gray*, just as an earlier account of 'man' in the same essay as 'the most complex of the products of nature' might almost be a self-description of Dorian's seducer, Lord Henry Wotton:

the mind of the race, the character of the age, sway him this way or that through the medium of language and ideas. It seems as if the most opposite statements about him were alike true; he is so receptive, all the influences of the world and of society ceaselessly playing upon him, so that every hour in his life is unique, changed altogether by a stray word, or glance, or touch. (p. 2)

Or possibly by the sight and smell of *lilas blancs*, so redolent for the ageing Lord Henry of his first encounter with Dorian. Nor is it just the differences between sensations that the decadent artist cultivates. The relative spirit has its moral side as well: it 'begets an intellectual finesse, of which the ethical result is a delicate and tender justness in the criticism of human life' (p. 26).

At the heart of this celebration of artistic endeavour is the concept of an intimate connection between 'moments of strange excitement' and 'an external, concrete form – a statue, or play, or picture' (p. 17), that is between 'the power of the understanding' and a 'logical process of construction'; and implicit in this is the conviction that formal relations in one system are reproducible – in technical terms they can be 'represented' – in others, and specifically that form in nature or art can be systematically related to form in thought and feeling. On this basis Pater can claim that art is a work of mind in the fullest sense – not something that merely grows spontaneously like a living organism, but something that is *done* by a unified and coherent agency with real knowledge of what it sees and of what it does with its experience.

But there are limits for Pater even to the autonomy of the cultivated mind, as references to Newman in the essay on Coleridge, and his other writings, make clear. Pater sees Newman as resisting, like Coleridge, the 'current of new life' (p. 1) signalled by relativism, and yet thereby, if unintentionally, disclosing 'the inmost delicacies' (p. 21) of 'the modern aspirant to culture'. The reason for this is that Newman, like Pater,

opposes the hegemony of empiricism. Newman figures even more significantly in *Marius the Epicurean*. When Marius recognizes, for example,
that a discourse on Stoicism could be easily reconciled with his own
Epicureanism, the following, avowedly anachronistic questions occur to
him: 'What really were its claims as a theory of practice, of the sympa-
thies that determine practice? It had been a theory, avowedly, of loss
and gain ... of an economy ... What did it lose, or cause one to lose?'
(II, pp. 14–15). This reference to the title of Newman's novel, and the
use of the term 'economy' in its Tractarian sense, confirm intimations,
in earlier references to 'conscience', 'reserve' and 'assent', that Newman's
Loss and Gain, and his writings generally, are being deliberately evoked.
The echoes of Newman persist. The Epicureans of Cyrene, for example,
are condemned as 'faulty economists'; with 'a little more of ... not
unreasonable "assent," ... they might have profited by a hundred serv-
ices to their culture'; Marius is the wiser 'economist' – the effect of his
wide reading in Epicurean philosophy is compared to that of Catholi-
cism on a convert from a narrow, non-conformist sect; as part of a
world-embracing system, a 'wonderful order, actually in possession of
human life', he even feels the need to limit his own freedom of action 'in
concession to ... that great crowd of admirable spirits' who engage in
the pursuit of this grand vision: 'he would be ... mistaken in his estimate of values, of loss and gain, and untrue to the well-considered
economy of life which he had brought with him to Rome ... if he did
not make that concession' (II, pp. 22–8).

What is going on here? In the first place, it seems clear that Newman's
term 'economy' is immensely useful to Pater. It exactly expresses the
ways in which the systems of difference, and the systems of systems of
difference, which make up Marius' world, are distinct from one another, and yet capable of synthesis. But the ultimate effect of the references
to *Loss and Gain* in *Marius the Epicurean* is to discriminate sharply
between incompatible views.

Both novels describe a young man's approach to, and apparent absorption by, the Catholic Church, but Newman's protagonist, Charles
Reding, is committed to conversion before meeting a single believing
Roman Catholic; his decision 'has been entirely the working of [his]
own mind'.[5] He does not even enter a Catholic church until the penultimate chapter, after he has become thoroughly acquainted with, and
convinced by, Catholic doctrine. Marius, by contrast, through his Christian friend, Cornelius, is introduced to Catholic worship in the house of
the widow Cecilia without ever entertaining a single Christian idea. He
is impressed by what he finds there, but only by the *structure*, the
harmony, of belief and feeling in the life and liturgy of a Christian
household, a literal *economia*, and thereafter he never once enquires

into, or receives instruction in, Christian doctrine. At the end of the novel, however, he is mistakenly imprisoned with a group of Christians. Out of purely natural affection, he lays down his life for his friend, Cornelius, by persuading the guard that the non-Christian among the prisoners is Cornelius and not himself. Later, he too is released, but only because he is dying; 'in his extreme helplessness' the country people, thinking he has been baptised, give him Communion and the Sacrament of Anointing, and bury him as a martyr (II, p. 224).

But he is a martyr only to friendship. The title of the chapter in which these events are related is 'Anima Naturaliter Christiana' – a contradiction in terms, as Pater well knew; for Christian doctrine is precisely that one cannot be 'naturally' a Christian, that the Christian condition is a 'supernatural' effect of Sanctifying Grace, and specifically of Baptism. But to be baptised, Marius would have had to make a declaration of Faith by reciting the Creed, to engage with Christian dogma; and in the essay on Coleridge Pater places 'all that is desirable in the world, all that is sympathetic to its laws' in 'trenchant' opposition to the dogmatic spirit ('Coleridge's Writings', p. 10). He never abandoned this view. Thus Marius never looks beyond his present life; it has been his 'deeper wisdom', 'with a sense of economy, with a jealous estimate of gain and loss, to use life, not as the means to some problematic end, but, as far as might be, from dying hour to dying hour, an end in itself – a kind of music, all-sufficing to the duly trained ear, even as it died out on the air' (*Marius*, II, p. 219). The dying Marius moves admittedly beyond this moral solipsism, but not much beyond it. Cornelius' ongoing life becomes for him a sign that 'a permanent protest [has been] established in the world ... against any wholly mechanical theory of [humanity] and its conditions' (II, p. 221). In effect, positivism and empiricism won't be left ruling the roost unchallenged after his death – and this assurance is all the future life Marius desires.

This modest protest against empiricist ideology clarifies the limits of the higher decadence. Pater affirms confidently and with rigour 'the unity, the strict identity with itself of the apprehending mind'. He attributes comparable objective unity to the structures of human utterance and the logical process of its construction. But he holds back from specific belief, from assent. This holding back is deeply characteristic. From time to time in the course of the novel Marius gazes at young men exercising, but he only gets into the bed of his pagan friend Flavian when the latter is dying, and he can do more than *look* at Cecilia whom he contemplates marrying – such are the practical limits of his affective life. He is capable of personal and responsible engagement only with his own perceptions, his own vision or '*theoria*'. And on the same principle he values 'economies' while avoiding specific beliefs. Entranced, as it were, by the beauties of so many *langues*, he shies away from engagement with specific *paroles*.

It is not surprising, therefore, that the relativist thinker Pater praises by name is Mansel. According to Mansel, 'I am immediately conscious of myself seeing and hearing, willing and thinking'.[6] The self, in other words, as disclosed directly in consciousness, is simply given. Hamilton's account is much more complicated. Since 'all that we know either of ... mind or matter is ... the different ... the modified', he argues, a knowledge even of the self is contingent on 'a conception of not-self' ('Philosophy of Perception', p. 165). To begin thinking, therefore, the mind must have, always already, what Hamilton calls primary convictions – however inchoate – in its own moral and intellectual coherence, even though that coherence is not immediately knowable and can never be conceptualised. Hamilton, in other words, believes in the *Anima Naturaliter Dogmatica*, the mind as that which positively affirms not God but itself. By contrast, all the mind has to do in the thought of Mansel, of Marius, and of Pater is to 'discover', to see itself.

Marius' life is accordingly dedicated simply to seeing. Had Pater read Newman more carefully, however, he would have recognized such seeing as, in Newman's words, rendering it 'impossible to discriminate between assent, inference, and assertion, on account of the otiose, passive, inchoate character of the act in question' (*Grammar of Assent*, p. 53). And such discrimination is essential.

> Doubt, Inference and Assent, are, with reference to one and the same proposition, distinct from one another ... For instance, in the case of Revealed Religion, according as one or other of these is paramount within him, a man is a sceptic as regards it, or a philosopher, thinking it more or less probable as a conclusion of reason; or he has unhesitating faith in it, and is recognized as a believer. If he simply disbelieves, or dissents, then he is assenting to the contradictory of the thesis, viz., to the proposition that there is no Revelation. (p. 27)

Marius the Epicurean is written in calculated opposition to this view. Marius does not question or infer, *he does not believe or disbelieve*. Instead he has others do the assenting for him as he looks on, which is why, no matter how exalted his aspirations, he remains, after all, a 'decadent' like his creator.

CHAPTER FIVE

Arnold and Newman: The Phenomenological Option

Noli foras ire, in te redi, in interiore homine habitat veritas.

I

I start with the quotation from St Augustine's *De vera religione* with which Edmund Husserl concludes *Cartesian Meditations* because I wish to examine potentially significant relationships between phenomenology, literature and the dogmatic principle. I concentrate on two writers, Matthew Arnold and John Henry Newman.

In Arnold's case the inner man of whom St Augustine and Husserl write is virtually inaccessible. Thus in 'The Buried Life'[1] Arnold hypothesizes a genuine self concealed within day-to-day experience; in moments of intense love 'the heart lies plain' (l. 86) and 'A man becomes aware of his life's flow' (l. 88), but even then he only

> thinks he knows
> The hills where his life rose,
> And the sea where it goes.
> (ll. 97–8)

The result is not just phenomenological fudge, but what Terry Eagleton calls a 'politically catastrophic vagueness' evident, for example, in 'The Scholar Gypsy' (78) and 'Thyrsis' (110).[2] The figure of the vagabond seventeenth-century Oxford scholar forever wandering the Cumnor hills in pursuit of 'the spark from heaven' (l. 171) which will disclose the Gypsies' secret knowledge of the 'workings of men's brains' (l. 46) encompasses both failures. The Gypsies' secret phenomonology is never disclosed, and the putative personal wholeness which the scholar embodies – 'Thou hadst *one* aim, *one* business, *one* desire' (l. 152) – and which the 'strange disease of modern life' (l. 203) prohibits, never has more than rhetorical adequacy. (Adequacy, according to Howard Foster Lowry, is a basic Arnoldian value.)[3] In 'Thyrsis' – Arnold's memorial to his dead friend, Arthur Hugh Clough – he is again in the Cumnor hills in pursuit of a vision of integration – this time an isolated elm tree, which he and Clough had taken as a signal that their 'friend, the Gypsy-Scholar, was not dead' (l. 29). A. Dwight Culler suggests that the central question in this poem is a 'loss of habit's power' that prevents Arnold from giving the landscape meaning as 'a region of the mind'.[4] This is also a political question, however, because the poem implies that Clough 'died' when he stopped looking for this region of mind himself, left Oxford and entered the hurly-burly of socially concerned good works (*Imaginative Reason*, p. 253). But if public engagement is a kind of dying, it is spiritually *and* politically important that the tree's reappearance – 'Bare on its lonely ridge, the Tree, the Tree!' (l. 160) – should represent an attainable goal. So is the 'adequacy' of Arnold's 'tact' in not taking possession of it – 'I cannot reach the signal-tree to-night' (l. 165). But the tree really only re-enters the poem as a grace, hope without work, another example of a poet only *thinking* he knows. The phenomenology of his intention is majestically ignored, which means that it is rendered politically nugatory also.

This objection cannot be met by claiming that while poetry, as Arnold put it in his correspondence with Clough, leaps over 'the articulations of the discourse' (*Letters to Clough*, p. 144), Arnold's prose develops a fuller account of how culture resists anarchy, both personal and social. Arnold, after all, claims only partial adequacy for his prose – as a criticism of life it yields to poetry. Adequacy, therefore, can *never* be made explicit, even by the fully qualified critic. It is not known 'in the abstract', but only when one is 'thoroughly penetrated' by the 'power' evident in 'specimens' of 'the very highest poetic quality'.[5] Eagleton condemns this celebrated '"touchstones" concept of criticism ... [as] an entirely intuitive response to some ghostly resonance supposedly common to a handful of poetic images ripped from their aesthetic and historical contexts' (*Criticism and Ideology*, p. 108). But Arnold's touchstones are not short cuts to sublimity – they can only function in minds that have engaged with the entire canon and have grasped both the whole work from which the touchstone comes and its bearing on the immense task which poetry has to perform. Always poetry must 'press forwards to the whole' (*Letters to Clough*, p. 124). Hence the inadequacy of the 'exquisite bits and images' (by definition incapable of becoming touchstones) which Arnold accused the Romantics of producing, and the wrongness of Clough himself striving heroically 'to get breast to breast with reality', before he had found an appropriate rhetoric, a 'natural mode of expression in poetry', in which detachment could flourish (ibid., p. 86).

It is in his development of the latter idea, however, that Arnold's real weakness discloses itself. An 'absolute propriety ... of form', he tells Clough, is 'the sole necessary of Poetry *as such*'. Propriety is determined by 'the world's general appreciation of naturalness' and takes precedence over 'the judgment of the mere thinker' and 'wealth and depth of matter' (pp. 98–9). Arnold's practice, both as a poet and a critic, suggests that he continued to believe that just such a 'worldly' sense of decorum is a condition of the subordinations proper to the grand style, of the part to the whole, of language to content, and of the temporary and provincial 'to the great primary human affections ... those elementary feelings which subsist permanently in the race, and which are independent of time'.[6] The detachment which facilitates appreciation of 'the whole' is thus crucially dependent on a stance determined by 'the world' or, more precisely, by a secularized Anglicanism: Arnold moves, Lowry suggests, 'along a *via media* ... towards that central quiet of the spirit which is the sign and seal of all abiding things' (*Letters to Clough*, pp. 51–2).

From this there develop distinctively Arnoldian versions of the tragic. John P. Farrell argues that Arnold sees tragedy as a 'doom visited upon ... noble and attractive men who are ... caught in a revolutionary climate in which the engaged forces become hardened and polarized into equally repugnant camps',[7] and 'in which access to the ideal is blocked by an antithesis that cannot be resolved', that is, because it resists resolution in terms of worldly propriety ('Tragic Vision', p. 117). Alternatively, J. Hillis Miller believes that in his pursuit of the immanent (the buried life), or of the transcendent (the unseen God of the mountain peak) 'Arnold finds that by separation from everything external he gets not possession of himself, but the final loss of life and joy'.[8] Arnold's only resource in either situation is apparently to make detachment, even in irresolution, heroically reflexive. So, despite the gloom of 'Empedocles on Etna' (47) which led Arnold temporarily to excise it from his works, the poem can be restored to the canon because its detachment places itself. 'Thyrsis', too, as an elegy, is properly about the mourner not the mourned, that is, about recovery in and through detachment and self-detachment. Similarly, at the end of 'The Buried Life', Arnold shifts from a collective first-person account of the epiphany of self – 'And what we mean, we say, and what we would, we know' (l. 87) – to an objectively cool, ironically cautious third-person account – 'And then he thinks he knows' (l. 96). 'Irony,' Miller suggests, 'like the stance of disinterestedness, is for Arnold a way of not being swallowed up by the world' (*The Disappearance*, p. 244).

But it remains a worldly form of detachment and puts 'the judgment of the mere thinker' firmly in its place. This conclusion is strengthened by a consideration of religious themes in Arnold's verse. On the subject of God, Arnold is casually inconsistent. 'Morality' (64), for example, moves from a nightmare of earnest self-denial to a vision of Nature blithely announcing her indifference to moral emotion, until she recalls a primordial experience of Morality's severe and earnest air:

> 'Twas when the heavenly house I trod,
> And lay upon the breast of God.
> (ll. 35–6)

Nature here has a personal intimacy with God like that of Christ and the beloved disciple at the Last Supper. In 'Empedocles on Etna', on the other hand, God is one with Nature and with Man; even railers whose understanding of the divine is inadequate to their bitterness are part of the Divine Being, though

> patiently exact
> This universal God
> ... quietly disclaims the cursings of himself.
> (ll. 297–8, 301)

Detachment, with the 'absolute propriety' necessary for 'the world's general appreciation', thus acquires exemplary and transcendent status.

Arnold's later theological works offer a possibly sounder defence, suggesting that his critics have missed an important element in his mature thought that may also be implicit in the poems. He refuses to pronounce God, identified as 'the Eternal not ourselves that makes for righteousness ... either a person or a thing'.[9] God may have conscious intelligence, but cannot be called a principle, or a unity, or an intention, or a revelation. The Divine is neither William Paley's watchmaker, nor the utilitarian moralist that John Stuart Mill adumbrates in his dispute with Sir William Hamilton. As 'eternal' and 'not ourselves', Arnold's 'God', like Hamilton's, is genuinely 'out of all relation' with the current and the contingent. Arnold the theologian thus tries to move beyond ideology – or at any rate to put all ideology under judgement.

His term for ideology is *Zeit-Geist*, and he was the most effective populariser of '*Weltanschauung* and *Weltanschauung* philosophy' in Victorian England. Husserl's account of this tradition[10] recapitulates all Arnold's leading conceptions – *Zeit-Geist*, culture, the pursuit of perfection, the free play of mind over the best that has been thought and said, and a high valuation of conduct and righteousness. The young Arnold professed to finding the 'uncertainty' entailed in the notion of *Zeit-Geist*, its incipient relativism, 'congenial' (*Letters to Clough*, p. 86), but he recognized also that in the 'confusion of the present times' a young writer would need 'a hand to guide him ... a voice to prescribe to him the aim which he should keep in view' ('Preface', p. 8). Relativism has its limits. '*Weltanschauung* philosophy', Husserl writes, 'teaches the way wisdom does: personality directs itself to personality' ('Philosophy as', pp. 143–4). But Arnold's hunger for a *current* voice, for presence, has to be placed in the context of his mature sense of the Bible as 'writing'. The mere act of inscribing, Derrida argues, liberates the words inscribed from the control of an author's intentions, even for the author as first reader. Arnold, too, finds that language, including biblical language, is 'in its very nature malleable'[11] and 'justifies *any* powerful and fruitful application of it'. The elements of Messianic prophecy, for example, 'belong of right to whoever can best possess himself of them for practice and edification' (*Literature and Dogma*, pp. 222–3). Scriptural language is 'thrown out, as it were, at certain great objects which the human mind augurs and feels after' (ibid., p. 243), at 'an immense reality not fully or half fully grasped by the writers' (p. 250). For Arnold, as for Derrida, there is no Leibnizian Book of the Universe, 'the earth's true Bible'.[12] For readers of Scripture, relativism is an opportunity, not an anxiety.

Textual relativization can be extended to Arnold's own works: I do not interrogate a poem such as 'Morality' as the utterance of a present and determining voice prescribing the aim I should keep in view; I encounter it rather as a text at play with the word 'God', and I make what fruitful applications of it I choose. I may even allow it to prescribe the aim I should keep in view. This assured proto-deconstructionism should enable Arnold to posit an 'Eternal' that really is out of all relation with the *Zeit-Geist*. Language is not tied systematically to the world in the prescriptive, law-governed manner of Locke and Mill. It therefore enables us to talk about 'God' without reference to any known system and the *Zeit-Geist* can be made subject to divine, even 'eschatological', judgement. In principle it may even be redeemed. Arnold, says Miller, believes in God, but not so that He can be spoken about; He 'transcends speech' (*The Disappearance*, p. 248). Arnold, says A.O.J. Cockshut, 'believed in Christ but could hardly believe in God'.[13] Both are right because Arnold's rejection of all propositions whatsoever concerning God constitutes a rejection of the powers of writing to specify religious truth. The free play of mind is not justified empirically as a way of encountering reality, but as a necessity determined by the contingency and relativity of all languages and all philosophies. Criticism is the free play of mind about the best that can be thought and said. The best that can be thought and said – quintessentially poetry – is itself criticism. The essence of this stance is its self-conscious circularity. Arnold, it would seem, is a proto-Nietzsche, or (at least if we follow Derrida) a proto-Levi-Strauss, engaging in 'the saddened, *negative,* nostalgic, guilty, Rousseauistic side of the thinking of play whose other side would be the Nietzschean *affirmation*' (*Writing and Difference*, p. 292).

Such comparisons have only to be made, however, to expose his inability to bear them. The detachment of the Eternal, not ourselves, is *unqualified*. But though Arnold's God does not relate to us, we must be able to relate to 'Him': 'righteousness', Arnold insists, 'is salvation verifiably' (*God and the Bible*, p. 230) – 'you verify [it] ... by experience! It *is* so; try it!' (*Literature and Dogma*, p. 370). But this surely creates phenomenological obligations for an Arnoldian theologian. *How* are we to try it? What will it be *like* to do so? Arnold never attempts an answer. The religious, the righteous life is located between two horizons, self and eternal righteousness, both of which must remain forever horizons. These limitations are clearly in evidence in his account of St Paul's attitude to the Resurrection of Christ. Arnold *knows* what St Paul consciously thought on this subject:

> if he had been asked whether he held the doctrine of the resurrection in the physical and miraculous sense, as well as in his own spiritual and mystical sense, he would have replied with entire conviction that he did ... But: –
>
> > Below the surface-stream, shallow and light,
> > Of what we *say* we feel – below the stream,
> > As light, of what we *think* we feel – there flows
> > With noiseless current strong, obscure and deep,
> > The central stream of what we feel indeed;
>
> and by this alone are we truly characterised.[14]

Important questions invite clear answers here. Is the *we* in the verse a poeticism for Arnold, or a real collective pronoun? If the latter, how do 'we' communicate with each other about the 'central stream' independently of speech and thought which in principle can never give adequate expression to it? On the other hand if it refers to the isolated subject, Arnold or the reader, the discriminations between speech, thought and feeling on which the entire argument depends are locked into a solipsistic mode of experience which renders detachment, criticism, meaningless.

'Modern *Weltanschauung* philosophy', Husserl writes, 'is ... a child of historical scepticism. Normally the latter stops short of the positive sciences, to which, with the inconsistency characteristic of every kind of scepticism, it accords real validity' ('Philosophy as', p. 130). This is Arnold's problem. Recognising modern thought as a mere emanation of the *Zeit-Geist*, he nevertheless stops short of denying objective validity to the empiricist norms which Enlightenment ideology endorses: *obviously* St Paul was wrong about the Resurrection. Hence Arnold's use of an ambiguous 'we', and his uncertainty about the place of the critic in the contemporary world. There is a crippling disparity between his urbanely facetious denigration of people and ideas which gives him lodgement as 'a mere man of letters' (*Literature and Dogma*, p. 239) in the European cultural scene, and the serious sense of nothingness which gives his critical, social and theological writings their importance. Unfortunately the gentlemanly worldliness with which he attaches himself to the world, while affecting to distance himself critically from it, dehistoricizes his prose. The society projected in his essays and the theological works, the world to which they are purportedly addressed, is perceived with vulgar superficiality.

It is great fun, of course, to write of bishops who 'talk of "doing something for the Godhead of the Eternal Son"', and who join 'the poor Bishop of Gloucester' in proclaiming 'the blessed truth that the God of the Universe is a PERSON"'(*Literature and Dogma*, pp. 280, 290); but in putting the matter so, Arnold falsifies contemporary theological debate and implicitly caricatures English society as well as the English Church. (Mill was at least prepared to *argue* with conservative Anglican theologians.) Arnold is even cruder in his treatment of Dissent, and, notoriously, English surnames such as 'Wragg'. But in not subjecting his own best thoughts to the discipline of effective dialogue with a widely disparate, sensitively perceived readership, he avoids having to treat any ideas really seriously.

The price he pays for this is severe. He makes it too easy for us *not* to think about his poems systematically, to read the 'Switzerland' poems, for example, as expressions of intense but passing feelings, not feelings that have provoked Arnold to think. Park Honan treats the sequence as if their sole interest for the biographer was the identity of Marguerite. But these are not poems, as Honan alleges, about a poet whose pride 'goads him to sexual conquest', and then defeats him 'by inhibiting his imagination'.[15] The first poem, 'Meeting' (34), speaks of Arnold's inability to commit himself *emotionally*, not of sexual conquest at all. It is not pride but 'a God' (l. 11) or 'guiding Powers who join and part' (l. 13) – pagan forms of the Eternal, not ourselves, with a curiously New Testament authority over marriage – who control and entrap him. Later, in 'Parting' (35), the Divine is apparently a person, then in 'To Marguerite – Continued' (37) once again remote and pagan. That 'moral desperado', Carlyle (*Letters to Clough*, p. 124), had denied 'God's' responsibility for the individual's isolation, but it is not enough to point out, as Honan does, that Arnold 'contradicts Carlyle's opinion' here (*Matthew Arnold*, p. 164). A disturbing emotional experience has forced Arnold to articulate the radical 'play' in his system of belief, uncertainties that are specific and public, and that stimulate him to a disturbed self-awareness – in 'A Farewell' (38) he is *feminised* by love.

> I too have wish'd, no woman more,
> This starting, feverish heart away.
> (ll. 31–2)

Yet it is easy to see why Honan does not give the poems this kind of attention. Their rhetoric conceals the nuanced character of the disagreement with Carlyle and the overtly insecure sense of self involved in it.

The instability in their vocabulary about the Divine makes the exact nature of our severance from one another ambiguous also. Isolation could be a datum of Empedocles' pantheistic universe, or it could be an interpersonal obligation laid upon us by the Eternal to accept each other's apartness. But this important, unresolved, tension is lost in Arnold's neutrally plangent lyricism.

Arnold, it seems, cannot leave ideas alone, but nor can he bring himself to rely on them. Remarkably, he does not adopt a liberal theology. He does not gloss the Incarnation, for example, in terms of what God has done in Christ. Arnold's Christ is a mediator only in the sense of being a remarkable teacher, whose doctrine is that righteousness is obligatory, that there is life in righteousness for those who try it, but that no revelation, no truth exists apart from that. In *Daniel Deronda*, George Eliot interprets the great Jewish doctrines of omnipotence, mercy, election, prophecy, law and messiahship in frankly humanistic terms. She thereby seeks to reinstate them. Arnold abandons them. He believes that 'the object of religion is *conduct*' (*Literature and Dogma*, p. 172), and that the Church must remain its principal agency (the Bishop of Gloucester notwithstanding). But he also requires the believer to do without opium. His God cannot be said to *do* anything, not even in Jesus, and his Jesus is terrifyingly alone. But this moving conception is lost even in the later works, because Arnold himself is not lost. He remains, precisely as a man of the world, detached still. It is a stance that enables him to admire and *place* Newman, and it prevents him from looking seriously at what the great doctrines of the Trinity and the Incarnation actually say.

II

The contrast with Newman in these matters is very striking. Newman always articulates ideas, his own and other people's, with care and exactness. He never shows a contempt for 'Protestants' like Arnold's towards the Dissidence of Dissent and the Protestantism of the Protestant Religion. He stands uncompromisingly behind the ancient credal formulations; he never leaps over the articulations of discourse; and he repudiates the claims of both empiricism and the *Zeit-Geist*. According to Arnold, it was an accident of birth only that prevented Newman from benefiting from the *Zeit-Geist*. Commenting on Newman's acceptance of the 'traditionary' ways in which the Church Fathers possessed themselves of Scriptural texts 'for practice and edification', Arnold writes: 'Born into the world twenty years later, and touched with the breath of the "Zeit-Geist," how would this exquisite and delicate genius have been himself the first to feel the unsoundness of all this!' (*Litera-ture and Dogma*, p. 377). Just twenty years, and what a difference! But that same exquisite and delicate genius *was* prepared to engage in phenomenological analyses which are profoundly at odds with Arnold's own phenomenological fastidiousness. For Arnold it is an agony that 'mortal millions live *alone*'; but Newman relishes the entirely private character of real assent shut up 'as it were in its own home' (*Grammar of Assent*, p. 83).

His confidence about the accessibility (though not the transparency) of the inner man suffuses the whole of *A Grammar of Assent*. He is as familiar as Arnold with difficulties arising from the limits of reason, private judgement, common consent and language itself, but he still uses reason, private judgement, common consent and language itself to place those difficulties in the broader context of human sensations, emotions, affections and powers. The three most important characteris-tics of this exercise are optimism, reflexiveness and dynamism. Human beings, Newman contends, can know and control their own lives; they can experience that knowledge and control as their own; and, at least in principle, they can make themselves into what they ought to be. This assurance is deeply and pervasively classical – it reaches back to Newman's master, Aristotle. And it reaches forward also towards a later phenomenology which was to declare itself the inheritor and the fulfilment of the Greek philosophical tradition.

But this involves the modern admirer of Newman in certain difficul-ties. Husserlian phenomenology is so brimful of its claim to be scientific that its incipient totalitarian character can hardly be concealed. In the 'Fifth Cartesian Meditation', Husserl writes that the 'systematic *unfold-ing of the all-embracing Apriori*' should be designated 'as the systematic unfolding of *the universal logos of all conceivable being* ... the true and *genuine universal ontology* ... that comprised in itself all regional exis-tential possibilities, and did so in respect of the *correlations* pertaining to them'.[16] The comprehensiveness of this claim suggests the excessive hegemonic ambition lurking in all phenomenology. Newman's work is similarly suspect. Like Husserl's, his ideas appear to claim a comprehen-siveness, clarity and unity in truth which a post-Nietzschean culture is bound to question. 'The embedding of transcendental phenomenology in the metaphysics of presence,' writes Derrida, 'the entire Husserlian thematic of the living present is the profound *reassurance* of the cer-tainty of *meaning*' (*Writing and Difference*, p. 60). Such suspect certainty seems to be Newman's also. He too rejects a *Cogito* that embraces madness and hyperbole.

Such a judgement, however, overlooks the fact that Newman's com-mitment to dogma is firmly grounded in the phenomenological principle of alterity. The perception of things, Husserl points out, necessarily involves a recognition that they have insides or outsides and certainly other sides which, from the very nature of *here* and *now*, are hidden. There is absolute certainty as to the thereness of the object as object – 'Husserl', writes Derrida, '... [takes] seriously the reality of the external world' – but as an intrinsic and necessary part of that thereness there is a hiddenness 'indicated only by anticipation, analogy and appresentation'. The alterity of objects, however, is not the same as the alterity of persons. What *here* and *now* conceal in an object can in principle be discerned *there* and *then*, but the alterity of another subject is absolute. I cannot experience another's here and now, Derrida notes, as something 'which is *mir eigenes*, which is *proper* to me' (ibid., p. 124). Newman discerns a comparable alterity in the dogmatic definitions of the early Church. Revelation is truth intentionally and effectively communicated, yet such communication is grounded in the alterity of God and what pertains to Him. Nor is it just the Divine that is communicated and concealed in this way. The same principle applies to the operations of intelligence, intuition and language. The said always implies the unsayable. Dogmas, certitudes, convictions, assents are provisional, insufficient and incoherent in their very assurance and indefectibility. Newman does not predicate a unitary Leibnizian Book of the Universe any more than Arnold does, just papyrus fragments of truth from separate, unknowably numerous scrolls and codices. He was neither surprised nor dismayed to discover a number of distinct and sometimes discordant voices in the Book of Genesis.

There is space in Newman's world, therefore, for inspiration in the exact sense that the word has for Derrida. In spite of the assured thrust of his sentences, Newman's is emphatically not the kind of writing that reductively knows where it is going. Like Derrida's, his conception of language allows writing to be genuinely '*inaugural*, in the fresh sense of the word, that is ... dangerous and anguishing ... [so that] no knowledge can keep it from the essential precipitation toward the meaning that it constitutes and that is, primarily, its future' (*Writing and Difference*, p. 11). This is because writing for Newman is an aspect of living, and to live is to bring the as yet unrealized – our 'inchoate and rudimental nature' – to completion and self-sufficiency (*Grammar of Assent*, p. 274).

We may turn to another writer in the phenomenological tradition, Maurice Merleau-Ponty, for a deeper appreciation of the relation of Newman's language to Newman's experience. Merleau-Ponty may seem a surprising thinker to cite in this context, since he actually denies St Augustine's assertion that truth inhabits 'the inner man': 'there is no inner man,' he insists, 'man is in the world, and only in the world does he know himself' (*Phenomenology of Perception*, p. xi). But he also writes of *returning to himself* (and so to a phenomenology sufficient for our purposes) 'from an excursion into the realm of dogmatic common sense or of science' and finding 'a subject destined for the world'. This, he maintains, is an essential move, for our existence 'is too tightly held in the world ... to know itself as such at the moment of its involvement'; 'in order to become acquainted with and to prevail over [the world's] facticity' we need 'the field of ideality' – the 'separated essences ... of language'. Language, however, does not separate essences from 'the ante-predicative life of consciousness' (ibid., p. xv). Even with language, the human being is not 'the universal thinker of a system of objects'. In responding to beauty, for example, we discover and enjoy our own nature. 'But,' Merleau-Ponty argues, 'if the subject has a nature, then the hidden art of the imagination must condition its categorial activity. It is no longer merely the aesthetic judgement, but knowledge too which rests upon this art, an art which forms the basis of the unity of consciousness and of consciousnesses' (p. xvii). Had he read his Newman, Merleau-Ponty would have recognized that his hidden art of the imagination is none other than Newman's illative sense, that instinctive logic of the inner being, in which the actual unity of consciousness and the potential unity of consciousnesses are disclosed.

Like Derrida, therefore, Newman would dismiss 'the notion of an Idea or "interior design" as simply anterior to a work' (*Writing and Difference*, p. 11) because such a conception would be inconsistent with his sense of life. At the same time, he would agree with Derrida that 'if creation ... is not the purely transparent expression of ... form, it is never the less, simultaneously, revelation. If creation were not revelation,' Derrida asks, 'what would happen to the finitude of the writer and to the solitude of his hand abandoned by God?' (ibid., p. 12). ('We mortal millions live *alone*.') For Newman, too, assenting human beings, at home in themselves, live alone, abandoned by God to finitude and to the law of their being which is to be responsible to and for the self, that is for and to conscience. Newman's God, as Judge, dwells *in interiore homine* precisely by a kind of absence, by a willed apartness which alone makes conscience possible, and in which is constituted the individual person's capacity to make a self out of an inchoate and rudimental nature, to be inspired both by divine grace and the hidden art of the imagination. Newman's Aristotelian phenomenology is as fully open to post-Nietzschean notions of inspiration and freedom as Derrida's.

And it is open also to what Derrida calls the '*sociality* of writing as *drama*' (p. 227). Unlike Arnold, Newman does not find solitude a curse because for him the solitude of real assent simultaneously gives us access to what Husserl calls '*the single community of monads*' – Merleau-Ponty's other consciousnesses – for whom 'there can exist *only one Objective world*' (*Cartesian Meditations*, p. 140). This shareable access to the objective order is grounded for Newman not in 'science' but in dogmas, in the great patristic formulations of the Trinity and the Incarnation, which Arnold thought 'incapable of application', and which he denied could ever 'have the force of an intuition' (*Literature and Dogma*, p. 298). For Newman, however, both in what they define and in the response which they predicate of the believer, they constitute the clearest possible articulation of what Charles Dessain identifies as the central principle of his thought, that 'True Christianity is the Presence of Persons'.[17]

So, on its various levels, is writing. For Newman as for Derrida, 'constituted–written–meaning presents itself as prerequisitely and simultaneously *read*', (*Writing and Difference*, p. 11), even if, again in Derrida's words, we 'would search the "public" in vain for the first reader: i.e., the first ... author who reads and ... the first reader who dictates' (ibid., p. 227). But in Newman's case we do not have to search the 'public', nor deploy the disciplines of the 'sociology of literature' to reach his readers. We have only to identify the sense of obligation inscribed in all he wrote. Obligation, argues Karol Wojtyła (Pope John Paul II) – a writer no less in the Husserlian tradition than Derrida – 'introduces the person ... into that characteristic drama enacted in the context of reality of which it makes ... him the subject ... Outside of [this] drama', the human being 'cannot live as a person'.[18] All Newman's writings, his sermons, lectures, letters, treatises, and even his notebooks, are in this sense dramatic, written under a precise and ineradicable sense of the obligations arising out of the presence of persons.

This is particularly evident in his contributions to that most paradoxical of forms, the written sermon or lecture. As writing, Newman's sermons and lectures confront us with the author uniting in himself the roles of preacher, of predicted congregation, of all subsequent readers of the printed text (friendly co-religionists, separated brethren, prejudiced antagonists, inquisitorial *monsignori*) and finally, though most immediately, the Just Judge Himself. In the presence of such persons, as constituted in and by his conscience, Newman is under immense and complex obligation; yet the alterity of all statements, however exact, and of all persons, however really present, prohibits simple, univocal, totalitarian responses to it. Newman cannot make ultramontanist claims for his text. Instead, in words that necessarily allude to the unsignifiable as well as to the signified, he has to address himself to men and women, whose here and now can never be his, about a world knowable only by anticipation, analogy and appresentation.

Such a task can only be undertaken by a mind actively interested in the details of a perceived world. It requires the kind of sensitive attention to circumstance which we have seen Arnold to lack, and which is possible only in minds capable of unconditional respect for other people. Hence the historical specificity of Newman's writing as against the political vagueness of Arnold's. *The Idea of a University*, for example, dramatises exactly the historical situation to which Newman referred in a conversation with Bishop Ullathorne when he complained 'that the bishops etc did not see the state of the Laity, e.g. in Ireland, how unsettled, yet how docile' (*Newman*, p. 114). Arnold, it is worth recalling, favoured repressive measures in Ireland; Newman appointed supporters of Young Ireland to chairs in his university. Moreover, as an address by an English, middle-class gentleman, a convert and a priest, to an audience of Irish middle-class gentlemen and gentlewomen, unsettled yet docile, which reveals and undercuts the ideal of gentlemanliness, and which simultaneously appeals to and qualifies papal and episcopal authority, *The Idea of a University* moulds itself to the contours of Irish social and political life in 1852 with a discrimination and expressive tact wholly missing from *Culture and Anarchy*.

This is why Newman's is a historically determined work in a far richer, more materialist sense than Arnold's, without being any the less intended. From a post-structuralist point of view, it is also more inspired and more dramatic. Thus the paradoxical lesson that Newman has to teach the literary theorist is that the phenomenological assurance which authentic writing requires is more securely founded in the great Trinitarian and Christological definitions and credal statements of the Patristic Age than on the 'science' which in their different ways Arnold and Husserl attempted to appropriate in the name of modernity. And if that is so, it follows that in literary criticism, as in so many other aspects of life, the words of St Augustine still apply: *Noli foras ire, in te redi, in interiore homine habitat veritas*.

CHAPTER SIX

Autobiography and the Illative Sense

I

Ludwig Wittgenstein begins *Philosophical Investigations* with the description in Augustine's *Confessions* of a child learning to speak: 'thinking primarily of nouns like "table", "chair", "bread", and of people's names', Wittgenstein tells us, Augustine does indeed 'describe a system of communication', but 'not for the whole of what [he was] claiming to describe', only for one of the many discrete language games learnt in infancy.[1] We cannot get outside these rule-governed games, Wittgenstein argues. It is an illusion of depth, a false pointing, to juxtapose one game with another, and imagine there is something further or deeper to be 'seen'. 'Think how many different kinds of thing are called "description": description of a body's position by means of its co-ordinates; description of a facial expression; description of a sensation of touch; of a mood' (*Philosophical Investigations*, p. 12). The mistake is to think there is something further about 'description' to be grasped in the light of its varied use when there is nothing to be grasped apart from the senses of the word as it is used, now here, now there. *Philosophical Investigations* is thus premised on the aphorism with which Wittgenstein ended *Tractatus Logico-Philosophicus*: 'What we cannot speak about we must pass over in silence' (p. 74).

John Henry Newman would have found this conclusion unreal. In fairness, it must be said that *Philosophical Investigations* focuses on the 'real' in a very Newman-like way, notably in its repeated assertion 'You could imagine ... ': Newman too appeals repeatedly to the imagination. It is only on the claims of language that there is potential for disagreement between them. But that disagreement is important, and there are seemingly powerful grounds, in the plenitude of *apologias pro vita sua* written before and after Newman's conversion, and culminating in, but not concluded by, *Apologia Pro Vita Sua* itself in 1864, for adopting Wittgenstein's and not Newman's view on the limits language imposes on mind. As we read Newman on Newman *in extenso*, distinctions between his life and his apologies for it get lost; the 'man' seems to disappear in the innumerable stories in which he constructs and reconstructs himself; we are left with writings and no remainder; and the feeling intensifies that any attempt to 'see' an essential Newman between the texts would be a case of false pointing.

All this seems to confirm the overwhelming acceptance in our culture of selfhood as an unstable illusion. We are, the theorists tell us, doubly deluded. In the first place the very notion of a self is at best a useful reference point. Daniel Dennett compares it to an object's centre of gravity. It is not, certainly, a fact about the human organism as a handle is a fact about a hammer, or a hard disc about a computer. The interactive systems which go to make up a human being, Dennett suggests, are given a single name, and together are capable of using pronouns, including the first person singular, but there is nothing 'in' these systems corresponding to the 'I' so used, not even their combined operations. Using 'I' would be difficult and confusing in these circumstances if it were not shadowed by a project which makes autobiographical material 'cohere into a single good story' ('Why everyone is', p. 1029), but this again is a delusion. The coherence of the fiction is as illusory as the centre it constructs.

Perhaps proponents of such views have in mind Wittgenstein's cryptic remarks on the problems of introspection:

> The feeling of an unbridgeable gulf between consciousness and brain-process: how does it come about that this does not come into the considerations of our ordinary life? This idea of a difference in kind is accompanied by slight giddiness, – which occurs when we are performing a piece of logical sleight-of-hand ... When does this feeling occur in the present case? It is when I, for example, turn my attention in a particular way on to my own consciousness, and, astonished, say to myself: THIS is supposed to be produced by a process in the brain! – as it were clutching my forehead. – But what can it mean to speak of 'turning my attention on to my own consciousness'? This is surely the queerest thing there could be! ... Here we have a case of introspection, not unlike that from which William James got the idea that the 'self' consisted mainly of 'peculiar motions in the head and between the head and throat'. And James' introspection shewed, not the meaning of the word 'self' (so far as it means something like 'person', 'human being', 'he himself', 'I myself'), nor any analysis of such a thing, but the state of a philosopher's attention when he says the word 'self' to himself and tries to analyse its meaning. (*Philosophical Investigations*, pp. 124–5)

Whether Wittgenstein can safely be called in aid of the Dennett model remains to be seen. What can be said is that that model is reflected in the endlessly repeated and modified tellings of his own story in which Newman indulges. To illustrate this I shall briefly summarize the history of the notorious *Tract 90* (1841) in which Newman argues for a Catholic interpretation of the Thirty-nine Articles of the Church of England, mainly on the strength of passages from the *Book of Common Prayer*, in particular the Visitation of the Sick, and of references in the *Book of*

Homilies to the Apocrypha and the Church Fathers. Even in its original version, Tract 90 engages in self-quotation and retelling, by quoting, in a discussion of the Eucharist, an earlier work of Newman's, published in 1838. Further self-quotation and retelling followed its publication. The huge controversy the Tract provoked led to Newman's writing public letters to Dr Jelfs and the Bishop of Oxford explaining his position and justifying his actions. In spite of these explanations, however, he did, of course, eventually leave the Church of England for the Church of Rome.

So matters rested for twenty years. Then in 1864, Charles Kingsley published a pamphlet bringing up the question of *Tract 90* once again. Kingsley insists that he never attributed 'intentional dishonesty'[2] to Newman. Newman was right, he says, to resist a Calvinist reading of the Articles – their framers had wisely made them ambiguous. But Kingsley does profess to being 'shocked' by Newman's commentaries on four Articles in particular, and he thinks that when Newman tries to show that a fifth Article, against '"the sacrifice of masses"', does not speak against the mass itself', he is in 'fearful danger' of destroying either his 'sense of honesty' or 'his common sense' ('What, Then', pp. 32–3). In the first Part of *Apologia*, Newman protests at this – Kingsley, he says, makes him seem bad or mad, if not 'a conscious liar and deceiver' (p. 63). Newman does not, however, there or later, specifically address the argument about the Mass. He focuses instead on the relation of the Articles to the Homilies and the Prayer Book, and the claim that, the intentions of the framers of the Articles being in general political and in detail unknowable, a true interpretation must fall back on Catholic tradition.

Thirteen years later, in 1877, while revising and republishing his works, Newman reprinted *Tract 90* in the two-volume *The Via Media of the Anglican Church*. Once again he engages in self-quotation and retelling. In a Prefatory Notice he asserts that both volumes 'contain various statements, which I … reproduce at the present time not without pain', and he quotes the Advertisement in his essays about 'the chance of [his work] being … used after his death' 'to benefit the cause it was intended to support at the time when it was given to the world', that is, Anglo-Catholicism, a cause he now opposes.[3] Another Notice, introducing *Tract 90*, states that its polemic has been weakened by deletion of quotations from the Homilies, but that this is 'better than the alternative … It is penance enough to reprint one's own bad language, without burdening it with the blatterant [anti-Catholic] abuse of the Homilies' (*Via Media*, II, p. 265). This clearly represents a hardening of view: *Apologia* refers to the 'eloquent declamation of the Homilies' (*Apologia*, p. 150).

It would seem then that Newman's texts constantly change status. First he makes a claim about a controversial topic, about patristic doctrine or the *Book of Common Prayer*. Almost at once, however, these claims acquire a second-order significance, as part of the Newman autobiographical record. In addition to what he said, the circumstances and good faith of his saying it become matters of controversy. In a later edition of *The Via Media* (1885), for example, immediately after his remarks about the language of the Homilies, he denies rather tartly the claim by a former fellow-Tractarian, William Palmer, that he never allowed his own Tracts to be revised by others: he often did so, he maintains, but emphatically not by Palmer. In the same edition, another Note, dated 'June 14, 1883', dismisses with contempt his original argument that Article xxxi does not condemn the Mass. 'What the Article abjures as a lie', Newman now announces, 'is just that which Pope and Council declare to be a divine truth' (*Via Media*, II, p. 351). No acknowledgement is made of the fact that this effectively confirms Kingsley's original remarks on the topic.

Traditional scholars would sift through this array of quotation, explanation and silence in order to identify the real Newman – saint, equivocator, sensitive, suppressed homosexual, or entrancing preacher, venerable Prince of the Church, and unreconstructed bigot. They might think, for example, that the attack by the Newman of 1883 on the Newman of 1841 for advancing a false argument about the Mass undermines the Newman of 1864 who was silent on the issue, even though it had been raised by Kingsley. Newman's defenders, however, could argue that *Tract 90* was a side-issue; that the text at the centre of Kingsley's offensive was the sermon of 1844 on 'Wisdom and Innocence'; and that the strong rhetoric of the later notes in *The Via Media* reflects Newman's age – he was 77 when he used the word 'blatterant' of the Homilies, and 83 when he wrote the note on Article xxxi.

But such approaches ignore the mind-crushing problem of quotation – and the omission which quotation always involves – in all the texts we have been considering. 'There is no such thing in nature as a naked text, without note or comment', Newman wrote in 1841 (*Essays Critical*, II, p. 252); but comment itself is text, and calls for further comment; context requires to be contextualised, and in this sea of relativism the possibility of definitive explanation vanishes. Thus Newman spent the later years of his life dressing up his Anglican writings in Catholic vestments; but they had never gone naked: the habit of self-quotation and retelling in an apparently unending pursuit of self-definition and self-explanation was with him when he wore the surplice. And as the poor Bishop of Oxford could have testified, the task was one which it was impossible to bring to any sort of conclusion.

Newman himself was familiar with the problem and saw only one way of resolving it. If 'truth' is 'vast and far-stretching', its advocate must resort to the 'economies' by which 'an historical narrative is converted into a tale' (*University Sermons*, p. 90). The numerous versions of Newman's Newman are just such tales, rounded off first one way then another, as honesty, self-interest or senility suggest. But would the Newman-story of a scholar–biographer be any the less 'an economy'?. In the end, it would seem, there is no canonical 'Newman', nor a canonical *Tract 90*, or canonical *Apologia*.

Dennett's model rationalises this conclusion. Newman's writings are continually revised for the purpose of self-definition because identity is always so constituted. Newman's assertions about theology and church history are made in earnest at one time, and repudiated with repugnance at another, but the issues at stake quickly lose their intrinsic importance, and the shifts of feeling in the mind proposing or re-presenting them become their principal significance. Virtually every note in the later editions of Newman's works is like this, supplementing and qualifying the already much-revised *Apologia*, without significantly helping us to reach a clear conclusion about Newman himself. The references to Palmer in 1885, for example, do not quite fit the Palmer of 1864, and we have no way of judging which better represents Palmer himself or Newman's 'real' feelings about him. But Dennett permits us to stop worrying about such matters. In his view, inconsistency between one autobiographical draft and the next is not only inevitable but essential, because the autobiographical impulse, in which, as he sees it, human subjectivity is founded, only gets going because the facts never do add up unless we force them to; and that can only be achieved on a strictly temporary basis, that is, until further redrafting is called for.

The problem with this model is the unconsciousness in the process it describes. The procedure would fail if its structure as fiction were always and immediately obvious – if we were all self-consciously Dickenses making ourselves laugh, making ourselves cry, and making ourselves wait. As Wittgenstein noted, one 'can mistrust one's own senses, but not one's own belief' (*Philosophical Investigations*, p. 190). But there is no point at which this unself-reflective element reaches its limit. As Dennett has come to realise, entailed in his 'multiple drafts model' of the fictional self is a 'multiple drafts model' of consciousness itself:

> In the world of publishing [he notes] there is a traditional ... distinction between pre-publication editing, and postpublication correction of 'errata.' In the academic world today, however, things have been speeded up by electronic communication ... [It] now often happens that several different drafts of an article are

> simultaneously in circulation, with the author readily making revisions in response to comments received by electronic mail. Fixing a moment of publication, and ... the *canonical* text ... becomes a somewhat arbitrary matter ...
>
> Similarly ... if one wants to settle on some moment of processing in the brain as the moment of consciousness, this has to be arbitrary. One can always 'draw a line' in the stream of processing in the brain, but there are no functional differences that could motivate declaring all prior stages and revisions ... unconscious ... and all subsequent emendations to the content ... post-experiential memory contamination. (*Consciousness Explained*, pp. 125–6)

Newman's autobiographical writings illustrate in a slowed-down version how these processes of mind might operate. Thus there are no functional differences between early drafts of Newman's writings and later revisions and omissions which enable us to represent the former as straightforward adjustments and the latter as 'post-experiential memory contamination'. But if the radical instability and inconclusiveness of the Newman narratives do indeed model 'consciousness', and the minute and intimate processes of *current* story-telling are in consequence always provisional, and in the continual flux of 're-vision', then it is not only Newman and the canonical version of his story that disappear, but the story-making process itself. Our consciousness of what constitutes a good story, of the rules of narrative coherence, must also be in process of continual redrafting, as indeed they seem to be in dreams. But this violates some of Wittgenstein's fundamental principles, that an 'intention is embedded in its situation, in human customs and institutions' – it cannot be improvised – and that 'to imagine a language means to imagine a form of life' – a foundation of some sort is a condition of any kind of utterance (*Philosophical Investigations*, pp. 108, 8). 'It is what human beings *say* that is true and false; and they agree in the *language* they use. That is not agreement in opinions but in form of life' (p. 88).

The rules of autobiographical selving must be based, therefore, on public agreement. The concept of a 'fictional' self – as distinct from a self closed to full introspective scrutiny – is thus, from Wittgenstein's point of view, surd. That part of me which is determined, not by what I think and say, but by my capacity to think and say it, cannot be opportunistically invented because it is shared with others. But there is an unspecifiable, yet necessary element of 'private language' in the multiple drafts model of the self, and that of consciousness entailed in it. The model, therefore, collapses solipsistically upon itself. If Dennett is right, 'I' have nothing in common with the Gardarene demoniac of the Gospels, 'clothed and in his right mind'; I am not even '"Legion", because we are so many'; even as I write, I am a herd of maddened swine rushing solipsistically into the sea. One is reminded of the editor–

narrator in Thomas Carlyle's *Sartor Resartus*, determined to generate the very presence of his hero, Teufelsdröckh, from 'fragments of all sorts; scraps of regular Memoir, College-Exercises, Programmes, Professional Testimoniums, Milkscores, torn Billets, sometimes to appearance of an amatory cast; all blown together as if by merest chance'[4] – yet terrified that he will produce no more than an optical shadow; or of Carlyle himself, unable to 'disenchant ... the imprisoned facts and secrets of heroes' languishing in seven folios of state papers.[5] Carlyle blew away his doubts with a blast of the Everlasting Yea. Newman's method was more drawn out, and in order to examine what might have been his response to the issues I have been raising, we must return to Augustine, whom Wittgenstein so grievously misrepresents. My second section will be based on a rereading of Augustine on language.

II

What, then, does Saint Augustine mean? Wittgenstein ignores a crucial phrase: 'Thus, as I heard words repeatedly used in their proper places in various sentences, I gradually learnt to understand what objects they signified; and after I had trained my mouth to form these signs, I used them to express my own desires' (*Philosophical Investigations*, p. 2). 'To express my own desires': 'the essence of language' for Saint Augustine is not, as Wittgenstein suggests, that 'individual words in language name objects', but that names are memorised to do the bidding of the will. Always already language presupposes the personal – memory, understanding and will. Wittgenstein, of course, believed this as well – his mistake was in not recognising that Saint Augustine did so also. Wittgenstein writes:

> 'We name things and then we can talk about them: can refer to them in talk.' – As if what we did next were given with the mere act of naming. As if there were only one thing called 'talking about a thing'. Whereas in fact we do the most various things with our sentences. Think of exclamations alone, with their completely different functions.
>
> > Water!
> > Away!
> > Ow!
> > Help!
> > Fine!
> > No!
>
> Are you inclined still to call these words 'names of objects'? (p. 13)

But does not Saint Augustine imply just such exclamations attaching to words such as 'Apple!' and 'Mother!'? He does not name objects either, he remembers their names, and the uses to which those names can be put in expressing his state of mind, and so he utters his desires to those around him, whom he has seen using language for similar ends. He has learned the rules of a game from forms of life, from the presence of other people.

But more is involved here for Saint Augustine than for Wittgenstein: memory, understanding and will, contemplating themselves and God, constitute for Saint Augustine an image of the Trinity.[6] His account of language is rooted in dogmatic theology, for it was in the doctrines of three Persons in One God and two natures in Christ that the Church Fathers clarified the notion of the human person. The Latin term, as they came to use it, combines the senses of the Greek words *prosopon* (character, aspect, appearance) and *hypostasis* (substance). The resulting doctrine is fundamental to Christianity. It is quite distinct from the much older doctrine of the soul. Plants, animals and the world were deemed to have souls, but the human being is a person; nor is it obvious that the personal condition necessarily entails ensoulment, at any rate in a sense stronger than Wittgenstein's.[7] Be that as it may, for Saint Augustine and for Newman, personhood is not a consequence of how the human being is perceived or perceives itself but the real foundation of all human life.

This concept was virtually a premise of medieval theology, renaissance humanism, the Reformation and the Enlightenment. But with the Enlightenment it lost its dogmatic underpinning, as Carlyle recognized. Forced by Reason to repudiate miracle and Revelation, Carlyle quickly discovered that there was also 'a fundamental infirmity, vitiating insufficiency, in all words' and therefore in Reason also (*Collected Letters*, 12, p. 165). So he opted for the will – 'man … can create as by a *Fiat*. Awake, arise! Speak forth what is in thee' (*Sartor Resartus*, p. 158): summon into existence, in other words, the 'wondrous agency of *Symbols*', through which a Teufelsdröckh or a Cromwell may be made present to you (p. 175).

In attacking Newman for failing to recognize the 'free play of the pure intellect … [as] the necessary and sufficient guarantee of all improvement of the race',[8] Sir Leslie Stephen ignores this problem of language raised by Carlyle, and relies on a traditional notion of the unified intelligence and a 'core of permanent knowledge [consisting] partly in those beliefs which can be expressed with mathematical precision … and partly in … the concurrent testimony of innumerable observers' ('Newman's Theory', pp. 213–14). There is no room for the will in Stephen's intellectual world, just as there is none in Mill's. Understanding reigns alone. Stephen in effect assumes the stance attacked by Marx in 'Theses on Feuerbach'; for him, 'the theoretical is the only genuinely human attitude', and the observer is 'superior to society' (pp. 69–70).

With Newman, Stephen tells us, 'we are knee-deep in the dust of the ancient fathers' ('Newman's Theory', p. 169), but in fact Newman moved smoothly between Carlyle's point of view at one moment, and Stephen's the next. Admittedly, Newman and Stephen disagreed about the uniformity of nature and the progress of the race; but Stephen could have abandoned both beliefs without sacrificing the claims of Locke and Hume, which are at the core of his thought, as they are at the core of Newman's account of notional assent and inference, that broad territory of shareable conceptions, from mathematics to ideology, which, as Newman describes it in *An Essay in Aid of A Grammar of Assent*, includes formal and informal inference, profession, credence, opinion, presumption and speculation. This is the terrain of discussion and argument, of demonstrable error, and coherence of view, of what can be said. It is also the basis of a university education and the formation of a gentleman. And for Newman it was not enough.

He proposed an alternative terrain, that of real assent, reserve and the illative sense. Real assents are convictions that are held unconditionally. We may have forgotten or repudiated our original grounds for holding them – that Great Britain is an island, that a friend is true, or that the promptings of conscience are crucial to the outcome of our lives – but we hold them none the less, and act on them. We may even be prepared to die for them. They provide the basis for certitude and the formation of saints and secular heroes. They 'are of a personal character ... They depend on personal experience; and the experience of one man is not the experience of another. Real assent ... is proper to the individual, and, as such, thwarts rather than promotes the intercourse of man with man' (*Grammar of Assent*, p. 82).

Real assents are thus among the things about which it is impossible to speak. Trying to explain his doctrine of 'Silence', Carlyle identified 'Self-renunciation' as one of its thousand senses. 'But', he warned, 'this too if we *talk* much of it will degenerate into an *ism*' (*Collected Letters*, XII, p. 164). Perhaps Carlyle's 'Silence' is the terrain of another of Saint Augustine's notions about language, his belief that 'when we utter what we know, a word is necessarily born from the knowledge which we hold in the memory, a word which is absolutely the same kind of thing as the knowledge it is born from ... a word that is neither Greek nor Latin nor any other language' (*The Trinity*, p. 409). Or, if this seems too Platonic, 'Silence' may be the terrain of Luce Irigaray's '"other meaning" always in the process of weaving itself, of embracing itself with words, but also of getting rid of words in order not to become fixed, congealed in them'.[9]

Newman, too, denies that language is 'the measure of thought'; 'judgement and action' are not driven by logic but by a 'multiform and intricate assemblage of considerations' that language can never capture fully (*University Sermons*, p. 230). The faculty which enables us to engage with these considerations is the 'illative sense', 'illative' denoting the inferential and so pointing to syllogism and language in regular ordered use, and 'sense' pointing to instinct and so to language which is figurative and exploratory. Irigaray might find this a significant conflation, and find, too, that Newman also recognized the dangers of becoming fixed, congealed in verbal formulae.

Three points need to be made about the illative sense.

The first is that the theoretical for Newman is emphatically not the only genuinely human attitude. On the contrary, even the dogmas of the Catholic Church are but 'faithful shadows of those truths, which unlearned piety admits and acts upon, without the medium of clear intellectual representation' (ibid., p. 65). The genuinely human attitude, in other words, is not that of theologians and philosophers, but of unlearned piety, which theologians and philosophers struggle to gloss. This is why, much to Stephen's disgust, Newman asserted that a peasant

> may take the same view of human affairs in detail as a philosopher ... such persons ... have clear and distinct opinions; they know what they are saying; ... they do not confuse points of primary with those of secondary importance; they never contradict themselves: on the other hand ... they use arguments which appear to be faulty, as being but types and shadows of those which they really feel. (Ibid., pp. 304–5)

Here we discover further common ground between Wittgenstein and Newman. Wittgenstein characterizes a false view of language as follows:

> What does it mean to know what a game is? What does it mean, to know it and not to be able to say it? Is this knowledge somehow equivalent to an unformulated definition? So that if it were formulated I should be able to recognize it as the expression of my knowledge? Isn't my knowledge, my concept of a game, completely expressed in the explanations I could give? (*Philosophical Investigations*, p. 35)

On behalf of his peasant, Newman would say to Wittgenstein's confused questioner, 'Knowledge of a game is *not* completely expressed in the explanations an individual can give of it.' A peasant who plays both football and hockey might know how goals are scored in both games, and act on that knowledge, while being unable to state the rules or their rationale with the completeness and accuracy demonstrated by his practice. Mastery of the practice is independent of mastery of the language games by which the rules governing that practice are expressed; and such mastery is knowledge. And what applies to games-playing applies much more compellingly to prayer. Thus if the notional supplies Newman with the equivalents for what Marxists call ideology and hegemony, the illative sense borders on traditional Marxist conceptions of praxis and class consciousness. Perhaps the only difference between Wittgenstein and Newman, therefore, is that Newman refused to be silent about the unarticulated dimensions of utterance. *A Grammar of Assent* is a carefully elaborated explication of them.

My second point is that for Newman it is 'the concrete being that reasons' (*Apologia*, p. 218), not Stephen's 'pure intellect'. 'Logicians are more set upon concluding rightly, than on right conclusions ... After all, man is *not* a reasoning animal; he is a seeing, feeling, contemplating, acting animal ... impressions lead to action, and ... reasonings from it. Knowledge of premises, and inferences upon them, – this is not to live' ('Tamworth Reading Room', p. 294), He 'asks me what I *mean*', Newman writes of Kingsley, ' ... about that living intelligence, by which I write, and argue, and act' (*Apologia*, p. 83). A recurring image in his work is the self-precipitating mind: to read the Fathers, a man must throw 'his mind upon their text, and [draw] from them their own doctrines' (*Essays Critical*, I, p. 94). 'To believe in Objective [that is, Revealed] Truth is to throw ourselves forward upon that which we have but partially mastered' (ibid., I, p. 34). The story of Newman's changing convictions is accordingly identical with Newman himself – not because we have nothing but text or texts without remainder, but because texts are *his* remainder, faithful shadows of a personal substance, his memory, understanding and will, fully and intricately engaged in the pursuit of certitude, and disclosed in his writing to the reader's illative sense. As he himself put it, 'the life and writings of Cicero or Dr. Johnson, of St Jerome or St Chysostom, leave us with clear and precise impressions of the intellectual and moral character of each of them' – even if we cannot put those impressions into words (*Grammar of Assent*, p. 96).

My third point, however, almost undoes the first two. Newman's system, so strategically superior to those of Carlyle and Stephen, so much more confident about language than Wittgenstein, is fatally self-subverting. In 1841, he wrote: 'we may surely take it for granted, from the experience of facts, that the human mind is at best in a very unformed and disordered state' ('Tamworth Reading Room', p. 263). This for Stephen was the ultimate scandal in Newman's thought, the conviction that every one of us 'is born into this world in a state of *death* ... under the bondage of an inborn element of evil, which thwarts and stifles whatever principles remain of truth and goodness in us, directly we attempt to act according to them' (*Parochial and Plain*, VI, pp. 76–7). By the fall, Adam's soul became a chaos, and needed a new creation, and so also his descendants:

> We are imprisoned in the body, and our intercourse is by means of words, which feebly represent our real feelings ... the best motives and truest opinions are misunderstood, and the most sound rules of conduct are misapplied by others. Even Christians are more or less strange to each other. We are [also] in the dark about ourselves. When we act, we are groping in the dark, and may meet with a fall any moment. Here and there, perhaps, we see a little; or, in our attempts to influence and move our minds, we are making experiments (as it were) with some delicate and dangerous instrument, which works we do not know how, and may produce unexpected and disastrous effects. The management of our hearts is quite above us. (Ibid., I, p. 173)

And consequently the management of our intellects and our words as well.

But what have we to do, Stephen asks, with such 'darker, deeper views'? – 'darker as deeper', he adds sardonically ('Newman's Theory', p. 173). Simply this – that Newman's vision of intellect corrupted transforms postmodernism into a drama. Postmodernism is a game, if it is confined to the realm of language and the notional. It becomes serious if it is real.

Newman was particularly contemptuous of Eusebius of Caesarea for holding out 'the ambiguous language of the schools' as an excuse for not being specific about doctrine (*The Arians*, p. 263). In teaching that orthodoxy consisted simply in adherence to scriptural terms, without regard to their interpretation, Eusebius corrupted 'the simplicity of the Gospel with an Eclectic spirit'. In Eusebius' world, the dispute with Kingsley about what Newman meant, and what the Articles may mean, would be unnecessary: there would be no wells to poison, just 'sensible, temperate, sober, well-judging persons' (as Newman put it in another context) 'moving through the channel of No-meaning, between the Scylla and Charybdis of Aye and No' (*Essays Critical*, I, p. 301). However, as he also pointed out:

> It is all very well for educated persons, at their ease ... to argue and speculate about the impalpableness and versatility of the divine message, its chameleon-like changeableness, its adaptation to each fresh mind it meets; but when men are conscious of sin, are sorrowful, are weighed down, are desponding ... [they] want to be assured that what seems to them true, is true; they want something to lean on ... more stable than their own minds.[10]

Eclecticism and scepticism are luxuries of the Academics. But if in real life things do not make sense, we – theorists and peasants alike – are on the edge of hell.

And making things add up is very difficult: 'each of us has the prerogative of completing his inchoate and rudimental nature, and of developing his own perfection out of the living elements with which his mind began to be' (*Grammar of Assent*, p. 274). I have pointed out elsewhere (*Milton and Free Will*, p. 3) how this description of personal formation is similar to Derrida's account of the formation of meaning: 'Meaning must await being said or written in order to inhabit itself, and in order to become, by differing from itself, what it is: meaning' (*Writing and Difference*, p. 11). Both definitions undercut Derrida's 'classical subject'.[11] But in the end Derrida is only talking about what can be said or written – he is a secular Eusebius – whereas Newman is talking about the real. The idea of a sentence always already being the future it has yet to become may amuse, intrigue or exasperate us, but having got the point we go on our way, check the time of this evening's showing of *Three Colours White*, and book the table for dinner. Not so, or at any rate not quite so, if it is we – rudimental, inchoate, our souls 'a chaos', the management of our hearts quite above us – who await our own thoughts and actions in order to inhabit ourselves, and in order to become, by differing from ourselves, what we already so perilously are: persons.

I conclude then with this suggestion. *Apologia Pro Vita Sua* may be fruitfully read in the light of its own insights and notions: that what we cannot speak about we are none the less incapable of passing over in silence; that the inchoate, the rudimental, the reserved and the personal are brought to texts by writer and reader alike – particularly by writers and readers who throw themselves into what they write and read – and that these things, about which we cannot speak, form part of the real outcomes of literature; that in consequence if a text is real it is also autobiographical; and that the whole process of writing and reading, of inference and logic in the world at large, as well as of real assent and certitude in the heart at home, is crossed and recrossed, diverted and thwarted, by what *Apologia* so eloquently calls 'some terrible aboriginal calamity' (p. 276) but which a less theologically minded age may more simply describe as the meaningless mess we get ourselves into.

PART TWO

Manifold and Complex Corruption

CHAPTER SEVEN

Celibate Men and
Angelic Women in *Oliver Twist*

Critics of *Oliver Twist* tend to assess either its psychological or its social truthfulness. The psychological critics focus on intuitive inspiration or compulsive fantasy. John Carey sees it as a reliving of the traumatic blacking factory episode in Dickens's youth: 'To the blacking factory, in one guise or another,' he writes, 'the evil spirits of the novel naturally flock.'[1] John Bayley suggests that Dickens's lack of modern self-consciousness accounts for his failure to distinguish between the truths of realism and those of fantasy. Dickens is 'all unknowing' about the effect of his work, his symbolism being involuntary and his greatest satirical effects unbargained for.[2] In arguments of this sort, the novel's strength is said to derive from direct communication between Dickens's pen and his unconscious, one consequence of which is technical crudity more deliberate writing would have avoided, along with factual uncertainties about the details of the workings of the Poor Law, and the legal penalties for receiving stolen goods. To compensate Dickens is said to generate, through a dream-like childhood fantasy of Gothic terror, that essential isolation of the individual which was the chief mark of developing industrial society (John Bayley, 'Things as They Really Are', p. 64.) or a mythical, Manichaean universe, in which the powers of good and evil are in eternal conflict (Graham Greene).[3]

Against such views we have the claim of the Preface that the novel attempts to report contemporary social conditions seriously. In Humphry House's judgement the Saffron Hill background had topical interest and, if allowances were made for domestic reading, the novel was realistic.[4] A.O.J. Cockshut, however, points to Oliver's unconvincing characterization, which he attributes to Dickens's traumatic childhood.[5] On this point, Carey sees the distinction between Oliver and the other boys as 'a hymn to the purity of the middle-class soul' (*The Violent Effigy*, p. 149), and, indeed, the novel's original effect was probably to reinforce complacency about the natural corruption of the criminally poor. But, argue the socially oriented critics, Oliver is not a 'character' like the Artful Dodger; he is a device for exposing social evils (Q.D. Leavis);[6] in depicting the poor pitted against bourgeois institutions, Dickens gives not details but the large movement of life (A. Kettle);[7] Oliver's 'very blankness brings into dramatic focus the social forces which dominate him' (Terry Eagleton, *Criticism and Ideology*, p. 128). Thus, like the psychological critics, the social critics offer us a Dickens too preoccupied with, or too occupied by, his 'real' subject to attend properly to the plot, the good characters, and the moral positives with which he proposes to counter the evils he describes so graphically. 'The ideology of the realist text', Eagleton argues, 'resides not in [a unitary] world view, but in the formal mutations and displacements which signify its attempts to subordinate other modes of discourse' (ibid., p. 126), and he offers a socio-historical rather than a psychological explanation for the fact that such effects are most obvious in Dickens's early novels. Their 'anarchic, decentred, fragmentary forms', he suggests, ' ... correspond to an earlier, less organised phase of industrial capitalism' (p. 130).

The good characters in the novel, however, including Oliver, are not quite as blank as some of these arguments imply. They can be categorized as celibate middle-aged men and angelic women and children, and while their engagement with evil may be unconvincing, they are too overtly extravagant to be explained away as the mere precipitates of contradictions disclosed in the writing process itself. In any case, there are different kinds of failure in the novel. Monks is more a device of plot than a character, whereas Dick, the angelic workhouse child, makes no contribution to the plot, and needs to be accounted for on different grounds. Rose's sickness is similarly gratuitous. The question is not what such supernumerary characters and incidents achieve but what, in their very awkwardness, they suggest about the ethical economy of the whole work.

This might not be thought very significant, since the traditional judgement has been, in C.B. Cox's words, that 'Dickens did not believe that moral issues are complicated'.[8] This fits in well with Greene's Dickensian Manichaeanism. Victorian critics especially linked these supposedly uncomplicated ethical perspectives with a simplified sense of personality and the art of caricature. Walter Bagehot argued that 'the embodied characteristics and grotesque exaggerations of Mr. Dickens' could never stand up beside the 'great works of the real painters of essential human nature', though he conceded that Bill Sikes came near to being 'a coherent man'.[9] George Henry Lewes[10] and Henry James[11] both felt that Dickens lacked knowledge of normal psychology, and it was long accepted that Dickens's rounded characters, such as William Dorrit, were few. Wilkie Collins, incidentally, thought Nancy successful in this respect (see *Charles Dickens*, p. 222). Even today there is a general assumption that, while there is real complexity in the work of the mature Dickens, his contemporaries were right to emphasize the lack of complication in his early work.

Victorian critics were not entirely logical, however, in attacking Dickens's allegedly simplistic characterizations since they were generally eager to enforce the reductive ethical perspectives associated with them. W.M. Thackeray argues that in properly censoring his account of the villains' lives, Dickens made them too attractive and therby encouraged vice.[12] R.H. Horne's remarkable essay on *Oliver Twist* objects to the chapters on Sikes's flight and death as too well written: 'We are with this hunted-down human being ... and we are *not* with the howling mass of demons outside.' Dicken has thus 'defeated his own aim, and made the criminal an object of sympathy'. Specifically Horne rejects the argument that we sympathize with the man not the murderer; such an approach creates 'a tough metaphysical contest' and 'it is never good to throw the feelings into a puzzle' (*Charles Dickens*, p. 72).

A tough metaphysical contest, however, is exactly what J.R. Kincaid finds in *Oliver Twist*,[13] but even he ignores the extent to which the 'successful' and 'unsuccessful' parts of the novel interact to a positive result. In particular, he pays no attention to the role of Oliver's benevolent bachelor saviour, Mr Brownlow, in the Sikes riot, even though, if carefully considered, it may strike the reader as disturbing. Like Kettle, Kincaid sets up a Dickens operating on contradictory levels. On the one hand, a complex pattern of image and ambivalent humour commits us to the cause of the outcasts; on the other, mere good fortune and an easy, reductive embodiment of benevolence (Mr Brownlow), give us access to 'a sanctified society' from which the poor, the criminal and the mad are 'naturally' excluded. Again, the formation of this dichotomy is allegedly outside Dickens's control. But if our sympathy during the riot is with Sikes and not Brownlow; and Carey is right to suggest that 'imaginatively' Dickens's was too (*The Violent Effigy*, p. 13); and if we adopt the working hypothesis that he was also bright enough to see and exploit such contradictions; then our sense of how *Oliver Twist* is organized may have to be re-examined. Perhaps its tensions and contradictions are more 'intended' than current criticism is inclined to admit even as a possibility.

That Dickens was indeed calculating his effects in the pursuit scenes is suggested by his decision not to name Mr Brownlow and Harry during them. Colin Williamson, arguing for a morally complex reading of the riot,[14] suggests that the excitement of Harry, 'the man on horseback',[15] is contrasted unfavourably with the self-control of Mr Brownlow, the 'old gentlemen' who offers fifty pounds to whoever will take Sikes alive (p. 346). But we already know that Mr Brownlow is 'in a fever of excitement wholly uncontrollable' (p. 338). It is true that he clings 'to the railing of the bridge ... to resist the force of the crowd' (p. 347) while warning those about him that Sykes is 'about to lower himself down', whereas Harry bursts 'through the crowd as if he were parting water'(p. 345) and offers twenty guineas to whoever fetches a ladder, but this hardly establishes a moral contrast between them, simply different physical capabilities. Both offer huge sums at random, and encourage the demonic pursuit of Sikes. On a second reading, moreover, most readers can be expected to recall Mr Brownlow's 'wholly uncontrollable' excitement in the pursuit of Sikes when they come to the earlier episode in which Oliver himself is the hunted thief and Mr Brownlow his rescuer. In the course of that incident, Dickens makes an important observation:

> There is a passion *for hunting something* deeply implanted in the human breast. One wretched breathless child, panting with exhaustion; terror in his looks; agony in his eye; large drops of perspiration streaming down his face; strains every nerve to make head upon his pursuers; and as they follow on his track, and gain upon him every instant, they hail his decreasing strength with still louder shouts: and whoop and scream with joy. 'Stop thief' Aye, stop him for God's sake, were it only in mercy! (p. 59)

It is because the good Mr Brownlow (just like Harry) is to become a hunter of this sort that the sharp ethical chiaroscuro implied by the term Manichaean is inappropriate to the novel.

It seems clear to me, moreover, that even though Mr Brownlow is a moral puzzle on this single occasion only, his being so is consistent with the way 'manhood' and male potency function in the novel's organization as a moral fable. Mr Brownlow is not the only eccentric, energetic old gentleman in *Oliver Twist*. The type has two other representatives, the absurd Mr Grimwig, by no means 'a bad-hearted man' (p. 91), but eccentrically suspicious of orange-peel and boys, and the doctor, Mr Losberne. Mr Losberne makes us feel particularly uneasy about irascible celibate benevolence. One celebrated scene, irrelevant in terms of the plot, suggests that Dickens was aware of Mr Losberne's ambivalence. It follows on Oliver's mistakenly pointing to a house as one used by the thieves. At once Mr Losberne exercises the privileges of his class and rushes in to investigate. But he meets neither the thieves, which would have been exciting, nor a London version of Mr Bumble, which would have been funny, nor the deserving poor, which would have been touching, but a malevolent old hunchback who *justifiably* shouts at him and makes him feel a fool:

> 'Now,' said the hump-backed man, who had watched him keenly, 'what do you mean by coming into my house, in this violent way? Do you want to rob me, or to murder me? Which is it?'
>   'Did you ever know a man to come out to do either, in a chariot and pair, your ridiculous old vampire?' said the irritable doctor.

'What do you want, then?' demanded the hunchback. 'Will you take yourself off, before I do you a mischief? Curse you!'

'As soon as I think proper,' said Mr Losberne, looking into the other parlour; which, like the first, bore no resemblance whatever to Oliver's account of it. 'I shall find you out some day, my friend.' (p. 346)

This absurd, unattractive intrusion of the rich into the life of the poor makes Mr Losberne seem uncomfortably like the monstrous magistrate, Mr Fang, who also exercises 'a summary and arbitrary power over the liberties, the good name, the character, almost the lives of Her Majesty's subjects, especially the poorer class' (p. 65). Williamson suggests that Dickens may originally have intended to reveal Oliver's whereabouts to the gang by means of this incident, but that he did not like Mr Losberne's generous impulse having so evil a result, and left the scene dangling. But in view of the moral complexity which Williamson has been so instrumental in revealing in the novel, it is just as likely that Dickens is showing how the emotions that make Mr Losberne an excitable enthusiast for justice and those which make Mr Fang a state-sanctioned sadist can be traced back to related sources in the mind and society.

One reason for suspecting this may be so is the theme of male celibacy in the novel. Both Mr Brownlow's interest in Oliver and Mr Losberne's eccentricity are linked to the circumstances that have left them unmarried. Nor are they the only benevolent male celibates in *Oliver Twist*. Mrs Maylie's servants are quite elaborately represented as being in the same condition. Jokes about the slow boy, Brittles, are part of a pervasive contrast in the book between sexual knowledge and experience on the one hand, and sexual ignorance and abstinence on the other. Oliver himself is often at the centre of such oppositions. Whether or not the Artful Dodger and Charley Bates have sex with Nancy and Betsey, at least they understand the girls' business, while Oliver remains almost stupidly ignorant of it. Noah Claypole similarly insults the memory of Oliver's mother from the position of the coarsened initiate. Dickens is not, however, setting up a complacent opposition between the purity of the middle-class soul and the degradation of the adolescent poor. Noah may be corrupt, but the Artful Dodger and Charley Bates are good-humoured and sociable in their knowingness. We identify and sympathize with them partly because of it.

The theme extends from adolescence into adulthood. Mr Bumble's unmanning is central to the comedy of the second half of the book. Following the loss of his beadle's cocked hat and his standing as the resplendent embodiment of masculine social authority, he becomes much more sympathetic. It was the artificial but real potency of his office, therefore, which made him loathsome in the first place. Similarly the melodramatically masculine Sikes is a figure of terror precisely when his considerable virility is most unrestrainedly in evidence. Yet the novel does not take a simply outraged attitude to these brutal manifestations of masculine power. It is Sikes's anarchic sexual potency which gives the mob's pursuit of him its demonic ambivalence and Sikes his status as a victim, while, even in the days of his glory, Mr Bumble has his moments of sexual pain, as in the vividly explicit scene in which he savagely lashes out at his ally, Noah Claypole, when he finds him kissing Charlotte Sowerberry. Carey sees this as expressing no more than the 'virtuous indignation' of a man incapable of feeling 'love or even lust'; but Carey insists that 'Dickens' main comic characters ... have no emotions', and that he is consequently unable to bring 'real suffering or real cruelty' within 'the scope of his comedy' (*The Violent Effigy*, p. 68). I think this simply wrong. Mr Bumble's sexual insecurity makes him human; but, equally, so do the Artful Dodger's cheerful knowingness, and Sikes's terrible sexual power. All contribute to the novel's discreet but sustained preoccupation with what it is to be a man.

This preoccupation is the context in which the celibacy of Mr Brownlow, Mr Losberne, and their absurd counterparts in the Maylie household, is placed. Both old bachelors, for all their benevolence, remain in touch with, and even energized by, the violent energies that erupt, so variously but so powerfully in Bumble, in Sikes and in the mob. They are not, therefore, *simple* embodiments of goodness. Moreover the novel's systematic attention to the issue of masculine knowledge and self-knowledge – the remarkable contrast between men in the thieves' kitchen and men in Mrs Maylie's – suggests that Dickens may well have calculated on his mature and knowing contemporaries recognizing just how the goodness represented by his single old gentlemen, substantial as it is, is closely related to being something less than a whole man.

The case seems somewhat different when we consider what it is in the novel to be a whole woman. Rose Maylie, after all, effortlessly transcends a fallen world:

> She was not past seventeen; cast in so slight and exquisite a mould; so mild and gentle; so pure and beautiful; that earth seemed not her element, nor its rough creatures her fit companions. The very intelligence that shone in her deep blue eye, and was stamped upon her noble head, seemed scarcely of her age or of the world; and yet the changing expression of sweetness and good humour; the thousand lights that played about the face, and left no shadow there; and above all, the smile; the cheerful, happy smile; were made for Home; for fireside peace and happiness. (*Oliver Twist*, pp. 187–8)

But even here there are advantages in assuming that Dickens saw and intended much more than is commonly assumed. He certainly did not anticipate this description passing unnoticed; and what it says is that Rose *is* unreal, unearthly, an angel; yet at the same time Dickens insists that she is necessary for earthly happiness. This paradox is central to a complex set of ideas and images in the novel associated with the word 'angel' which are as persistent and varied as its preoccupation with male celibacy.

The word is associated more with death than domesticity. When Mrs Corney goes to the dying Mrs Thingummy, for instance, we are ambushed by some unexpectedly solemn prose:

> Alas! how few of Nature's faces are left to gladden us with their beauty! The cares, and sorrows, and hungerings, of the world, change them as they change hearts; and it is only when those passions sleep, and have lost their hold for ever, that the troubled clouds pass off, and leave Heaven's surface clear. It is a common thing for the countenances of the dead, even in that fixed and rigid state, to subside into the long-forgotten expression of sleeping infancy, and settle into the very look of early life; so calm, so peaceful do they grow again, that those who knew them in their happy childhood, kneel by the coffin's side in awe, and see the Angel even upon earth. (p. 152)

It is worth repeating that this rhetorical surge is prompted by the death of the disfigured Mrs Thingummy. To understand its significance, it is helpful to recall an earlier death-bed scene, that of the dead pauper woman whom Oliver helps Mr Sowerberry to lay out. Dickens makes two relevant observations in the course of this episode: first, that even the rats in the neighbourhood are 'hideous with famine' (p. 31); and second, that Oliver is frightened of the living, not the dead, that is, of the dead woman's grief-stricken mother and husband, because they seem 'so like the rats he had seen outside'. In childhood and death, human beings are angels; in life, even good people are like rats. (Dickens was to reuse this idea in a striking passage in *Little Dorrit*.)

But that is too stark a contrast. Dickens's sense of non-angelic ordinariness, which melts away in death to reveal the angelic original, is also evident in the comedy surrounding Mrs Thingummy's parting:

> 'Did she drink the hot wine the doctor said she was to have?' demanded the first [old woman].
>
> 'I tried to get it down,' rejoined the other. 'But her teeth were tight set; and she clenched the mug so hard that it was as much as I could do, to get it back again. So *I* drank it; and it did me good!'
>
> Looking cautiously round, to ascertain that they were not overheard, the two hags cowered nearer to the fire, and chuckled heartily.
>
> 'I mind the time,' said the first speaker, 'when she would have done the same, and made rare fun of it afterwards.' (pp. 153–4)

Perhaps she did the same at Agnes Fleming's death-bed, when she made her celebrated remark, 'Think what it is to be a mother, there's a dear young lamb, do' (p. 2).

Both the maternal and the angelic condition, therefore, exalted as they are in Dickens's rhetoric, are yoked, sometimes with violence, to the comedy of *Oliver Twist*. Mr Bumble declares Mrs Corney to be 'a angel'; and it is in this complicated context of 'rats', 'rare fun' and Mrs Thingummy's ideal of motherhood, of the Artful Dodger, Charley Bates, Sikes and Fagin – messy, cruel, sexual and alive – that Rose functions in the novel. And here the difference between her kind of goodness and that of the old bachelors becomes important. They suffer a kind of deprivation by being not wholly involved in life: as lonely, celibate and sometimes absurdly violent men, they exhibit that 'deformation of character' (p. 299) – as the Artful Dodger puts it at his trial – which twists the other characters out of true. Neither shortcoming applies to Rose. She is neither deprived of life nor distorted by it. Instead she embodies 'woman's original nature', of which a little survives in Nancy – Dickens insists on the similarity between Nancy's love for Sikes and Rose's for Harry – but which has been totally obliterated in the prostitutes in The Three Cripples. Rose does not represent the normal, therefore, against which the eccentric can be measured; still less does she represent some kind of agency by which the problem of evil might be overcome. Rather, precisely as an 'angel' she reinforces our sense that deformation of character is the inevitable condition of of those who are simply human.

Caricature, in other words, is the only, the normative way of depicting non-angelic ordinariness. Far from representing a socially isolating example from some comfortable human norm (say the middle-class soul), it signifies the chief bond between people. Our world is Bumble's, Mrs Thingummy's, Mr Losberne's, Mr Grimwig's and Fagin's, not Rose's or the *dead* Mrs Thingummy's. This applies especially to Fagin and his gang. Fagin is a grotesque, oddly affectionate devil-father in an otherwise completely human brotherhood of grotesques. He and they are proof that the universe is not Manichaean, that stark divisions into black and white belong either to the vulnerable perspectives of childhood, or to the brutal righteousness of beadles and magistrates. The gang's cheerful, companionable acquiescence in the corruption of the world; their brotherly defiance of collective helplessness at the trial of the Artful Dodger; and, above all, Fagin's tender, witty and cruel presidency over their laughter and vice; all this constitutes both a detailed documentation, and an archetypal generalization of a world in which the deviant is the ordinary. Fagin becomes a terrifying, nightmarish monster, yet there is a masterly reversal of this at his trial, when the devil who haunts Oliver's dreams becomes in his turn a compulsive dreamer. And his dreams come horribly true. The account of his last meeting with Oliver fails badly; but we do see during his trial that he is not a devil at all, but 'an old man ... a very old, old man', whose neck is about to be legally broken. His substantial humanity, moreover, is evident precisely to the extent that it is not 'sound' but twisted frantically out of true.

But if Rose is not of this world, why doesn't she die as Dick does? What sense is there in her gratuitous recovery? The answer is to be found, I suggest, precisely in that gratuitousness. In the 1841 Introduction, Dickens claims that his purpose was to show 'the principle of Good surviving through every adverse circumstance, and triumphing at last'. He does not talk of Good overcoming Evil, just of its surviving, and it is this which gives significance not only to Rose's recovery, but also to Oliver's apparently psychologically vacuous passivity. Thus on one of the few occasions when the generally helpless Oliver could have contributed to the victory of Good by rousing the Maylie household during the burglary, everything conspires, in Mr Losberne's words, 'to prevent his doing any good for himself' (p. 199). But helplessness, and its moral correlative, passivity, are not mere negation, as the drama of Rose's illness makes clear. 'The suspense:' Dickens writes when Rose is near to death, 'the fearful, accute suspense: of standing idly by while the life of one we dearly love, is trembling in the balance; the racking thoughts that crowd upon the mind ... the desperate anxiety *to be doing something* to relieve the pain, or lessen the danger' (p. 218 – italics mine). But, he adds, 'we have no power to alleviate' the evils that thus beset us. The fierce desire to act is urgent and honourable, but also dangerous and probably futile. This is a difficult and self-wounding conclusion for a man of the temperament described by Carey. Significantly Mr Brownlow and Mr Losberne are ensnared in puzzling moral entanglements when they are driven into importunate activity by 'the desperate desire to be doing something' or 'the passion for hunting something'. Nor is it irrelevant that the two most feverishly active characters in the novel are Fagin and Sikes.

In obvious ways Dickens's commitment to the principle of passivity in the organization of *Oliver Twist* has unhappy consequences, notably in the fortuitousness of the plot and the shadowiness of the hero. However it is not forced on an unwitting Dickens, as Eagleton implies, but is central to the novel's intelligent grasp of social problems, which Kettle and Eagleton accurately identify. The novel is notably exact about the locations of injustice. The first number began with a fiercely facetious description of workhouses, the last with the physical hideousness created by commerce itself:

> Near to that part of the Thames on which the church at Rotherhithe
> abuts, where the buildings on the banks are dirtiest and the vessels
> on the river blackest with the dust of colliers and the smoke of
> close-built low-roofed houses, there exists, at the present day, the
> filthiest, the strangest, the most extraordinary of the many locali-
> ties that are hidden in London, wholly unknown, even by name, to
> the great mass of its inhabitants. (p. 338)

The deformation of character which the novel finds in people, it finds
also in places. Nor can the invidual human will challenge either. The
novel, therefore, avoids reliance on anything as easy as a change of
heart to put the world to rights. Even the heart of a Mr Brownlow can
be suspect, and society is too twisted out of true to be capable of self-
scrutiny. Of course Dickens believes in, and campaigns for, the reform
of workhouses, prisons and slums; but even his good characters point
to his sense that comprehensive solutions are illusory.

Hence Rose's deeply improper presence in the text. Precisely as 'an
angel', she is outside her proper sphere, even though she is exactly what
the world needs. The problem is only compounded by the fact that the
novel itself operates by worldly means, the devices and excitements of
caricature. She is included none the less, not as any kind of 'solution' to
the problem of human deformation, but rather as a light by which the
darkness is able to disclose itself. Exactly the same imaginative economy,
but far more richly developed, operates in *Little Dorrit*. Quite as improper and as neccessary as Rose's presence is the novel's ending – the
retirement of the good party *en bloc* out of life and into a rural heaven.
The logic underlying this unabashed escapism is quite tough, and like so
many other improprieties in *Oliver Twist*, it suggests how seriously the
young Dickens tried to specify and enlarge the tragic complexity at the
heart of his comic gift. There is simply nowhere else for them to go, and
nothing else for them to do: the ending is a logical consequence of the
historically shaped, concretely realised and penetratingly understood
feeling of helplessness symbolized in the celibate Mr Brownlow and the
angelic Rose.

CHAPTER EIGHT

The Radicalism of *Little Dorrit*

I

To understand the strategy of *Little Dorrit* proper recognition must be given to the plot, which can easily be undervalued. John Wain maintains that it is 'in essence, a plotless novel. For all the scurry of event on its surface, it never for a moment suggests genuine movement',[1] and Raymond Williams writes of the action being 'properly one of collision, of chance, of unlooked for connection and involvement'.[2] Both recognize that coincidence, mystery, and mechanical connection between characters suggest specific views of human life, individual and social – but they give the impression of a limited story-telling technique being put to unexpectedly good use. A more positive treatment of the story-telling in *Little Dorrit* requires the mystery element to be distinguished from the rest of the action. There *is*, of course, an important element of chance and unlooked-for connection in the novel, but for nine-tenths of the book it remains fixed. The secrets of Arthur Clennam's birth, of Mrs Clennam's connection with the Dorrits, and of Blandois's association with Flintwich's brother and Miss Wade, reassure the reader that some, at least, of the novel's problems can be solved by persistence on the reader's part and ingenuity on the author's. But Pancks's search for the Dorrit money (the details of which are never mechanically revealed), or the fear felt for Amy at the prospect of her father's marrying Mrs General, generate a different kind of suspense. The right blend of predictable and unpredictable events in the action (Fanny's marriage, Arthur's speculations) make it impossible to dip into *Little Dorrit* as one might into *The Pickwick Papers* or *Martin Chuzzlewit*. The novel must be read in sequence because the main action unfolds freely and yet with controlled inevitability – damming up and then releasing the reader's mental energy by turns in ways that must, if the novel is to have any value at all, relate to its meaning.

Dickens's own accounts of the action's formation suggest growth rather than mechanical contrivance. Decisions about it occur late. He is well into the novel before deciding to make Amy 'very strong' and (tentatively) to overwhelm the Dorrits with wealth;[3] and though his plans for Merdle and the Circumlocution Office develop early, with Mr Merdle's complaint emerging 'as the last drop in the silver cream-jug on Hampstead heath', it is not until June 1856, when he is working on the ninth number, that he is able to write: 'The story lies before me, I hope, strong and clear. Not to be easily told; but nothing of that sort IS to be easily done that *I* know of' (*The Life*, p. 600). But the cover-design of the first number indicates the main themes of the novel,[4] which suggests that in Dickens's mind there was clarity and confidence about the ideas he wanted to deal with, and an exploratory, tentative approach to the action. The book comes alive for him only when action and theme fuse, and the novel *as a story* lies before him strong and clear. He can then see his way to a prolonged and complex manipulation of the vast public awaiting each number as he wrote it; and it is as a carefully organized assault on the consciousness of a historic readership that *Little Dorrit* is meaningful.

The experience of writing *Little Dorrit* was very much tied up with feelings of political despair, particularly about the maladministration revealed by the Crimean War. But it is not just about political problems in the 1850s (though set in the 1820s). Because Dickens and his public, in each other's presence, as it were, and over a period of some nineteen months, experience the complex pressures of a tensely told story with a political theme, *Little Dorrit* works as an organized political event in the society it describes. Its representations of, and judgements on, society are only comprehensible in terms of an intimate and *developing* relationship between book and public. This means, of course, that *Little Dorrit* must reflect and acknowledge the values and experiences of its readers – that is, by and large, the English middle class. But it must also be against those same readers; it must disconcert their literary expectations, trap, surprise and frustrate, as well as gratify their bourgeois narrative aesthetic. And because it is centrally about politics, its attempts to disconcert them even in literary terms will necessarily involve disconcerting them morally and politically as well. The question is how strong these opposing tendencies are. When at last the story lay before Dickens, strong and clear, some of the effort it called from him required a strengthening of the political and social attitudes he shared with his readers, an intensification of their intimacy; but some involved challenging those conventions and so, directly or indirectly, the social, economic and political order in which the novel itself was selling so successfully. How radical this literary and political challenge was can be seen only through an examination of *Little Dorrit* as a sequence of experiences; and this of course involves taking it seriously as a story.

II

I have suggested that the world Dickens writes about and wrote for is his world. This is why, as George Orwell rightly points out, *Little Dorrit* lacks historical perspective.[5] Middle-class values are therefore fundamental to Dickens's activity as a writer. There are relatively super-ficial signs of this – the careful use of Maggy as chaperon and non-chaperon for Amy ('So, at last, Clennam's purpose in remaining was attained, and he could speak to Little Dorrit with nobody by. Maggy counted as nobody, and she was by'[6]), or the happy tolerance of Mr Meagles's philistinism. But middle-class commitments and habits of thought and feeling contribute to the novel at a deeper, darker level also. When the landlady of the Break of Day dismisses 'political philan-thropy' with the words 'there are people who have no human heart, and who must be crushed like savage beasts and cleared out of the way' (p. 121), the themes of frustration, violence and repression which work so intensively in the text endorse a position uncompromisingly hard and anti-intellectual. There is no doubt about the kind of mind this remark will appeal to, nor about Dickens's own pleasure in it.

To say that *Little Dorrit* is a middle-class novel, moreover, is not to deny it an effective radicalism in the Bright and Chamberlain tradition. There is nothing incompatible with middle-class values in Dickens's anti-Sabbatarianism or his anger at Westminster landlords. And even if this sort of radicalism can become a source of self-congratulation (it is the special achievement of our century and our class that we think scientifically and act energetically on matters of public health and hous-ing), it gives rise also to a thoroughly satisfying rhetoric.

> Ten thousand responsible houses surrounded him, frowning as heavily on the streets they composed, as if they were every one inhabited by the ten young men of the Calender's story, who black-ened their faces and bemoaned their miseries every night. Fifty thousand lairs surrounded him where people lived so unwholesomely, that fair water put into their rooms on Saturday night, would be corrupt on Sunday morning; albeit my lord, their county member, was amazed that they failed to sleep in company with their butcher's meat. (p. 29)

The anger is accurate and directed at a real political enemy. Dickens and his readers know that they think and feel differently from both aristocratic members of parliament and tenants of slum property. They know also that their opposition to restrictive Sabbatarian legislation is generous, humane and just.

Hence the confidence in the tone of certain parts of *Little Dorrit*, Dickens's easy conviction that what he says and how he says it will be popular. The attack on the county member, for instance, could have gone into *Household Words*, just as the famous 'Nobody, Somebody, and Everybody' article[7] could have found its way into *Little Dorrit*. Whatever he happens to be writing – letter, article, or novel – Dickens has the power to drop all doubts about what he is saying and how it will be received, and to press forward in prose at times almost violent in its simplifications. Whether he is writing laudatory letters about the sturdy no-nonsense rebelliousness of the Swiss,[8] or, ten years later in *Little Dorrit*, describing Merdle as '*simply* the greatest Forger and the greatest Thief that ever cheated the gallows' (p. 691, italics mine), the effect is the same: he presents an articulate and sophisticated version of Mr Meagles's rage at the Circumlocution Office. And though there is a great deal more to be said about his handling of Merdle's death, this talent for the simplifications of energetic belief is one of the dominant – and essentially middle-class – features of *Little Dorrit*.

It combines with a disturbing confidence in the values of that class. One of the most disconcerting instances of this occurs in a passage of some importance in view of its anticipation of the closing paragraph – Amy's conversation with Arthur about her feeling that Mr Dorrit ought not to have to pay his debts 'in life and money both' (p. 409). Unhesitatingly Dickens calls this moving and justified reaction a 'taint' in Little Dorrit, the first and last Clennam ever sees 'of the prison atmosphere upon her'; and he makes this judgement in spite of his having given us earlier the careful translation, 'Forgive us our debts as we forgive our debtors' (p. 45), in order to show up the contradictions in Mrs Clennam's religious views. He recognizes, of course, that financial obligations cannot and should not be paid in the currency of 'life', and that forgiveness of debts is a virtue in creditors, but he denies that remission of money-debt is ever a *right* in debtors. It is thus wrong to think of Arthur's sense of obligation about his own debts as having mainly symbolic importance, or psychological significance. In writing *Little Dorrit*, Dickens is committed to the view that debts represent inalienable obligations. The commitment is inextricably a part of the vision and energy of the whole work.

The dogmatism which marks the expression of such opinions finds further expression in Dickens's readiness to type and classify his characters. This is a habit which many of the characters themselves indulge in; it helps to establish a stable world, in which the problems facing society can be concretely represented in simple terms. The process is typified in Mr Meagles's remarks about the French: 'They're always at it. As to Marseilles, we know what Marseilles is. It sent the most insurrectionary tune into the world that was ever composed. It couldn't exist without allonging and marshonging to something or other – victory or death, or blazes, or something' (p. 15). Mr Meagles makes his world coherent by reducing and simplifying revolution and insurrection to a matter of 'allonging and marshonging'. In the same way the world of the novel is secured by the reduction and simplification of representative characters, Mr Merdle's Chief Butler, Bar, Physician, Bishop, and the Barnacles, as well as the more detailed studies of Mrs Gowan, Mrs General, Mr Casby, and the Plornishes. Mr Meagles's efforts in the art of characterization in terms of type, however, hardly show its limits; nor is it to criticize the mode adversely to suggest that it offers the reader fixed, generally reassuring and familiar categories of good and evil, truth and error, right and wrong, dramatically polarized in figures like Cavalletto and Blandois. It is here that Dickens establishes a confident common ground with his readers; and though the judgements implicit in, say, the portrait of Mr Casby may be complex, causing a middle-class readership some discomfort, the laughter such readers are betrayed into, in spite of their opinions and interests, arises out of an aesthetic in which basic moral categories (love, patience, duty, debt) and basic social facts (riches, government, poverty, crime) are as fixed and familiar as the caricatures involved in the action.

The flexibility of this technique is considerable; it can even stand the strain of self-parody (with brilliantly funny results), as in the description of the ladies in Mrs Merdle's drawing-room: 'the file of beauty was closed up by the bosom. Treasury said, Juno. Bishop said, Judith' (p. 244). More significant is the splendidly unpleasant 'Patriarch', Mr Casby. His choice of a fixed role for himself suggests the secured smugness such an approach can lead to. But an even greater challenge to the habit of simplifying human beings into fixed roles and types is suggested by Blandois. Thinking in such terms is at the heart of his wickedness. In choosing the role of 'cosmopolitan gentleman' for himself and imposing on others roles that suit his convenience, he identifies life with acquisitiveness: 'If you try to prejudice me, by making out that I have lived by my wits – how do your lawyers live – your politicians – your intriguers – your men of the Exchange?' (p. 10). His grotesque division of human beings into strong and weak, gentlemen and servants, exposes in an extreme form the inhumanity inherent in reducing men and women to types. Yet this is all he is himself – a crudely typed villain-figure. Nevertheless it is through him that Dickens signals his keen awareness of the moral limitations inherent in this method of presenting character. The question arises, however – is there more than just self-diagnosis here? Did Dickens merely recognize the limitations of his method or did he rise above them? Critics have generally stuck to the view that Dickens rarely gives us anything but 'fixed figures, in phrase and appearance, "grossly and sharply told"' (as Raymond Williams puts it); his characters, 'isolated by their fixed public appearance' are thereby limited in their relations with each other to the arbitrary interconnections of chance and coincidence ('Social Criticism', p. 219). Williams insists that Dickens's 'view of society is not available for reduction or detachment from his whole view of life', and that for him 'what others call an "interest" in society or sociology is a directly personal energy and commitment' (ibid., p. 214); but he does set a limit, none the less, on Dickens's whole approach to the novel and therefore on the vision of human beings and their social world which arises out of it. Everything that is hidden or falsified by 'fixed figures, in phrase and appearance' must be hidden and falsified in a Dickens novel. Nor will it do to argue that those obscurities and falsifications are what Dickens wishes to expose. The question put by Henry James in his review of *Our Mutual Friend* has to be met: 'Who represents nature? Accepting half of Mr. Dickens's persons as intentionally grotesque, where are those exemplars of sound humanity who should afford us the proper measure of their companions' variations?' (*House of Fiction*, p. 51). If Dickens does confine himself to fixed grotesques, if he never brings book and reader into contact with humanity unfixed and free, then his view of people and society is necessarily limited. Edmund Wilson would be right to argue that Dickens's 'concrete way of looking at politics' makes him 'sometimes actually stupid about society';[9] and a similar link would be established between Orwell's suggestions, that Dickens's characters are 'finished and perfect', and that his view of society is of an unchangeable natural order ('Charles Dickens', pp. 82, 37). In other words the traditional judgement, voiced by James and accepted by critics as influential as Wilson and Williams, that Dickens gives us only grotesques and no 'exemplars of sound humanity' places Dickens as ultimately conservative in his social attitudes and judgements. Certainly he can only be considered a truly radical writer if he breaks out of his grotesqueries. Equally, because this grotesquerie was just what so many of his readers wanted from him, it is necessary to show that he was ready to risk a really thorough-going radicalism if James's judgement – that he is a *superficial* novelist – is to be resisted.

The Meagles household suggests how the problem can be met. Mr Meagles is a good man; the failures, therefore, in his approach to life – of controlling the world by categorizing it – bring the novel into contact with dangerously unfixed human experiences. His insufficiencies go beyond the mere failure of intelligence which makes his estimate of Doyce so inadequate; his failure with Tattycoram points to a complete breakdown in understanding and charity between the classes. What the well-intentioned, warm-hearted Meagles family cannot admit is their inability to give Tattycoram equal human status with Pet. The ugly fact is disguised in a funny name, and glossed over in a show of eccentricity, by tricks in fact which are distinctively Dickensian. Mr Meagles constructs his home life as if it were a Dickensian comic scene. Tattycoram can be appropriately read, therefore, both as the representative of all Dickens's other grotesques rising in violent revolt against their author for giving them silly names and fixing them in phrase and appearance, and as the representative of a servant-class outraged by cosy, middle-class paternalism. Dickens in short recognizes the close relation between his fixed comic world and his fixed bourgeois attitudes – and arranges for both to blow up in the faces of his readers and poor Mr Meagles at the same moment.

Tattycoram's rebelliousness is thoroughly unsettling. We are not merely faced with irreconcilable claims on our sympathy (which both the Meagleses and Tattycoram may certainly make), but with a dangerous loss of all moral perspective as well – especially in relation to Pet:

> 'Oh, Tatty!' murmured her mistress, 'take your hands away. I feel as if some one else was touching me!'
> She said it in a quick involuntary way, but half playfully, and not more petulantly or disagreeably than a favourite child might have done, who laughed the next moment. Tattycoram set her full red lips together, and crossed her arms upon her bosom. (p. 191)

Nothing here is certain. Tattycoram's feelings towards Pet are ambiguous – 'I hate her! They make a fool of her, they spoil her' (p. 25) – and her resentment reflects an adult intelligence which enables her to see the mistakes the Meagleses are making. But she *touches* Pet, and Pet feels as if the touch were Miss Wade's, which thoroughly unsettles all easy interpretations of the incident. It is impossible to decide which reaction (Pet's to Tattycoram's unwanted touch, Tattycoram's to Pet's rudeness) is the more human. What becomes clear, however, is that both are alive in ways which cannot be contained in their roles of child–mistress and child–maid. They are altogether different from the sort of human beings suggested by the silly names a loving, sentimental, insecure and pre-eminently Dickensian Mr Meagles has given them.

Tattycoram's rebellion leads to Miss Wade. In spite of Dickens's expressed hope that 'The History of a Self-Tormentor' (II, xxi) would integrate smoothly with the rest of the novel (*The Life*, p. 626), it is an excellent thing that it does not. Its awkwardness cannot be explained away as the tidying up of loose ends (like the hurried account of Mrs Clennam's past sins). Instead it intrudes as something gratuitous and ugly, which cannot be ignored. And by thus calling attention to itself, it challenges the domestic security of all the Meagles-type households in which the novel is being read, possibly aloud. The autobiography, apparently, of a bisexual, who is first engaged to a pleasant, middle-class

young man, then runs off with his aristocratic friend, and finally se-
duces the maid-servant of her ex-lover's wife, it defies the whole range
of literary and domestic decorums which the domestic reading of novels
in middle-class families assumes. It is consistently ambiguous – 'Upon
that, the aunt fondled her ... '; motives are sullied – 'The mother was
young and pretty. From the first, she made a show of behaving to me
with great delicacy'; 'I saw directly, that they had taken me in, for the
sake of the dead woman'; ordinary habits of mind are bitterly scruti-
nized – 'I have an unhappy temper, I suppose.' 'I did not say that.' 'It is
an easy way of accounting for anything' (pp. 645–8). Dickens expects
us to be shocked and angered by Miss Wade, and though he also elicits
judicious sympathy both for her and for Tattycoram, he does not allow
us to reject the good represented by Mr Meagles. But neither does he
allow us to fool ourselves into imagining that Mr Meagles has an
effective way of coping with Miss Wade's bitterness of heart. Dickens
takes his stand firmly in the Victorian sitting-room, but with an adult
consciousness of raw, uncontrollable human fact which is incompatible
with all Mr Meagles stands for. This recognition is thoroughly 'radical'.
It puts a strain on his confident relations with his readers, between his
insights and their sensibility, between shared laughter in a safe world
and shared humanity in an unsafe one.

It is because the novel shifts between secure fixtures, clear judgements, confident assertions, and middle-class values on the one hand,
and unfixed dangers and ambiguities on the other, that its narrative
development is so important. Its readers must first be made familiar
with a solid world in which the broad facts of human life are fixed in
controllable categories; only then can the break-up of that world challenge their sense of personal and social security. Yet Dickens remains, in
part, committed to the fixed world. The tensions are as present for him
as for his readers; readers and author experience them in each other's
presence. Mr Meagles, Dickens and his readers are all one, just as the
aesthetic, psychological and social contradictions which the novel deals
with are all one. The effort for Dickens was almost unbearable. Significantly, perhaps, he became obsessed with setting an entire story 'on the
top of the Great St Bernard', just as, two years earlier, he had longed to
break out of his own world, and live 'above the snow-line in Switzerland' (*The Life*, pp. 638–9). The strain of belonging and not belonging
was too great.

The position of Arthur Clennam in the novel is thus like Dickens's
own as author. Throughout the book Arthur has to revise or withhold
judgements about the people he meets – Pancks for instance; he is
unable to relax in the certainties implied by fixed phrase and appearance. He is equally tentative in his general ideas, anxious not to project

his own depression on to the world, yet constantly finding that the world reinforces his private anxieties; he is confident on matters of principle, uncertain about life itself. Both Arthur and Dickens are actively and dangerously *inside* the situations they observe with detachment; and, like the reader, they need to see the world in the reassuring terms of fixed phrase and appearance as well as to feel the dangers and learn the lessons of finding that it is not fixed or fixable at all.

Both Flora and John Chivery are relatively simple instances of how these tensions reveal themselves. Initially they are comic formulas: Flora, the 'moral mermaid', is a caricature of the middle-aged Maria Beadnell; John – 'great of soul. Poetical, expansive, faithful' (p. 206) – a caricature of the young Dickens who loved her so extravagantly. But they are not left as puppets whose antics are only a sign of the puppet-master's energy and vision. When John approaches Amy on the bridge, she backs away from him 'with an expression in her face of fright and something like dislike' (p. 210) – an understandable but wounding dislike which modifies our sense of his passion as something merely comic. The ground is thus prepared for his great encounter with Mr Dorrit's feeble snobberies on the latter's visit to London; John's vulnerability makes his point of view, and not merely Dickens's or our own, important. In the same way Flora comes generously alive at the wedding of Amy and Arthur. Without losing their fixed phrases and appearances – John his inventiveness as a composer of epitaphs, Flora her free-associating garrulity – both break out of their comic shells as a challenge to their fellow-characters and the reader alike. As John Holloway points out, this happens to a large number of characters in *Little Dorrit*.[10] It is, moreover, a central element in the treatment of class and wealth in the novel.

Throughout *Little Dorrit* the class system is seen in terms of the imposition of roles on other people. Mrs Gowan assimilates the Meagleses by confining them to roles in which she can patronize them. William Dorrit does the same to his 'pensioner', Old Nandy. Fixing the world's appearance hides uncomfortable social realities. It obscures human truths and obligations. It is corrupt, evasive, and – in Mr Dorrit – sad:

> The Father of the Marshalsea had never been offered tribute in copper yet. His children often had, and with his perfect acquiescence it had gone into the common purse, to buy meat that he had eaten, and drink that he had drunk; but fustian splashed with white lime, bestowing halfpence on him, front to front, was new.
>
> 'How dare you!' he said to the man, and feebly burst into tears.
>
> The Plasterer turned him towards the wall, that his face might not be seen; and the action was so delicate, and the man so penetrated with repentance, and asked pardon so honestly, that he could make him no less acknowledgement than, 'I know you meant it kindly. Say no more.' (p. 66)

When the fixities of the class system break down, Dorrit and Plornish have to face their common humanity: they quickly retreat. The whole strategy of *Little Dorrit* is to confront its readers with a similar break-down and to cut off their retreat, so that they have to face the full implications, social, political and personal, of being human.

These tensions – between fixed and unfixed positions and defensive and challenging social and political attitudes – explain the ambiguity in the novel's symbolism. Only rarely is a challenging symbol simple: Doyce, for instance, is a fixed figure who survives the clumsier attempts of Mr Meagles and the Circumlocution Office to categorize him in ways that suit themselves; but apart from Amy he is in this unique, a point of firm, confident affirmation. Generally in *Little Dorrit* the imaginative catego-ries in which Dickens thinks are shifting and ambiguous. The great images (prison, river, journey, labyrinth and so on) may seem to have the solidity not of symbols but of established phenomena; yet they are very hard to grasp and judge. The accoutrements of the soldiers in Italy hanging on the buildings, for instance (Dickens was thinking of Napo-leon III's occupying forces, though the dates of course are wrong) seem 'like hosts of rats ... (happily) eating away the props of the edifices that supported them' (p. 453). Rats here might seem a simple enough image if the first mention of them in the novel had not referred to 'other unseen vermin in addition to the seen vermin, the two men' (p. 2). One of these men is Blandois, whose association with the rat-like detritus of tyranny might seem appropriate, but the other is Cavalletto, who can be seen as a 'rat' only from a class position which is disablingly myopic. Even more striking is the description of Covent Garden at night: 'where the miser-able children in rags ... like young rats, slunk and hid, fed on offal, huddled together for warmth, and were hunted about (look to the rats young and old, all ye Barnacles, for before God they are eating away our foundations, and will bring the roofs on our heads!)' (p. 159). 'Rats' have become a complex and distinctively political symbol, relating to that larger vision of the poor suggested by the hangers-on round the Marshalsea:

> As they eyed the stranger in passing, they eyed him with borrowing eyes – hungry, sharp, speculative as to his softness if they were accredited to him, and the likelihood of his standing something handsome. Mendicity on commission stooped in their high shoul-ders, shambled in their unsteady legs, buttoned and pinned and darned and dragged their clothes, frayed their button-holes, leaked out of their figures in dirty little ends of tape, and issued from their mouths in alcoholic breathings. (p. 87)

D.H. Lawrence describing miners on strike could not be more acute and uncompromising. The phrases and appearance of mendicity – static, sullen, impersonal – discover and identify a social evil. As in the rat images, Dickens's readers are faced with *fact*, and simultaneously their own reactions are exposed with disconcerting concision: anger at injustice mingles disturbingly with distaste for its victims and fear of them. Like Mr Meagles, Dickens thinks about society in fixed, solid categories – 'Doyce', 'rats', 'mendicity' – but unlike Mr Meagles (or William Dorrit, or Mrs Gowan) he does not always do so for his own or the reader's comfort.

In contrast, the treatment of the upper classes, high finance and the civil service in *Little Dorrit* may seem brash and mechanical – in spite of Lionel Trilling's suggestion that the novel's 'finest power of imagination appears in the great general images whose abstractness is their actuality, like Mr. Merdle's dinner parties, or the Circumlocution Office itself'.[11] Terry Eagleton argues that 'Dickens is forced in his later fiction to use as aesthetically unifying images the very social institutions (the Chancery Court of *Bleak House*, the Circumlocution Office of *Little Dorrit*) which are the object of his criticism' (*Criticism and Ideology*, p. 129). This is another version of the fixed characters 'grossly and sharply told' praised by Raymond Williams, and the cumulative effect of writing of this sort is certainly impressive. Sharpness of telling is as important as grossness. That Dickens should describe Bar, for instance, as 'in reference to KF, a suggested likeness in ... many touches' (*The Life*, p. 625) indicates how detailed these great abstract images were for him. The overall effect, however, is not one of close observation but of an abstract satirical construction, of inflexible imaginative fixity, signifying the oppressive inhumanity of a whole social system. The individual is reduced to a function. Bar and Bishop lack even Affery's individuality; mere cardboard figures, they surround stiffly the oozy nothing of Merdle's wealth. It is a brilliant image – and yet, beside the complexity of the great images in the novel of journeys, prison, and the family, it seems remote from the passionate, difficult, questioning engagement with society in the descriptions of the Marshalsea, or the frozen figures in the St Bernard Pass. It is, in short, satire Mr Meagles would too easily see the point of; but it is also the most overtly political element in the novel. Is it then the case, as Eagleton implies, that when it came to attacking the actual political and economic structures of English society, the radicalism of Dickens's imagination faltered, and the reader's imagination was left morally and politically unharassed?

In this connection, however, the emergence of Mr Merdle, from the abstractly modelled world against which he is presented, is crucial. To begin with he is just another fixed figure, perpetually taking himself into custody. Then the following exchange takes place between him and Mrs Merdle, and for the first time we sense the man himself, lonely, jaded, detached from life:

'You don't want me to scream, Mrs. Merdle, I suppose,' said Mr.
Merdle, taking a chair.

'Indeed I don't know,' retorted Mrs. Merdle, 'but that you had
better do that, than be so moody and distraught. One would at
least know that you were sensible of what was going on around
you.'

'A man might scream, and yet not be that, Mrs. Merdle,' said
Mr. Merdle, heavily. (p. 387)

He reappears in this mood in that singularly oppressive chapter 'The
Evening of a Long Day' (II, xxiv). The reader knows why he wants the
tortoiseshell-handled penknife, knowledge which makes the lonely emptiness of his exchange with Fanny so terrifying. It is all part of the
tremendous build-up before the long-expected crash which follows
Merdle's suicide and which overwhelms all the major characters. The
desire for Merdle to kill himself, for the crash to come, and for the
relief, that must follow it, of just and vigorous anger at corruption and
fraud in high places, intensifies unbearably. And when it does come it is
gratifyingly complete. In a great wave of impassioned, angry prose,
Dickens, on behalf of small investors everywhere, couples 'the name of
Merdle ... with every form of execration' and declares him to be 'simply
the greatest Forger and the greatest Thief that ever cheated the gallows'
(p. 691). Yet the image of Merdle in Fanny's vexed watery eyes, going
to his death and appearing 'to leap, and waltz, and gyrate, as if he were
possessed by several Devils' (p. 683), calls the whole simplification into
question.

The key to the problem is provided by Physician. Dickens heightens
the tension before the suicide by dawdling over this enigmatic figure
who finds his way into life's 'darkest places', 'like the rain, among the
just and the unjust', and yet who is also an attractive man: 'Where he
was, something real was', and the guests at his dinner table 'came out
so surprisingly ... they were almost natural' (p. 684). It is in the company of this ally of the natural that we are led, in the middle of the
night, to the dead Merdle: 'There was a bath in that corner, from which
the water had been hastily drained off. Lying in it, as in a grave or
sarcophagus, with a hurried drapery of sheet and blanket thrown across
it, was the body of a heavily-made man, with an obtuse head, and
coarse, mean, common features' (p. 686). Merdle, who according to Mr
Dorrit had been 'the name of the age' (p. 469), is now 'carrion at the
bottom of a bath'; but dead flesh under the frock-coat of a financier is
precisely the reality, 'the monstrous impropriety' (p. 684), which Physician has known and faced throughout his professional life. The reader
has been drawn by narrative excitement and the anticipated pleasures
of righteous anger to face something every bit as indecorous as the sins
of Miss Wade – the naked blood-drained corpse of a bankrupt suicide.

The novel's great abstract images of power and class, finance and government, with their stiff and abstract anonymity, their comfortingly obvious failings, their reassuring fixity in ridiculous postures, collapse; like Tattycoram bursting out of her silly name, Physician's reality – humanity stripped – breaks out of the fixtures of phrase and appearance which Dickens has lured the reader into accepting; and the full range of human, sensuous activity which Merdle's grey naked body at once suggests and denies is seen to stand in frightening opposition to the *whole* world of the novel, to the respectable domestic intimacy of Dickens's relations with his readers as well as to the imperturbability of Bar, Bishop and the Barnacles. The point comes over more impressively if we think of Mrs Merdle's comically marble bosom, her comically unchucked chin, and her vaunted envy of 'Savages in Tropical Seas'. Cold flesh is no longer funny. In both the Merdles it points to areas of dangerous truth which a whole society is bent on suppressing.

Ten years earlier, Dickens had attacked the Malthusian economists with their 'politico-economical principle that a surplus population must and ought to starve ... There is a sense and humanity in the mass, in the long run, that will not bear them ... Not all the figures that Babbage's calculating machine could turn up in twenty generations, would stand in the long run against the general heart' (*The Life*, pp. 412–13). 'Physician's reality' is this 'general heart', the humanity which Merdleism and Barnacleism deny. It enforces an astonishingly profound radicalism. Having first allied himself with his middle-class public in caricaturing and ridiculing the posturings of the great and powerful, Dickens suddenly presents them with this image of a 'face and figure ... clammy to the touch' and a white marble bath 'veined with a dreadful red' (p. 686), with an image, in short, of humanity denied which is as shattering to their own peace of mind as it is to the system which they have felt free to criticize. By, as it were, compelling Mr and Mrs Meagles to accompany Physician to the bath-house, *Little Dorrit* breaks out of its own imprisoning ways of thought and feeling, out of that formal solidity which Eagleton judges it to collude with; and because those ways of thought and feeling have successfully signified the political, economic and social structures of nineteenth-century England, to break out of them is to assert that England itself is a prison.

III

But if *Little Dorrit* enacts its own liberation at the level of form, revolution should also be one of its main themes. We may certainly regard Arthur Clennam's fantasies, when he is accidentally locked up inside the most inflexible fixture in the novel – the Marshalsea – as having precise political as well as psychological significance: 'As to escaping [he wonders], what chances there were of escape? Whether a prisoner could scale the walls ... alight on a housetop, steal down a staircase, let himself out at a door and get lost in the crowd. As to Fire in the prison, if one were to break out while he lay there?' (p. 85). Fantasies about an individual's liberation lead spontaneously to frightened fantasies of the whole prison structure going up in smoke. But terms like 'individual' and 'society' are hardly applicable. Social, political, and economic tensions in conflict with human freedom merge into psychological tensions. Writing to Layard while at work on *Little Dorrit*, Dickens described the mood of the poor as 'extremely like the general mind of France before the breaking-out of the first Revolution, and is in danger of being ... turned into such a devil of a conflagration as never has been beheld since'; he longs for the people to 'stir themselves in the vigorous national manner'.[12] In another letter he describes writing *Little Dorrit* as a blowing off of steam 'which would otherwise blow me up' (*Dickens at Work*, p. 226). Dickens was thus intensely conscious of the imprisoning nature of social institutions, the violence implicit in them, and the need for, and yet the dangers of, a decisive conflagration 'breaking out'.

It would be a mistake, however, to see the violent Dickens as the most revolutionary. The impatience of his radicalism, his tendency to smash his way out of difficulties, has affinities with the authoritarian ferocity of the landlady at the Break of Day. Besides, the novel invites identification with a respectable kind of middle-class violence, like Mr Meagles's in the Circumlocution Office. More disturbing, perhaps, is our implied approval of Frederick Dorrit, breaking out of his fixed condition of being 'dead without being aware of it' (p. 231), and charging down the footman who, he thinks, has insulted Amy, 'and threatening to trample him to death' (p. 444) with his mule. This delight in outbursts of righteous rage cannot be dissociated from Dickens's tendency to assert, 'in the vigorous national manner', strong-armed, simple-minded solutions to complex human problems, to think in the idiom of *A Child's History of England*, the kind of thinking represented by the anti-climactic collapse of Mrs Clennam's house, an amusingly and carefully prepared red herring in the plot, but as a piece of symbolism altogether too crude. Certainly, if, as T.A. Jackson suggests, it prophesies 'a like fate awaiting the Circumlocution Office',[13] the gesture is politically simplistic. Violence of this kind is part of the indignant, 'Meagles' side of Dickens which seeks arbitrary solutions to particular problems rather than risk the viability of the whole structure, the sort of approach, indeed, which Dickens satirizes in the rich, senile William

Dorrit's memories of the Marshalsea: 'I – hum – I caused you to be respected there, Amy. I – ha hum – I gave my family a position there. I deserve a return. I claim a return. I say, sweep it off the face of the earth and begin afresh. Is that much? I ask, is *that* much?' (p. 464). There could be no acuter exposure of the deficiencies of a certain kind of radicalism. It is another, more complex radicalism which is at the heart of the novel's political vision.

The problems posed by violence are central to this complexity. Dickens evidently recognized that violence already existed in the structures of capitalism and possibly in human nature also, and that the problems posed by non-violence were as complex as those posed by violence. The former point of view is clearly suggested in the excesses endured by Affery at the hand of Flintwich, and in 'Mr. F's Aunt', with her blackly comic paroxysms of formless hatred against Arthur Clennam. It is easy enough to see the violent malice in Blandois, Henry Gowan, Miss Wade and Tattycoram as something *added* to their personalities, the product of choice or of stress; but the violence in 'Mr. F's Aunt' is a fact of nature. On the other hand, in Doyce, peacefulness too looks like a fact of nature. Doyce offers a definite norm of steadiness: his 'composed and unobtrusive self-sustainment' (p. 186) is based on 'a calm knowledge that what was true must remain true'. (Ironically, Charles Babbage, on whom Doyce is partly based, was a man of self-destructive irascibility.) Dickens is too complex a writer, however, to rely on such a simple antithesis. Beside the repose of Doyce there is Mr Casby, at whose table 'everything ... promoted quiet digestion' (p. 149), but who is in truth 'a mere Inn signpost without any Inn – an invitation to rest and be thankful, when there was no place to put up at and nothing whatever to be thankful for' (pp. 141–2). Peace, the absence of the fierce energies which arise out of repressed instinct and feeling, is as ambiguous as the violence it replaces.

Doyce and Casby are 'peaceful' in their public functions as inventor and landlord. So is Mrs General, 'delegated on her mission, as it were by Church and State' (p. 436). Her peace, and that of her cathedral-city rentier class, is secured by a wilful blindness to all that might disturb it, and since the serenity she thereby secures comes near to injuring Amy, it is perhaps the unloveliest condition the novel describes. It is based on sweeping economies with the truth: 'Accidents, miseries, and offences' (p. 438) are not to be mentioned before her; 'Passion ... [must] go to sleep' in her presence. That passion is the enemy of her way of life becomes vividly obvious whenever she is sent to dream dreams ' – if she had any – ' that 'ought to have been varnished ... lying asleep in the arms of the good Saint Bernard, with the feathery snow falling on his house-top' (p. 439). It is not revolution as such which threatens Mrs General's world, but the insurrections of ordinary human feeling.

The theme of passivity has thus the deepest and most disturbing implications for the whole novel. In the Marshalsea, indeed, it is a disease: 'Elsewhere [says the doctor who delivered Amy], people are restless, worried, hurried about, anxious respecting one thing, anxious respecting another. Nothing of the kind here, sir. We have done all that – we know the worst of it; we have got to the bottom, we can't fall, and what have we found? Peace. That's the word for it. Peace' (p. 63). Dickens understands the degeneration involved in passive submission to social evil. He has also a profound sympathy for those who submit, debtors in the Marshalsea, blank-faced musicians in cheap theatres, old drunks stumbling back to the workhouse, even the imprisoned Arthur Clennam. But above all in William Dorrit he confronts us with a humane study of both violent and peaceful impotence. In his worse moods Dorrit turns on Amy with a feeble cruelty that only invented dignities for himself and promises of like dignities for her can soothe, allowing him to lie down 'with wet eyelashes, serene, in a manner majestic, after bestowing his life of degradation as a sort of portion on the devoted child upon whom its miseries had fallen so heavily' (p. 224). In the Marshalsea there is no question of resorting or not resorting to violence: society has deprived its debtors of any adequate response, passive or enraged, to the conditions in which it has placed them.

This is the context for the two major studies of 'rebellion' in the novel, of Pancks against Casby and of Fanny against Mrs Merdle and Mrs General. Casby's corrupt passivity obviously contrasts with Pancks's explosive restlessness, and yet from the start Arthur Clennam is doubtful about Pancks. His manner, unlike that of the other grotesques, makes it very difficult to pass even preliminary judgements on him. He is benevolent and sinister, especially in his savage self-satire. '"Here am I," said Pancks ... "What else do you suppose I think I am made for? Nothing. Rattle me out of bed early, set me going, give me as short a time as you like to bolt my meals in, and keep me at it. Keep me always at it, and I'll keep you always at it, you keep somebody else always at it. There you are, with the Whole Duty of Man in a commercial country"' (p. 154). This is more than an attack on Samuel Smiles. As in his insistence that in helping the Dorrit family he is only doing 'business', and in his terrible question, 'What business have I in this present world, except to stick to business? No business' (p. 269), Pancks here points to a level of pain only the greatest satire touches. Yet he is himself dangerous: 'a shadow on [Arthur's] papers caused him to look up for the cause. The cause was Mr. Pancks.' The world 'cause' is cruelly reiterated. Significantly, he is virtually repudiated (just as he is preparing his triumph in bringing the Dorrits to a fortune) by Amy herself: 'looking musingly down into the dark valley of the prison', she doubts 'if he could tell many people, even their past or present fortunes'; when Maggy asks if he could have told 'the Princess' or 'the tiny woman' theirs, Amy, 'with the sunset very bright upon her', answers firmly 'No' (pp. 286–9).

It is of course Pancks who gives Arthur 'the dangerous infection with which he was laden' (p. 565) – Merdleism – and in doing so outlines the case for cooperating with the Merdle system:

> 'One word more, Mr. Clennam,' retorted Pancks, 'and then enough for to-night. Why should you leave all the gains to the gluttons, knaves, and impostors? Why should you leave all the gains that are to be got, to my proprietor and the like of him? Yet you're always doing it. When I say you, I mean men such as you. You know you are. Why, I see it every day of my life. I see nothing else. It's my business to see it. Therefore, I say,' urged Pancks, 'Go in and win!'
> (p. 567)

Pancks here is rationalizing. He hates his infatuation with business, and his plea to Arthur is an attempt to get round what his own compulsion illustrates, that business and human feeling are incompatible. Distrusting himself, he looks to Arthur for the right combination of business success and human motivation. The attempt fails. Arthur is imprisoned, and Pancks has to face his dilemma on his own: so he turns on his proprietor, the serene Patriarch, and symbolically castrates him by cutting off his hair. It is a savage gesture, but it achieves nothing in practice and leaves an after-taste of ugliness and futility. Typically and sadly, Pancks, who is a good, brave man, can only give the reader a slightly alloyed pleasure.

Fanny offers a similarly paradoxical study in the pains and penalties of rebellion. Generosity and selfishness, pride and self-abasement, integrity and self-betrayal are continually at war in her. Trilling argues that Fanny is among those characters whom the novel condemns for sharing its own 'social bitterness' (*The Dickens Critics*, p. 287), but this is to miss the fact that rage is frequently the measure of her integrity. Her fierce hatred of patronage wins our sympathy, for instance, in her first encounter with Mrs Merdle, though what she says is clearly 'wrong' and painful to Amy. She insists on making Mrs Merdle 'pay for it, you mean little thing. What else can you make her do? Make her pay for it, you stupid child; and do your family some credit with the money!' (p. 238). The name-calling of Amy is especially disarming; it is clearly affectionate and a disguised admission of guilt. Fanny is an intelligent, self-knowing woman. Her dilemma is adroitly suggested in this exchange with Mrs General:

> 'I should think so,' observed Miss Fanny, with a toss of her head, and a glance at her sister. 'But they would not have been recalled to your remembrance, I suspect, if Uncle hadn't tumbled over the subject.'

'My dear, what a curious phrase,' said Mrs. General. 'Would not inadvertently lighted upon, or accidentally referred to, be better?'

'Thank you very much, Mrs. General,' returned the young lady, 'no I think not. On the whole I prefer my own expression.'

This was always Miss Fanny's way of receiving a suggestion from Mrs. General. But, she always stored it up in her mind, and adopted it another time. (p. 467)

Fanny's arrogant toss of her head is part of her integrity in resisting Mrs General and convention, but it is followed by capitulation. And in her equal determination to pay Mrs Merdle back, she again compromises her own position by adopting the standards of the enemy. Just as she stood up for good prose only to make the choice of bad prose her own, so a wilful integrity marks her choice of Edmund Sparkler for a husband. Like Pancks, she is drawn irresistibly to what she despises.

Her marriage emphasizes the similarities between her and Becky Sharp. It also points to Dickens as a far more serious and responsible artist than Thackeray, even at his best. Becky's marriage in *Vanity Fair* is a well-organized narrative *coup*. 'Taking Advice' (II, xiv), the chapter in which Fanny decides to marry Sparkler, is not nearly so dramatic – yet Fanny's account of her decision, proud because it is hers, shamefaced because she is telling Amy, is outside Thackeray's range: '"Short time or long time," interrupted Fanny, "I am impatient of our situation. I don't like our situation, and very little would induce me to change it. Other girls, differently reared and differently circumstanced altogether, might wonder at what I say or may do. Let them. They are driven by their lives and characters; I am driven by mine"' (p. 573). For Dickens to represent internal energy as having the compulsiveness of fate is impressive enough. For Fanny to grasp it is astonishing. She is at once free and enslaved: 'the way she had chosen lay before her, and she trod it with her own imperious self-willed step' (p. 578). Fanny's freedom, moreover, like Pancks's energy, relates impressively to the major social and political themes of the novel. At the heart of her choice is a profound protest against all that Mrs Merdle and Mrs General stand for: 'And the dancer, Amy, that she has quite forgotten – the dancer who bore no sort of resemblance to me, and of whom I never remind her, oh dear no! – should dance through her life, and dance in her way, to such a tune as would disturb her insolent placidity a little. Just a little, my dear Amy, just a little!' (p. 574). 'Dancing' here is vitality, instinct, the general heart, everything marble-smooth Merdleism petrifies into bodiless role-playing. Fanny intends to disturb (just a little) the placid inhumanity of the rich. And yet, marrying Sparkler will take the dancing out of her own life. Her integrity, like Pancks's, savages itself as well as her enemies; her wilfulness is brave, stupid, wrong, and inevitable. A strong will is not necessarily a free one.

Fanny and Pancks live at the heart of the social, political, and human dilemmas which the novel enacts. Their head-on encounter with high finance, high society and Westminster slums force them into complex complicated distortions of phrase and appearance, which they can break out of only at great cost. Their natural violence, the integrity and energy with which they live, drive them at times into open rebellion, at times into subversive cooperation with the system, but in the end it is all self-defeating and corrupting. They are as helpless, finally, as William Dorrit.

IV

Little Dorrit, then, in its complex rejection of violent insurrection, makes a comprehensive statement of political despair. A problem remains, however, with Amy; her goodness seems a compromise, a sentimental attempt to assuage the pain. She is certainly difficult to get into focus. The sunlight is too likely to bathe her in symbolic glory, her line in allegory too feebly imitates Andersen's. And yet, unexpectedly, she is a success. When some notable misconceptions are set aside, like John Wain's suggestion that her relationship with her father leaves her 'in a permanently disabled psychological state' ('*Little Dorrit*', p. 176), she emerges as one of Dickens's most sensitively presented woman characters. Her loneliness in Rome has a delicacy the opposite of sentimental. Yet intimations of sentimentality remain, all summed up in her nickname. It is, as Flora says, 'of all the strangest names I ever heard the strangest, like a place down in the country with a turnpike, or a favourite pony or a puppy or a bird' (p. 265); or like Little Nell or little Em'ly. But to read 'Little Dorrit' in this way would be to miss the point more thoroughly than Flora does, because the name and Amy's childish exterior are intentionally misleading. She is fixed in the role of a child, but only by phrase and appearance, in a calculated repudiation of Dickens's earlier faith in female immaturity. The middle-class sentimentalizing of grown women into little girls produces Pet Meagles, not Amy Dorrit. The point is made repeatedly in phrases like 'the Child of the Marshalsea began her womanly life' (p. 70), and 'she passed to and fro ... shrinking now, with a womanly consciousness that she was pointed out to every one' (pp. 75–6). Arthur Clennam's failure to recognize this 'womanly consciousness' in her feelings towards him is a source of great pain. All the other characters (except Maggy) fail in this respect even more than Arthur; and when the prostitute runs away from her on finding she is not a child, she is simply joining the other characters in deliberately refusing to accept the scrutiny of *adult* goodness and innocence.

But Amy also relates impressively to the novel's main themes. Against both the negative passivity of Casby and Mrs General, and the doubtfully altruistic rebelliousness of Pancks and Fanny, her mature calm and social usefulness are obviously important. Twice in coming out of the Marshalsea Arthur carries her 'quiet with him into the turbulent streets' (p. 410), once after their conversation about Mr Dorrit's debts, once in the closing paragraph of the novel. She is thus centrally relevant to the great problems of peace and violence, and yet it is difficult to see her as anything but a self-indulgence on Dickens's part, to relate her intelligently to the Circumlocution Office, and the Merdle empire. She seems, after all, to be out of place, a detached fantasy functioning tendentiously as a solution to the novel's problems. Paradoxically, however, this invented quality points directly to her significance.

The working class, Marx argued, 'can no longer lay claim to a historical status, but only to a human one'.[14] That is all Amy lays claim to as well. The comparison, obviously, is awkward, but there are other elements in *Little Dorrit* which support it. Casby is exactly the 'self-satisfied private property' of Marx's *Holy Family*, enjoying his '*semblance* of a human existence'; Pancks, Casby's dialectical opposite and the disturber of Bleeding Heart Yard and his own peace, is 'the *negative* side of the antithesis, its restlessness within its very self'.[15] (There is a subtle variation of this dialectic in the household and personality of Mr Meagles.) Again, the relations of Casby and Pancks with the Plornishes are echoed in the Marxist claim that the bourgeoisie had destroyed 'all feudal, patriarchal, idyllic relations' – symbolized perhaps in Mrs Plornish's 'counterfeit cottage' (p. 556) – leaving 'no other nexus between man and man than naked self-interest, than callous "cash payment"'. Certainly Marx's description of the bourgeois epoch as a time of 'everlasting uncertainty and agitation' matches the turbulent streets of *Little Dorrit* and the turbulent lives of its characters.[16] At the very least, Marx and Dickens share an overall sense of their times as being especially inhuman, and both set against them simple humanity, without traditional status.

Marx, however, believed that the proletariat would first have to undergo 'a complete loss of humanity', thereby making necessary and possible 'a *complete redemption of humanity*' ('Towards a Critique', p. 73). Amy suggests a different approach. Without explanation she is simply introduced into an unredeemed world as a rebuke both to smug quietism and the distortions of revolutionary anger. She is at the centre, in other words, of a literary rather than a practical appreciation of intransigent political and human problems; through her they are felt and judged; but she is not an instrument of change, a solution to the novel's problems. On the contrary, as Fanny acutely says, 'the virtues of the precious child [are] of that still character that they require a contrast – require life and movement around them, to bring them out in their right colours and make one love them above all things' (p. 676). There is thus no question of her reconciling us to the world of the novel. Rather she stands out against it, quietly in contrast to 'the noisy and the eager, the arrogant and the forward and vain', as they fret and chafe and make 'their usual uproar' (p. 802); and because she does so peacefully and gratuitously, in delicate poised adulthood – not like Little Nell, though perhaps as an immensely subtle reworking of Rose in *Oliver Twist* – the novel finally asserts the complete incompatibility between a humanity which lays claim not to traditional but to full human status, and nineteenth-century Western Europe.

Lionel Trilling suggests that 'the whole energy of the imagination in *Little Dorrit* is directed ... to the search for the Will in which shall be our peace' ('*Little Dorrit*', p. 293). I hold on the contrary that the novel was directed towards disturbing its original readers with the knowledge of an unbridgeable gap between humanity and their own institutions. It led them away from partial condemnations of specific evils, which fixing people and institutions in rigid, convenient categories makes possible, away from the kind of anger they were used to, and towards the kind they were afraid of. It also lured them into affection and sympathy for Amy, and then challenged them with the implications of her final happiness. And it did so effectively because it 'took place' within the situation it described; writing and reading the novel were public events; its tensions were not externally observed, but internally enacted and uncompromisingly acknowledged. And it is because Dickens was within his situation, with his readers and therefore without historical perspective, that *Little Dorrit*, far from leading us to 'the Will in which shall be our peace', continues instead to establish grounds for our perpetual disquiet.

PART THREE

Luminously Self-Evident Beings

CHAPTER NINE

The Feral Children of Haworth: Charlotte and Emily Brontë

I

Terry Eagleton's account of the Brontës in *Myths of Power* is ostensibly historical: Haworth, he writes,

> was close to the centre of the West Riding woollen area; and their lifetime coincided with some of the fiercest class-struggles in English society. The years of their childhood were years of ruination for thousands of hand-workers ... Their childhood witnessed machine-breaking; their adolescence Reform agitation and riots against the New Poor Law; their adulthood saw the Plug strikes and Chartism, struggles against the Corn laws and for the Ten Hours Bill.[1]

The effects of this on the Brontë sisters were not superficial. Eagleton writes:

> history entered, shaped and violated the inmost recesses of their personal lives ...
> In ... [their] unique imaginative formation ... social, sexual, cultural, religious and geographical issues fuse ... [and] we can trace in their very 'eccentricity' the contours of a common condition ... a general grammar. (Ibid., pp. 7, 9)

In the 1970s, this emphasis played its part in dismantling New Criticism, which Eagleton claimed severed 'one particular nerve between text and history' (p. 7) by the trivial basis of its rejection of 'a disreputably Cartesian notion of intentionality'.

The Cartesianism to which Eagleton refers is well described by Maurice Merleau-Ponty. For centuries, he alleges, science and philosophy took 'perception' to be the opening of 'a window on to things', and endorsed the 'tacit thesis ... that at every instant experience can be co-ordinated with that of the previous instant and that of the following, and my perspective with that of other consciousnesses – that all contradictions can be removed, that monadic and intersubjective experience is one unbroken text'. This appeared to make 'intention' coherent and practical, but actually extended the principle of coordination from the world into the mind. It resolved 'being-in-the-world ... into a series of causal relations ... [reduced] to third person processes that particular way of dealing with the world which we know as behaviour ... and [converted] the living body into an interiorless being' (*Phenomenology of Perception*, pp. 54, 55).

A similar reduction is also the vice of a third critical stance which Eagleton objects to – vulgar Marxism. By regarding the author as 'some anonymous "class representative", the passive, replaceable bearer of historical forces', the vulgar Marxist 'fails to understand the dialectics whereby an individual life actively transforms the historical structures which determine it into a unique artistic product' (*Myths of Power*, p. 7). Eagleton thus confronts the 'problem of the *author*' as a crucial link between text and history, while seeking to replace 'intention' with an historically constituted 'individual life' as the agent of artistic transformation.

We can clarify the problem of author as intermediary between text and history by considering Eagleton's disagreement with Q.D. Leavis. Leavis presents Emily Brontë as a 'responsible novelist'[2] whose interests were neither 'superficial nor theoretic', but had 'specific and informed sociological content'. This is an excellent example of traditional critical practice. The text is perceived as the outcome of 'varying intentions', including a historical project, which need to be sorted out 'in order to decide what *is* the novel' ('A Fresh Approach', p. 87). *Wuthering Heights*, Leavis argues, is set 'at a time when the old rough farming culture, based on a naturally patriarchal family life, was to be challenged, tamed, and routed by social and cultural changes that were to produce the Victorian class consciousness and "unnatural" gentility' (ibid., p. 99). Dates therefore matter. The novel is 'deliberately built on the opposition between ... two different cultures' represented materially by the two houses, and the land around them.

> The whole social pattern provided for us by the farm-house at the Heights, with its house-place shared by master and man, is created for us as something to be respected, and regretted when it is superseded, whatever its limitations ... by the new gentility of Thrushcross Grange – where servants live in their own quarters and know their place (unlike old Joseph whose scolding voice can never be avoided) and where children are kept from the realities of life. (p. 133)

Among the questions which critics ask from such a perspective is 'Did Emily Brontë get her history right?', and the same sort of questions may subsequently be asked of them: 'Was Leavis factually correct, for example, in suggesting that Emily Brontë envisaged "several alternative conceptions of Heathcliff ... and ended by keeping and using them all"?' (p. 96). This approach, Eagleton implies, is ultimately reductive.

Consideration of Leavis's argument is also bedevilled by her use of the word 'patriarchal' to designate how households are organized, not how women are oppressed. The word signifies, in Leavis's understanding, the father's government of both sexes and all ranks, a sense which persists and creates problems for recent feminists. Sandra Gilbert and Susan Gubar, for example, recognize the implication for younger sons as well as daughters of a system in which paternal power passes to the eldest son. This leads, in their terms, to the feminisation of younger and illegitimate sons: for them 'Heathcliff is "female"'.[3] Heathcliff, it should be remembered, beats his wife, brutalizes, physically abuses and bullies children, tortures animals, and forces two adolescents into a farrago of a marriage. The term 'patriarchy' clearly has limitations if its logic leads to such a figure being called 'female'. I propose supplementing it, on the model of biblical narrative. The patriarchal order of Abraham, Isaac and Jacob in the Book of Genesis is *less* oppressive to women than that of the fraternal band which succeeds it, when the twelve sons of Jacob take responsibility for their sister Dinah's honour in defiance of their father (Genesis 34). Thereafter the status of women in the Bible changes radically: Dinah, Tamar (Genesis 38), the Levite's concubine, the virgins of Jabesh-Gilead and the Daughters of Shiloh (Judges 19–21) are a few examples of biblical women who are much worse off than the wives and even the maidservants of the Patriarchs.

Be this as it may, Leavis's treatment of history in *Wuthering Heights* differs markedly from Eagleton's. For him, history is not realistically *depicted* in the text but loosely signified in character and incident. The adolescent Heathcliff, for example, represents, in his 'freedom' from culture, 'those at the bottom of the class structure' (*Myths of Power*, p. 103), but later he becomes 'the atomic capitalist to whom relational bonds are nothing, whose individualism is ... enslaving rather than liberating' (ibid., p. 111). He functions ambivalently, therefore, as 'caricature of and traditionalist protest against ... agrarian capitalist forces'. Later he becomes 'a type of the ascendant world of capital' in 'an imaginatively transposed version of that contemporary conflict between bourgeoisie and landed gentry which ... is central to Charlotte's work' – Yorkshire from 1812 to the 1840s (pp. 113–15). Eagleton concedes that this 'relationship holds in no precise detail since Heathcliff is not literally an industrial entrepreneur', but argues that the 'complex of class-forces' of the later period is 'reproduced' in the novel, which dramatizes 'its "metaphysical" challenge to society only by refracting it through the distorting terms of existing social relations, while simultaneously, at a "deeper" level, isolating that challenge in a realm eternally divorced from the actual' (p. 117).

Both approaches have weaknesses. Confidence in Leavis's historiography is not enhanced by her suggestion that the ethos of the Heights 'evokes the England of Squire Western ... a fact that suggests that a historical eighteenth-century rural society is the author's aim' ('A Fresh Approach', p. 133). Besides, her 'sociological novel' lacks a sociological dynamic. A narrative depicting 'social and cultural changes that were to produce the Victorian class consciousness and "unnatural" gentility' needs to show the forces which brought this about. Eagleton's limitations are no less clearly seen when he criticizes a text adversely. Some convoluted remarks about Charlotte Brontë's *The Professor* make the point:

> The novel's crass insensitivity to its hero's complacency ... signifies ... what the book has to sacrifice ... Like all Charlotte's protagonists, Crimsworth must make himself invulnerable to others ...
> ... it is certainly difficult ... to imagine the book's straight-faced endorsement of William's bloodthirsty urge to whip the old Adam out of his son. But neither is it true that the treatment is ironic; the novel seems instead to inhabit some third, less easily definable category. The smugly unselfcritical way in which Crimsworth is presented seems itself an act of half-conscious defiance on the novel's part. (*Myths of Power*, pp. 78–9)

Besides misrepresenting the chapter in which whipping children is discussed, the transfer of epithets from writer to text ('crassly insensitive', 'straight-faced', 'smugly unselfcritical', 'half-conscious') denies Charlotte Brontë responsibility for her own work and reduces her to 'a case'.

Where this leads in critical practice is illustrated in James H. Kavanagh's study of *Wuthering Heights* in a series of which Eagleton was General Editor. Introducing Kavanagh's book, Eagleton rejects the idea of a 'single, distinguishable human faculty known as "the imagination", as enduring and identifiable as the left foot or the right cortex'.[4] Kavanagh goes further. Following Catherine Belsey, he holds that subjectivity itself is best understood as 'a set of partial, dispersed subject-positions around which the text is organized and to which it appeals' (*Emily Brontë*, p. 13). That characters in novels are only 'virtual human subjects, and [that] historical events [unfold] within the illusory coherence of a virtual time and space' (ibid., p. 31) is uncontroversial. But what are the subject-positions to which a text *'appeals'*? Readers, presumably, including the author as reader. Kavanagh thus effectively abolishes the category 'person', which leaves him free to personify 'social and psychological tendencies' (p. 32), 'sexuality', 'the patriarchal power of the Law and the Word' (p. 42), and of course 'the text'. The result is an uneasy rhetorical–theoretical mix: 'From the outset,' Kavanagh writes, 'the text seems at once fascinated with rebellion and worried that the disruption of the repressive mechanisms of culture will tend towards mindless anarchy' (pp. 20–21). It has 'a set of unconscious fears, desires and tensions' (p. 15), 'a libidinal project'

(p. 77); and an 'I' which cries for sympathy along with Nelly Dean (p. 63). It is rescued, however, from incipient emotional instability by 'objective narrative tasks, imperfectly related to any character's illusory subjectivity or intention' (p. 53), and forcibly effected 'by narrative determinations' – this in reference to Heathcliff's instinctive move to save Hareton when dropped by his father, Hindley. Characters and text are allowed 'feelings' but only if outcomes and actions are 'objectively' determined – never 'intended'.

The major difference, then, between Kavanagh's study and *Myths of Power* is that Kavanagh discovers 'a general grammar' in novels, not authors. That this is a fruitful approach is demonstrated both by his book, and by Eagleton's recent *Heathcliff and the Great Hunger*,[5] which explores ways in which Heathcliff 'figures' Irish cultural experience *after* the publication of *Wuthering Heights*. But there is a price for thus freeing up the relation between text and history. Nelly Dean, Kavanagh tells us, 'is the female figure who wields the phallic tools of the symbolic order, of language and culture, and ... becomes an agent of patriarchal Law' (*Emily Brontë*, pp. 39–40). She exemplifies the 'social intruder ... It is the servant or household worker, the paid intruder, whether male or female, that makes for a "hole in the cell", a point of contact between family and social world that threatens the family's imaginary sense of integrity' (ibid., p. 55). There is truth in both claims, but they override chronology, for Nelly is also a 'character' in 'history'. Her mother breast-fed Hindley Earnshaw, and she herself rears Hindley's son with cow's milk. She is therefore in Leavis's terms not an intruder at all, but a member of the original Earnshaw household or *familia*. An intruder is what she becomes in the Grange – the paid servant, living below-stairs. However, she does not 'smoothly [transfer] her fealty to her new Linton "master"', as Kavanagh maintains (p. 56). She remains as ambivalent in her new role as in her old. If Gilbert and Gubar are undiscriminating in calling her 'patriarchy's paradigmatic housekeeper' (*The Madwoman in the Attic*, p. 291), they are right to emphasise that she 'survives'. She is the only character in the novel to make the transition into modernity, from 'foster-sister' to 'career-woman'. She may 'figure' woman as the instrument of male domination; but her story also illustrates how a woman could make her own way in a man's world between 1760 and 1802. The validity of all this, of course, depends on whether or not Emily Brontë got her facts right about late eighteenth-century Yorkshire.

And factual accuracy is no less important when a critic is writing of 'authors' rather than 'characters', which is why *Myths of Power* runs into trouble. Eagleton's account of the Brontë family history is based on assumptions which recent biographers suggest are inaccurate. There is no evidence, for example, that the Brontë sisters 'were forced to endure an especially brutal form of ideological oppression – Calvinism' (*Myths of Power*, p. 8), at least in their own home. How and what they assimilated of their father's anti-Calvinist Evangelicalism cannot be measured, but Patrick Brontë's was certainly not 'grimly hostile to the creative imagination' (ibid., p. 11). Again, we might ask whether the biographical record does not show Emily Brontë herself as a successful 'capitalist', and how this affects a reading of Heathcliff as 'atomic capitalist'. In author-centred criticism, therefore, even when freed from 'discredited' intentionalism, a coordinated, sequential narrative seems unavoidable, but the result, in the absence of intention as a category of explanation, is uncomfortable. References to 'one particular nerve between text and history', and the history that 'entered, shaped and violated the inmost recesses of their personal lives', make Charlotte and Emily Brontë not just 'subject-positions' in a psycho-historical process, but victims of a kind of rape. Eagleton fails to negotiate the gap between empirical guesses about processes and the personal experience of writing.

II

The differences, then, between 'A Fresh Approach to "Wuthering Heights"' and *Myths of Power* are less than first appears. Each needs the support of external evidence, and when one is working on the Brontës, this is to be at a disadvantage. It is worth recalling what happened to the Brontë literary remains after Charlotte Brontë's death. M. Héger tore up her letters but his wife recovered them and they surfaced at the beginning of this century. The remaining manuscripts were carried off to Ireland by Revd Arthur Bell Nichols, who for the rest of his life regarded them as 'tender keepsakes concerning none but himself'.[6] He was consequently an easy target for the forger, T.J. Wise, who got his hands on the manuscripts through an intermediary, and cut them up for clandestine resale, so making scholarly pursuit of them very difficult. One of Emily Brontë's 1844 Notebooks, though photographed in 1926, and reproduced in facsimile in 1934, has disappeared, and the Angrian stories of Charlotte and Branwell are only now being published. These developments are not fortuitous. The heirs of best-selling authors usually know the market for surviving papers. With other writers, therefore, Wise resorted to forgery, but the Brontës left no literary executors, university librarians or prosperous publishers to guard the hoard. This was partly the result of Charlotte Brontë's having committed flagrant exogamy by marrying outside the literary world, partly of the family's ignorance of the world, and the world's of them.

Wise, however, was preceded in his depredations by Charlotte and Emily themselves. They cooperated in elaborate secrecy and complicated editorial manipulations in preparing their poems for the press, and Charlotte Brontë continued the habit when editing her sisters' posthumous works. Moreover, edited and unedited, the texts themselves indulge in wilful reticence – on the question of Heathcliff's origins, or the family histories of William Crimsworth and Lucy Snowe. In the late nineteenth and early twentieth centuries, conventions of factual uncertainty became available even to inexperienced writers, the perspectives of British culture being then informed by a pessimistic, conservative relativism which foregrounded opacity and disconnection; but in the 1840s such attitudes and techniques were unorthodox in English, if not American, fiction. If uncertainty surrounds the Brontës' work, it is of their own making, an expression of ignorance or self-conscious difference. Of all great writers, with the exception perhaps of Blake, they come nearest to relying on a private language.

I find myself, therefore, in the embarrassing position of preferring the approach implicit in Edmund Gosse's verdict on Charlotte Brontë, to Leavis's, Eagleton's, or Kavanagh's. 'All her career,' Gosse wrote,

> was a revolt against conventionality, against isolation, against irresistible natural forces such as climate and ill-health and physical insignificance ... Her hatred of what was commonplace and narrow and obvious flung her against a wall of prejudice which she could not break down. She could only point to it by her exhausting efforts ... Hence, to the very last, she seems ... to be forever ruffled in temper, for ever angry and wounded and indignant, rejecting consolation, crouched like a sick animal in the cavern of her own quenchless pride ... a certain admirable ferocity is the notable feature of her intellectual character.[7]

This effort to find 'the author' in the text is, I suggest, at least as responsible as Eagleton's. Gosse's remarks, moreover, evoke one of the great recurring images in the works of both Charlotte and Emily Brontë, that of the caged or cornered or uncomprehending savage, or animal, or fairy-child. They thus point to the most important common factor in the lives and works of Charlotte and Emily Brontë, the tensions of a confrontation between the civilized and the feral.

The two most famous examples of children as estranged outsiders in the Brontës' fiction are Heachcliff's account of how he and Catherine 'ran from the top of the Heights to the park'[8] – Catherine barefoot – to creep through a broken hedge, grope up a path and peer through a window at the Grange, and Jane Eyre's description of her young self looking at her reflection in a glass:

> All looked colder and darker in that visionary hollow than in reality; and the strange little figure there gazing at me, with a white face and arms specking the gloom, and glittering eyes of fear moving where all else was still, had the effect of a real spirit: I thought it was like one of the tiny phantoms, half fairy, half imp, Bessie's evening stories represented as coming out of lone ferny dells in moors, and appearing before the eyes of belated travellers.[9]

In Charlotte's work the feral is usually concealed within the civilized, and the confrontation less vivid but more complex than in Emily's. Frances Henri in *The Professor*, for example, compares her life to that

> ' ... of a – that little animal subterranean – une taupe – comment dit-on?'
> 'Mole.'
> 'Yes – a mole which lives underground.'[10]

Contact between the wild and fantastic and the social and rational is most painfully internalized for Charlotte Brontë when childhood and adulthood meet in late adolescence. 'At that time – at eighteen, drawing near the confines of illusive dreams, Elf-land lies behind us, the shores of reality rise in front.' Such at any rate is Caroline Helstone's case in *Shirley*.[11] Profounder because more adult possibilities are suggested (if imperfectly realized) in the affinity between Louis Moore and Shirley Keeldar, symbolized in the movement of the ruffianly dog, Tartar, from one to the other.

But perhaps the most extraordinary of the many feral images in the novels is that contained in Shirley's school-exercise, '*La Première Femme Savante*'. Echoing an earlier allegory by Shirley about 'a woman-Titan ... [who] speaks with God ... Eve ... Jehovah's daughter, as Adam was his son' (*Shirley*, pp. 360–61), it tells the story of a primitive tribe ('their nature is our nature, – human both') among whom lives a neglected child: 'None cares for this child: she is fed sometimes, but oftener forgotten ... Forsaken, lost, and wandering, she lives more with the wild beast and bird than with her own kind.' But she grows up 'straight and graceful. You see in the desolate young savage nothing vicious or vacant; she haunts the wood harmless and thoughtful: though of what one so untaught can think, it is not easy to divine.' At the climax of the story her isolation is total; she has 'lost all her tribe'; she sits, 'her body still, her soul astir occupied, however, rather in feeling than in thinking, – in wishing, than hoping, – in imagining than projecting ... Of all things, herself [seems] to herself the centre, – a small, forgotten atom of life, a spark of soul ... burning unmarked to waste in the heart of a black hollow.' Desperately she asks whether she is 'thus to burn out and perish, her loving light doing no good, never seen never heeded', and at last, unlike her Miltonic precursor, she receives a mystical communication directly from God rather than through her husband: she is 'Eva', and she is to become the bride of a 'Son of God', 'that Seraph on earth, named Genius' (pp. 548–51).

This overblown allegory has a doubly autobiographical significance. It is by 'Shirley' and about 'Shirley', that is, as an imitation of her *devoirs* for M. Héger, it is 'by' and 'about' Emily Brontë. It *may* be appropriate, therefore, to read it as an 'incestuous Byronic love story' in which the figure of Genius is a 'Byronic/Satanic god of the Night' (*The Madwoman in the Attic*, p. 208). However, Gilbert and Gubar also judge it to be less directly identified 'with the assertive Satanic principle' than is the allegory of the woman–Titan (ibid., p. 207), in which case it may be read as a 'conservative' story by and about Charlotte Brontë – it is after all *her* fiction. This gives its Biblical references, which are much more specific than the Byronic ones, a special significance: like Mary of the Annunciation (traditionally the second Eve), the young woman's response is to call herself 'handmaid' of the Lord (*Shirley*, p. 551). Like Mary also, she is overshadowed by the Holy Spirit under the denomination 'Comforter' (John 14:26), and her divine bridegroom (presumably her Muse) is accorded the Christological title 'Dayspring from on high' (p. 552 – see Luke 1:78). Here, then, is a Charlotte Brontë who publicly sanctions a Byronic, radically feminist *rewriting of Scripture*, but who has also undertaken a startlingly conformist mission. For while the word 'Genius' may be legitimately applied to both women, it is Charlotte who performs the historical task of the feral child by re-entering the life of the tribe.

One reason why stories about children raised by wild animals, or Gypsies, or elves, have such mythic power is that feral children are not kitted out with the structured knowledge which turns most adults into productive, future-oriented members of society. We are drawn to their freedom from history – like Romulus and Remus, they can start afresh. In the case of fictional feral children, this is, of course, an illusion; his jungle nurturers introduce Kipling's Mowgli into an intensely ideological social order. But the case of the real-life 'feral' child is different. To be brought up by a father and a maiden aunt, that is in an unsexed household, and by adults as culturally estranged from their community as Revd Patrick Brontë and his sister-in-law – it is worth recalling that when Charlotte Brontë went to school she spoke with an Irish accent – is to forego a fundamentally important conditioning into common humanity, which no amount of reading about the Duke of Wellington can compensate for. It is to grow up marooned from history, blocked from access to work and love.

On this basis I wish to supplement the model of the artistic process as overdetermination developed in *Myths of Power*. A host of subsidiary factors, Eagleton suggests, often purely private, are fused in the production of literary texts by processes akin to the displacement and condensation of the Freudian model of dreamwork, into representations and reflections of the complexities and tensions of a major historical conflict. In the Brontës' case, he believes this conflict to have been the struggle 'between landed and industrial capital' (ibid., p. 8), but he fails to account for the continuing fascination of this long-decided and local contest. If what finally holds the attention are the overdeterminations themselves, the conflict disclosed in them is reduced to a triviality. On the other hand, if class conflict remains the issue, then Eagleton's discriminations – roughly for Emily Brontë and against Charlotte – become tendentious judgements about political correctness. These deficiencies can only be met, I suggest, by complementing the concept of the overdetermined text by that of 'feral' authors, whose social underdetermination discloses the most important attribute of all major writers – a capacity to give effect to identifiable intentions.

Among the four Brontë children, underdetermination was most marked in the lives of Branwell and Emily. As adults neither worked nor loved successfully, though Branwell made vigorous efforts at both. Emily Brontë's case is different. She ran the Haworth household, and controlled the family finances. She also wrote *Wuthering Heights* and a number of mature and passionate poems. If she was socially underdetermined in girlhood, the persistence of that condition into womanhood was thus apparently her choice. I shall begin to fill out the concept of underdetermination, therefore, by examining Emily Brontë's writing as the record of a poet and novelist who anticipated the thought of Edmund Husserl by willing herself into a condition of phenomenological abstraction.

III

The intentions of Emily Brontë's with which I am concerned have nothing to do with either Gondal or mysticism, as consideration of the following poem, perhaps the best of her early verse, written apparently late in 1837, will show.

> I'll come when thou art saddest
> Hid alone in the darkened room
> When the mad days mirth has vanished
> And the smile of joy is banished
> From evenings chilly gloom
>
> I'll come when the hearts real feeling
> Has entire unbiassed sway

And my influence oer thee stealing
grief deepening joy congealing
Shall bear thy soul away

Listen 'tis just the hour
The awful time for thee
dost thou not feel upon thy soul
A Flood of strange sensations roll
Forunners of a sterner power
Heralds of me (143)

This poem is written on a sheet of paper with another completed poem, in which a speaker of unspecified sex cannot or will not go somewhere in a snowstorm, and a fragment in which another speaker is unable to sing a love-song. Fannie Ratchford read it in the context of Augusta Geraldine Almeda's 'loneliness and remorse' after she has regained the throne of Gondal;[12] Derek Roper thinks the speaker appears to be 'a spectre' (*The Poems*, p. 273), but it could as easily be the voice of 'the Genius of a solitary region ... [addressing] his wandering and wayward votary' which Charlotte Brontë offered as an explanation for three other poems by her sister: 'Shall Earth no more inspire thee' (84), 'The night wind' (79), and 'Aye there it is! It wakes tonight' (85) (ibid., p. 252). Clearly the poem changes fundamentally if is about a man addressing a woman, or a woman a man, if it concerns friends of the same sex, the dead and the living, or god and mortal; nevertheless its most serious meanings are constituted by its status as a fragment denying answers to such uncertainties.

There is a danger in endowing the fragmentary with a fortuitous interest. Discreteness, however, is formally inherent in the lyric. Lyrics are self-isolating, organized to achieve a moment of unmediated communication through their own internal movement and precluded from rationalizing their moment of closure. In the case of 'I'll come when thou art saddest', this formal reticence is clearly readable. The first line ends on a half-rhyme. This for the period is a minor technical flaw – not that half-rhymes were unacceptable, but to open with one was unusual. This subtle irregularity lays the foundation for the more flagrant break-up of the established verse-pattern in the final stanza, with its truncated first line, broken by the heavy pause after a trochaic first foot, its additional line and third rhyme. The speaker is thus established as dominating the poem's form. This reinforces the power play between 'I' and 'thou', 'me' and 'thee'. There is a reduction here to the bare egos of the two consciousnesses in the poem – or rather of the single consciousness with which the reader chooses to identify; for not only does the poem parenthesize distinctions of gender, it leaves the reader free to adopt the point of view either of the speaker's powerful controlling consciousness or that of the threatened, controlled person addressed. Abstracted from all imaginable contexts, sexual, social or ideological, the speaker is the centre of power in the poem, the principle of its organization and its 'sense' or direction. This exercise of power gives effect to the authorial will, even if that will is to be, not the possessor, but the possessed. We are thus confronted – as Denis Donoghue decisively demonstrates – with a solipsistic autonomy in the poet to match that of the lyric mode itself.[13] On this basis Donoghue argues that Emily Brontë is the God within her own breast, and that that God, and the entire universe, are indistinguishable from her and each other.

But this surely misses the sophistication and authority of a performance in which Emily Brontë discloses her capacity as a writer to become what Husserl calls

> the attentive Ego ... [which] practises abstention with respect to what [it] intuits ...
>   This universal depriving of acceptance, this 'inhibiting' or 'putting out of play' of all positions taken toward the already-given Objective world and ... those concerning being, illusion, possible being, being likely, probable etc ... this 'phenomenological epochē' and 'parenthesizing' of the Objective world ... does not leave us confronting nothing. On the contrary ... what we (or, to speak more precisely what I, the one who is meditating) acquire by it is my pure living ... The epochē can ... be said to be the radical and universal method by which I apprehend myself purely: as Ego. (*Cartesian Meditations*, pp. 20–21)

But this provisional bracketing of 'all existential positions' – time, place, gender, everydayness – does not collapse God, the self and the universe into a holistic blob, as Donoghue maintains; for as Husserl argues and Emily Brontë exemplifies,

> I must first explicate my own as such, in order to understand that within my own, what is not my own likewise receives existential sense ... The illusion of solipsism is dissolved, even though the proposition that everything existing for me must derive its existential sense exclusively from ... my sphere of consciousness, retains its validity and fundamental importance.

Thus 'I'll come when thou art saddest' constitutes two selves, and therefore real intersubjectivity, precisely because either of the persons can be the sphere of consciousness in and by which the poem is constituted.

We may accordingly reject Donoghue's version of Emily Brontë's solipsistic pantheism, and restore her to the ordinary world. We may doubt, for example, whether her religious convictions were particularly heterodox. We certainly have no evidence that they were. On the other hand, the will to self-abstraction in the poems does suggest that the claims of Leavis and Eagleton that the success of *Wuthering Heights* derives in substantial part from its sociological and historical sugges-tiveness should be approached with caution. J.F. Goodridge has pointed out that we do not find in *Wuthering Heights* 'the same interest in social changes, or the life and work of rural England, as we find in Hardy. The Heights is seldom thought of as a farm; neither the topogra-phy of the Dales, nor their way of life, have the same *kind* of relevance to *Wuthering Heights* as the West Country has to Hardy's novels, or the Potteries to Arnold Bennett.'[14] He adds, however, that 'the moors iso-late and divide, and only the strong passionate individual survives', but it is Emily Brontë who does the isolating and dividing, who refuses to write about shared life at all, about the dramas of class, gender or community, and insists on thinking of and through individuals.

Moreover, with the exceptions of Lockwood and Nelly, those indi-viduals are reduced to bare consciousnesses driven, for example, by the needs of gender without the appetites of sex. Domestic life in the novel is without intimacy, except between children. Even its more convincing marriages, between Hindley and Frances, and between Edgar and Catherine (the latter convincing as a dysfunctional marriage) are pre-sented in hostile terms, from the point of view of the pre-adolescent Catherine who registers the loss of vividness in the lives of adults but has no sense of what sexual maturity has given them in recompense, though as Gilbert and Gubar observe, she 'understands its relevance to her' (*The Madwoman in the Attic*, p. 270). Marriage in *Wuthering Heights* is thus emotionally arbitrary, the book carrying least conviction in its account of Heathcliff's marriage to Isabella and the younger Catherine's to Linton. The latter in particular seems completely indiffer-ent to the physical as well as the psychological traumas involved. A related example of this indifference to adult and historical realities is the arbitrary way in which Heathcliff accumulates a substantial for-tune, a sophisticated vocabulary and considerable *savoir-faire* in the two years he is away from the Heights. The transformation is mythical, like the deaths of the first generation of Earnshaws and Lintons. In the same way the begetting of Linton and his later marriage (at seventeen) are designed merely to create situations, without regard to the emo-tional (never mind the sexual) dramas they imply.

More significant than the novel's lack of interest in marriage is its representation of masculine experience. Gilbert and Gubar maintain that Edgar has 'specifically patriarchal ... feelings toward Heathcliff', that he 'does not need a strong, conventionally masculine body, because his mastery is contained in books, wills, testaments ... all the parapher-nalia by which patriarchal culture is transmitted from one generation to the next' (ibid., pp. 280–81). However, like the novel itself, they fail to address the issue of the transfer of power from the patriarch to the fraternal band. Edgar is manifestly not the 'man' his father-in-law was; he is to Earnshaw what the indecisive, guilty Reuben is to his father Jacob in Genesis, but unlike Reuben he has no fraternal band to help him conceal his weakness. Nor has any other male character in the novel. The Heights after Nelly leaves is a parody of masculine society; it has the coarseness and sadism of the fraternity house without its self-interested, collusive power-politics. As a result both Catherines and Nelly achieve an autonomy which an authentically historical narrative, with a dominant fraternal band, would have denied them.

This blocking of adult and historical perspectives in the novel is not, ultimately, a 'failure', however. Admittedly it leaves us with an awkwardly desocialized Catherine and Hareton in possession of both houses at the end of the novel, but in other respects it forces us to impose our own sense on the narrative and its outcomes. Events in *Wuthering Heights* are not available for 'perception', our own or anybody else's, not even Nelly Dean's – on the contrary, like the poems, it forces the work of its completion on its readers. The issues which these labours raise for us are, moreover, metaphysical (or mythical) rather than social and historical. What is the nature of the bond between Catherine and Heathcliff, as children, as adults, after Catherine's death, after Heathcliff's death? We cannot find definitive answers to these questions, as the narratives of Nelly Dean and Lockwood try to do – Nelly's after Catherine's death, Lockwood's in the closing paragraph of the novel – by coordinating experience 'at every instant ... with that of the previous instant and that of the following'. As Eagleton admits, 'The relationship of Heathcliff and Catherine ... seems ... to transcend the personal into some region beyond it' (*Myths of Power*, p. 107). But his premises force him to account for this deterministically, to suggest that 'society' projects the central character 'to the periphery ... into myth' (ibid., p. 109). But this is to leave Emily Brontë's will out of account. It is she, not 'society', who does the pushing, who chooses to ignore the adult world of men and marriage so that she can retain the privileges of pre-adult imagination.

This is why Georges Bataille's perverse essay on her in *Literature and Evil* contains a truth Eagleton fails to acknowledge:

> In *Wuthering Heights*, as in Greek tragedy, it is not the law itself that is denounced: what it forbids is ... [a] domain made for man. [This] forbidden domain ... is tragic ... or, better still ... sacred ... The lesson of *Wuthering Heights*, of Greek tragedy and, ultimately, of all religions, is that there is an instinctive tendency towards divine intoxication which the rational world of calculation cannot bear ... to which the instincts of childhood are closely related, [and which] is entirely in the present.[15]

This at least helps to explain why Emily Brontë's representation of the struggle between local landed and industrial capital still holds the attention. The normal processes of ideological formation having failed in her case, she is free to quit the historically determined 'rational world of calculation', and enter the terrain of 'divine intoxication'. The price of this self-exclusion from everydayness is childishness, an internalized sadism which only a writer of Bataille's psychopathology could embrace with unqualified glee. Nevertheless Bataille is justified in claiming that the world (constituted, as I see it, by Emily Brontë's *epochē*) is 'a domain made for man', not because it is forbidden, as he claims, but because it is the product of *her* intelligent refusal to conform, to accept the imposition of a 'general grammar' on her life.

The novel thus opens to us moving possibilities of willing in history. Emily Brontë's rebellion is uncompromising. Heathcliff is not allowed to participate in society's material and ideological reproduction of itself – to be an adult, to be a man among men. In this he is supported by Catherine, even in the throes of her severe and exactly observed mental disorder. Both pay the price: they are reduced to the status of ghosts, to myth, even in each other's minds. But myth, while it can interpret the world, cannot change it. The 'problem-solving' function attributed to it by Gilbert and Gubar (*The Madwoman in the Attic*, p. 256) would actually compromise the tragic seriousness of the narrative. Emily Brontë, true to truth, refuses to offer us the weak consolation of merely mythical resolutions. Instead, she lays her ghosts, if not in the quiet earth, at least in the persons of the younger Catherine and Hareton, to work the defeat of that very spirit of rebellion with which she willed herself into myth in the first place. It is not a mere text, then, which stands athwart the ideological current and rejects 'an illusory resolution of real contradictions' (*Myths of Power*, p. 97), but a woman's will.

IV

Like her sister, Charlotte Brontë reached adulthood in a relatively underdetermined condition, but then chose to enter the world more or less on its own terms. Thus if Emily Brontë's *epochē* is significant as an act of rebellion, Charlotte Brontë's thrust in the opposite direction inevitably appears reactionary. The weakness of rebellion, however, is that it quits history in disgust, and opts heroically for extinction. Revolution, on the other hand, can only take place in the real world. Briefly, the ideologue wills the reproduction of society, the rebellious mythographer its extinction, and the revolutionary artist its transformation. Consequently, if any of the Brontës can claim the latter title, it must be the sternly Protestant enthusiast for the Duke of Wellington and implacable foe of the Luddite rioters. I shall therefore attempt to show that Eagleton is wholly wrong in representing her novels as 'ideological in a precise sense – myths' (p. 97).

In Charlotte's case, intention is as important as in her sister's. Because she, too, was ideologically underdetermined, she could only incorporate herself into society by her own efforts. She was thus by choice what most of us are by conditioning, which meant that she could not be like the rest of us after all. Her relationship to the world was that of a spy in a strange land, willing her own invisibility, at least until she had learnt its ways. But the use of adult powers to achieve this orthodoxy meant that her assimilation of ordinariness stimulated her critical powers instead of allaying them. In effect the acquired skills of belonging to society reconstituted on a more mature basis the condition of estrangement which made their development necessary in the first place. But the skills required to make a late entry into ordinary life can be adapted for literary purposes. Charlotte Brontë's novels achieve a disturbing intensity when those adaptive skills depict their own formation in a biographical or autobiographical narrative. Hence the identity between novel and protagonist in her work. Jane Eyre IS *Jane Eyre*, Lucy Snowe IS *Villette*, William Crimsworth IS *The Professor*, whereas Emma is only a constituent of (Jane Austen's) *Emma*, and Heathcliff of *Wuthering Heights*.

The three defining notes of Charlotte Brontë's writing are orthodoxy, secrecy and rationality, and it is the second – reserve, watchfulness – which ensures that the interaction of the first and the third is openly revolutionary. To clarify this claim, it will once again be necessary to inspect the workings of a writer's powers of decision by looking at a text using some of the techniques of New Criticism, a task made more difficult in Charlotte Brontë's case because instead of a poem we must examine an extract from a novel. What follows presupposes a careful rereading of chapter nineteen of *The Professor* (pp. 166–90).

William Crimsworth begins this chapter tendentiously. 'Novelists', he writes, 'should never allow themselves to weary of the study of real life', and should avoid 'vivid contrasts of light and shade', rapture and despair. He next uses this supposedly normative evenness of life and art to justify an ideal of ruthless self-suppression. A rational man may of course be totally and unexpectedly impoverished, but if he is sensible he will do no more than stagger, recover and try again. Pain may make him writhe, death root up all he loves, but he knows – 'Religion' assures him – that there are consolations in Eternity. These thoughts are prompted by Crimsworth's recalling a loss not quite so serious as life everlasting, but serious enough – that of his best pupil. The disappearance of

Frances Henri was something 'a steady, reasonable man' such as he could cope with. All he had to do in the daytime was put his feelings 'on the silent system', though he concedes that at night those 'morose nurslings ... in revenge ... sat on my pillow, haunted my bed, and kept me awake with their long, midnight cry'.

The reader is given quite as much work to do by this passage as by anything in *Wuthering Heights*. 'Reason' functions in the Crimsworth world, along with its ally, 'Religion', as the principal means by which the mature human being becomes reconciled to the contradictions of experience. They are ideological and savagely repressive – the laconic image of the Benthamite 'silent system' for prisons is extremely telling. Is Crimsworth the naïve bearer of this ideological apparatus, or is he bitterly ironic? Is he aware of the contradiction in his denigration of extremes and the melodramatic image with which the third paragraph concludes? Does he see what we see, that the subversion of his explicit message by the images deployed to express it mirrors the interaction of powerful social forces to which his own socially marginalized status as a teacher in a foreign land have alerted us? How sophisticated an ironist is he? Does his irony (selfconsciously or unselfconsciously) signal his own secret autonomy in a world otherwise bearing heavily down upon him?

In the light of such tensions, it is hard to see what Eagleton means when he finds, in what he calls the 'smugly unselfcritical way in which Crimsworth is presented ... an act of half-conscious defiance on the novel's part' (*Myths of Power*, p. 79). We are after all given nothing *but* Crimsworth's self-presentation. How can 'the novel' distinguish 'its' way of presenting Crimsworth from 'his'? Eagleton's accusation can only make sense if *both* narrator and author have not the faintest notion of what they are about, if the reader occupies a position superior to the text, and the academic's is the only genuinely human attitude. Eagleton assumes that 'we' can see the blindness which author and narrator unwittingly inflict upon their narrative, that, as an agent in its own right, the text effects a 'smooth exclusion of other values', and that this is a 'structural irony, an essential rigour which we must take or leave' (ibid., p. 80). By this self-privileging prosopopoeia, Eagleton effects the smooth exclusion of all questions raised by the text which might point to the intentions of Charlotte Brontë and her narrator.

The remainder of the chapter requires us to identify the conflicting values which it brings into play, and to make sense of where Crimsworth, Charlotte Brontë and the reader stand in relation to them. Having held his peace for a week, Crimsworth asks Mlle Reuter about Frances's whereabouts, and is repulsed. Even when he receives a letter enclosing money for the lessons he gave Frances, and for which he has already been paid by the school, he is unable to trace her. The letter notes that it is 'easier to write about a severe duty than to perform it', but the bearing of this on what Crimsworth has himself just written for us is not made explicit. Still ignorant of Frances's whereabouts, William haunts various Protestant churches in the city, and, ever the outsider, makes caustic observations about English dress as he does so. Eventually he discovers Frances in the Protestant cemetery where her aunt has recently been buried. This lovers' meeting in necropolis requires the male lover to put on his spectacles to see his beloved. Nevertheless his stealthy approach to her is, he declares, 'a wonder in her heart'. She calls him '*mon maître*'. He describes her as 'penniless and parentless; for a sensualist charmless' but for him the 'personification of discretion and forethought ... of self-denial and self-control ... model of truth and honour, of independence and conscientiousness ... silent possessor of a well of tenderness, of a ... more dangerous flame [that] burned safely under the eye of reason'. The obvious irony here – surely 'seen' by the 'writer' – is that two social misfits and atypical lovers, meeting stealthily in a graveyard, give life to the socially sanctioned values of self-control and love which are so inadequately represented in the thoroughly socialized Mlle Reuter and M. Pelet. Unchaperoned, and without any sense of impropriety, they go to her apartment, and she wastes her small ration of fuel making tea. He admits with feelings of mortification that he has never had a home, and that the task of making one has yet to begin. He describes how he watched her too closely, and was pleased by the neat movements of her body (in spite, presumably, of her lack of sensual charm). After tea they control their embarrassment by playing the roles of master and pupil, and in spite of Crimsworth's supposed preference for the literature of everyday life, Frances proposes that they read *Paradise Lost* together – and he takes the opportunity when correcting her intonation of gazing at her 'without exciting too warm a flush' – whether in her, or in himself, or in them both is tactfully not disclosed. He then abruptly takes his leave. He wants to give her the money she has unnecessarily given him, but much-praised Reason stops him doing so. Impulse gets the upper hand, however, and he slips back, and like a man of the world paying a courtesan, secretes the money in an ornamental tea-cup. Finally he walks home, and the rational moralist, who believes in the evenness of life and art, and dislikes 'vivid contrasts of light and shade', confronts, and confronts the reader with, a rococo display of colour in the florid evening sky, from which he draws the laconic moral, 'Hope smiles on Effort'.

For all the elaborate explanation and rationalization on its surface, this is a narrative method and, in so far as the text is Crimsworth's, a consciousness, which refuses to explain or rationalize. But, unlike a poem by Emily Brontë, neither is abstracted from 'the world'. The text carries the world with it into all its operations on itself, without declaring its relationship with the world – and this, paradoxically, is itself to effect and make specific such a relationship. The text (or the consciousness deemed to have written it) effects a dramatic play between paraphrasable sense and implicit contradictions, and achieves (as truly as any poem subject to the scrutinies of New Criticism) a unity which does not find 'its sanctions in the ordinary logic of language ... [but] in the dramatic contest, and ... there alone'.[16] The drama is essentially one of anomalousness hiding itself in, and perhaps sanctioning a flaunted subservience to, the letter of the law. The narrative deploys the skills of the feral child unobtrusively attaching itself to the ranks of orthodoxy to tell the story of William Crimsworth and Frances Henri doing the same thing, and becoming lovers in the process.

This applies generally, I believe, to almost all of Charlotte Brontë's work, at least in prose, and particularly to *Shirley*. Eagleton writes of *Shirley* that it 'veers unsteadily between Romantic conservatism and progressive liberalism, bringing them finally to synthetic resolution' (*Myths of Power*, p. 86). But this denies a signifying function to the unsteady and synthetic elements in the text, even though the most conservative and complacent readers must notice them. Thus one of the major awkwardnesses in the narrative is Shirley's refusal to tell her friend Caroline the true state of Robert Moore's feelings for her and the identity of Mrs Pryor. Tom Winnifrith attributes these silences to Charlotte Brontë's 'inability to communicate with her readers',[17] but the problem is surely not that she can't but that she won't. Narrator and character are silent on principle. Shirley is reserved about the real state of feeling between Robert and herself because those feelings are inseparable from her love for his brother, Louis, and secrecy, the self-protective reserve of the feral spy in the strange land of the historically commonplace, is the heart and foundation of their love. This is why it is mistaken to compare the mastery of Louis over Shirley, as Eagleton does, with Robert's over his workers. Sado-masochistic and magniloquent as the love-scenes between Shirley and Louis may be, they constitute an unmistakable critique of dominance and submission in the industrial worlds and the Helstone household. Thus while Shirley's romantic–conservative interventions on Robert's behalf are indeed a repressive involvement in the economic and political system, the emotional ground for that involvement is a radical personal independence from the commonplace, Trollopian world in which Sir Philip Nunelly would be regarded as a suitable husband for Shirley.

The whole book is energized by such movements and counter-movements. Charlotte Brontë refuses, for example, to allow evangelical

Anglicanism perform the socially assuaging function of myth which theory suggests she should. She applies it instead almost randomly to her narrative with the clear logic of an adult and the improper insistence of a child, notably in the account of the attack on the Mill and the events leading up to it, the School Feast and the battle between the Church party and the Dissenters. The chapter describing the latter bristles with the recognition that there can be no steadiness, no moral or social resolutions, in the world of the novel. A fat Dissenter is left sitting in the ditch, a spirit merchant by trade, who drinks more water that afternoon than he had swallowed before – the vignette reeks of the scornful snobbery of squire and parson, represented by the hearty, self-congratulatory alliance of Shirley and Mr Helstone. But the next sentence reads: 'Mr. Hall had taken care of Caroline, and Caroline of him: he and Miss Ainley made their own quiet comments to each other afterwards on the incident' (p. 342). When Mr Hall, the one authentically religious clergyman in the novel, is seen in alliance with Miss Ainley and Caroline and in opposition to Shirley and her allies, we are reminded of distressing issues raised in the chapter entitled 'Old Maids', and particularly of Mr Helstone's shortcomings as a husband, a parson and an uncle. Shirley's romantic war-games are accordingly exposed as a morally questionable charade.

Her alliance with Mr Helstone, moreover, quickly collapses. As news of the imminent attack on the Mill hardens, Robert Moore and Mr Helstone are reconciled; Messrs Wynn, Sykes, Armitage and Ramsden gather in a close circle around them; and Shirley is excluded from the band of brothers – she is not 'iron-souled enough to be trusted in a crisis' (p. 353). Evidently religious rivalries were only a game to the clergymen, a game in which women could join, but defending property is the real thing. Yet by means of the School Feast battle which arbitrarily precedes and parodies the struggle for the Mill, feminist and theological issues are thrust gratuitously into the drama and subvert the unqualified reconciliation between Romantic conservatism and progressive liberalism which the repulse of the Luddites is supposed to enforce. During the riot, Eagleton complains, we do not see the rioters. 'At the point of its most significant presence in the novel, the working class is wholly invisible' (*Myths of Power*, p. 49). But by recounting the incident through Shirley and Caroline's experience of it, and as a sequel to the School Feast, Charlotte Brontë adroitly exposes the fissures, contradictions and confusion in the perspectives of the land- and mill-owning classes at the very moment of crisis when, faced with a violent challenge to their authority, they are themselves least conscious of those contradictions, and most in need of unquestioning class solidarity.

All Charlotte Brontë's endings are odd. (Why does *Jane Eyre* conclude with the apocalyptic martyrdom of St John Rivers?) In the last dialogue between principal characters in *Shirley*, Robert Moore, with brutal masculine relish, tells his bride Caroline of his plans for the industrialization of rural Yorkshire: 'the beautiful wild ravine shall be a smooth descent; the green natural terrace shall be a paved street: there shall be cottages in the dark ravine, and cottages on the lonely slopes: the rough pebbled track shall be an even, firm, broad, black sooty road, bedded with the cinders from my mill: my mill, Caroline – my mill shall fill its present yard' (p. 737). The gentle Caroline is shocked, but Robert discloses the other side of his dream – 'the houseless, the starving, the unemployed shall come to Hollow's Mill from far and near', and there will be day-schools and Sunday schools for Caroline and Shirley and Miss Ainley to run, and 'treats' once a quarter (p. 738). At this, Caroline surrenders to his kisses. The state of affairs after rather than before the attack on the Mill is thus confirmed. Shirley's title of 'Esq.' is transferred to her husband, Louis; the proper sphere of women is defined, and is rewarded with husbandly ardour (Charlotte Brontë has a keen sense of the interpenetration of the politics of production and of gender – it is as much his Mill as Robert himself that makes love to Caroline), and the future state of society, the Victorian reader's present without the inconveniences of Chartist disorders, is represented as the dream of an honourable entrepreneur.

It would be a mistake to patronize any part of this vision. Establishing day-schools and Sunday schools (for both sexes) was one of the great achievements of Patrick Brontë's ministry, and his daughters were proud of their own part in it.[18] In what amounts to an epigraph to the novel, the narrator *in propria persona* refers to Robert's day-dreams as 'prophecies', and they clearly echo the Book of Isaiah:

> They shall feed in the ways and on all bare heights shall be their pasture ... And I will make all my mountains a way, and my high ways shall be exalted. Lo these shall come from far: and, lo, these from the north and west; and these from the land of Sinim. (Isaiah 49:9; 11–12).

But is Robert an authentic or a false prophet? Is Caroline's husband, and what he represents – the industrial foundation of Victorian prosperity – finally blasphemous? In Isaiah the levelling of the hills, the building of the high way, and the call of the poor is the work, not of a man, but of the Lord, and there is a disturbing incontinence in Robert's atavistic insistence on his ownership of the Mill. The narrator calls its chimney as 'ambitious as the tower of Babel' (p. 739) – symbol of human pride and social chaos – and the old housekeeper ends the novel with recollections, first of the building of the old Mill (the one defended against the Luddites), and then of the Hollow as it used to be when her mother was frightened out of her wits by 'a fairish' there, forty years before:

'A lonesome spot it was – and a bonnie spot – full of oak trees and nut trees. It is altered now.'

The story is told. I think I now see the judicious reader putting on his spectacles to look for the moral. It would be an insult to his sagacity to offer directions. I only say, God speed him in his quest! (pp. 740–41)

The celebrated novelist, living a life of desolating loneliness in her odd childhood home, her brother and sisters, her aunt and her old house-keeper dead, her father dumb with grief, has done her work. If her story is read as an awkwardly synthetic resolution of contradictory impulses towards Romantic conservatism and progressive liberalism, that is the reader's doing, not hers. She has too odd and accurate a view of the world and of how novels should be ended to believe her fiction could reconcile anyone to anything.

CHAPTER TEN

Fragments of Consciousness:
The Poems of Emily Brontë

Even with the recent publication of three scholarly editions of her poems,[1] Emily Brontë's achievement as a poet remains confused. There are four reasons for this: disorder of the manuscript sources; scholarly emphasis on chronology at the expense of Emily Brontë's own editorial work on the texts; uncertainty about printed and manuscript sources; and the desire to read the poems as proleptically post-Christian – witness Katherine Frank's biography.[2] Barbara Lloyd-Evans, it is true, prints the Ashley MS and the two Notebooks begun in 1844, but her edition has many misprints, ignores other manuscript sources, and downgrades the version of the poems published under the name of Ellis Bell in 1846. Janet Gezari gives definitive status to the latter, but prints the other poems chronologically, thus confusing the record of the Notebooks. Derek Roper prints neither printed nor manuscript versions of the 1846 poems but an eclectic text, and he too regiments the poems chronologically. In an attempt to introduce some order into the discussion – it is difficult to follow even as clear and perceptive an account of them as Lyn Pykett's in the *Women Writers* series[3] – this essay will briefly describe the manuscript record; outline differences between the poems in manuscript and the Ellis Bell poems of 1846; outline in general terms the themes and perspectives opened up by the poems, and their technical resources; and finally, using key formulations by Edmund Husserl, Maurice Merleau-Ponty and Georges Bataille, it will attempt to summarize what Emily Brontë achieved as a poet, particularly from 1844 onwards.

The most important sources of the poems are a mutilated Notebook into which Emily Brontë transcribed a large number of poems written between 1837 and 1839, and two Notebooks into which, in February 1844, she began transcribing selected poems, often noting the date of original composition as she did so. The 1844 Notebooks are 'edited', making 'the final division ... between her Gondal poems ... copied into one notebook and clearly marked "Emily Jane Brontë. GONDAL POEMS", and the poems which were not about Gondal copied into another',[4] Gondal being, of course, the imaginary Pacific island about which she and her sister Anne had been writing prose and verse since 1831.

The organisation of the first half of GONDAL POEMS was clarified by Mary Visick in 1958.[5] There are forty-five poems in the Notebook, twenty-seven being dated before February 1844. Five are dated between March and May 1844, and there are no further entries for that year until November. May, therefore, was the month in which the task begun in February of transcribing a selection of existing Gondal poems seems to have been completed (117 extant poems were excluded from transcription).[6] Three poems were finished in May. Of these the first, 'The Death of A.G.A.', is dated January 1841 and May 1844. Emily Brontë evidently returned to it with the purpose of including it in the Notebook. It is the poem which, according to Visick, is the key to understanding the twenty poems preceding it.

The first two poems in the Gondal Notebook are in reverse chronological order. We read first of a woman called Augusta G. Almeda soliloquizing over the tomb of her lover, Alexander Lord of Elbe; in the second Alexander is 'Parted from Gondal', 'on a desolate sea' and doomed to die if not already dead. The next six poems present another lover of Augusta's, Lord Alfred of Aspin Castle. Of these, one (104) was written for the Notebook on 'March 2d 1844'. Augusta proves an unfaithful lover to Lord Alfred, but now mourns his death. Finally, an unknown speaker meditates on three portraits in Aspin Castle, of Lord Alfred, whose ghost has returned from exile, of a child Lord Alfred never saw, and of the 'idol queen' for whom he became a damned soul.

The next four poems involve different characters. In the first, a story is told by the fireside of a man called Douglas escaping from horsemen seeking to avenge their 'sovereign's gore'. In the second, also a fireside story, a man called Gleneden recalls the death of a comrade called Arthur in a venture intended to secure peace for his people. In the third, Gleneden, in prison, awakens in delirium to discover that Gondal has lost her liberty – the assassination of a tyrant has proved futile. In the fourth, a woman called Rosina also wakes from delirium to recall the murder of Julius Brenzaida, King of Gondal.

There follow two groups of three poems each. The first three are about Julius and a woman called Geraldine. In the third of these, Geraldine is in a cave with a single attendant and Julius's child; she is certain the child will go to heaven, falls asleep and apparently dies herself. The next three poems are about Augusta. She addresses a guitar and revives memories of a former love. Her lover, Fernando, then expresses his undying desire and hatred for her.

In the context of the Notebook, the next two poems are more obscure. In the first, former students of 'The Palace of Instruction' recall the loss of comrades in battle; in the second, a place called Zalona falls to forces fighting under a crimson flag. On external evidence we know that the Palace of Instruction is in Gondal and that Julius's standard is red, so the first poem refers to his conquest of that country. Zalona is in the southern island of Gaaldine, where Julius began his career, so again the chronology is reversed. Without this information, we only get a general sense of battles lost and tyranny resisted.

At this point Emily Brontë transcribed 'The Death of A.G.A.' (81). It is in four parts. In the first Douglas seeks the love of Angelica; both are in 'savage attire'; Angelica reminds Douglas of her previous lovers, and recalls a childhood friend who wronged her and someone dear to her; in the latter's company she subsequently suffered a long exile, but now, 'in these regions wild', she has discovered the traitress, alone, and she urges Douglas to kill her. The second part concerns the deaths of 'fair Surry' and Lord Lesley, who dies praying for his 'Sovereign' and 'her' ultimate victory. The third part shows Douglas with Augusta, whom we may assume is Angelica's enemy; she is of 'Gondal's royal race' (and so presumably Lesley's 'Sovereign'); she is repentant, drinks from a well, faces her murderer, and wounds him. By nightfall, however, she lies alone, though earlier Angelica left Douglas to die alongside his victim. In the fourth part, a Lord Eldred sends his men to track a trail of blood across the snow – presumably Douglas's – and meditates on Augusta's tragic life.

'The Death of A.G.A.' resolves uncertainties in the poems preceding it. The fireside poems (it is now clear) recall two assassinations, Arthur dying after Julius's, Douglas escaping after Augusta's. Since Gleneden wakes in prison after Julius's assassination, there must have been a quick counter-coup, led presumably by Augusta. She at any rate must have succeeded him – her royal title in the last Lord Alfred poem was not just a metaphor. The other sufferer in the delirium poems, Rosina, cannot therefore be the same person as Augusta, as has been suggested. Rosina and Geraldine were Julius's lovers, just as Alexander, Alfred and Fernando were Augusta's. Surry and Lesley, murdered with Augusta, presumably by Douglas, were originally in attendance on the Queen during her perambulations in the 'regions wild'.

Visick demonstrates that the Notebook began as an arrangement of poems designed to facilitate the construction of an elaborate story. The narrative conventions and procedures of ballad govern the workings of each poem, the relations between the poems in the groups, and the groups themselves. Disconnected facts are baldly referred to, and knowledge of other facts is assumed. The reader has to hypothesize explanations and suspend judgement about apparent inconsistencies, but the procedure is ultimately self-elucidating. The Notebook might even be an experimental attempt to eliminate the need for a prose history of Gondal.

If that was Emily Brontë's original intention, the scheme broke down in the summer of 1844. Six of the eight poems following 'The Death of A.G.A.' were written before February 1844, which suggests a continuing process of selection, but apart from two further early poems the remaining completed poems in the Notebook were written between March 1844 and October 1845 and transcribed in order of composition. We know from Emily's diary paper of 31 July 1845 that she was working on a prose account of 'the First Wars'.[7] Possibly more than one work on Gondal was written during this period. In any case, a year later, Emily Brontë used the Notebook for the rough draft of a long poem about a civil war which she made a desultory attempt to rewrite in 1848.

The nine poems in the second half of the Notebook, transcribed before the end of May 1844, refer to characters and events in the first half, but lack discernibly significant order. Four later poems also refer to the first half, two about Julius and Augusta in prison, one an address by Douglas to a woman named Gleneden about a projected act of treason, and one a lament by Rosina beside Julius's grave fifteen years after his death. Some poems involve new characters, possibly children of the participants in the earlier action. Others refer to battles and imprisonments omitted from the earlier scheme or taking place after the death of Augusta. Some, perhaps, were relevant to prose narratives being written concurrently, though their separate transcription remains unexplained. The Notebook's later use for the purposes of composition confirms the impression of a project abandoned.

All this has been recognized for some time. What has not been examined is the possibility that the second 1844 Notebook might have been similarly organized, at least initially.

The first eight poems clearly tell a story of some kind. In the first four, the speaker recalls summer on the moors, and anticipates being reunited with loved ones. In an oppressively busy life, she finds time to day-dream, and though she sometimes enjoys a calm December evening her anguish returns and she longs for spring and for the bluebell. In the fifth poem the much-longed-for summer has come, yet she is still companionless and full of yearning; but Hope rebukes her, and promises a more divine return. In the sixth 'a lonely dreamer' (presumably the speaker of the previous poems) is rescued by Nature from 'fond idolatry' in 'regions dark'. The Night Wind then invites her to come and play with flower and young tree, but she prefers her own 'human feelings', and the wind warns her of the loneliness of the grave. In the final poem, she decides to follow her own heart to the end of her days.

The impact of the first seven poems read in sequence is not markedly different from their effect in the form in which they were later published. They may reasonably be read as about Emily Brontë herself. However, if the sequence is a considered meditation, assembled from poems written on various occasions, the concluding poem is remarkably cool-headed, and (as we shall see) acquires a completely different complexion in a different context.

The next group of (up to seven) poems cannot be autobiographical because, together, and in some cases separately, they refer to a love-story of some kind. In the first, the speaker addresses an ecstatic companion whose 'prisoned soul' will experience comparable ecstasy in death. Charlotte Brontë suggested that in 'these stanzas a ... gale has aroused the sleeper on her pillow: the wakened soul struggles to blend with the storm by which it is swayed'. This is incorrect: 'the Tempest' is referred to in the third person, and a second person is addressed. It simply does not have the autobiographical character usually attributed to it. In any case, on the assumption that lovers *are* involved, one of whom is facing death and the other bereavement, the next poem makes excellent sense. The beloved's death will not be a cause of weeping because the world is best left behind. The third poem is a prayer to an absent angel, an idol, to return (from the dead?) and offer comfort. The fourth is a lament for an absent 'Dream', from whose 'angel brow' the light decayed. But consolation is at hand: in the next poem, the speaker decides not to 'nurse that dream again'; morning has come, and there are no more visions, but the 'darling shade' will be cherished as a memory of youth. Restless fantasies return, however, in the sixth poem, bringing not consolation but bitterness, though this is unexpectedly assuaged by the prospect of a second love, a change of mood confirmed in the last poem: friendship is deemed preferable to love, and the sequence (if such it is) ends with a mourner being told to 'journey onward not elate,/But never broken-hearted.' This cool conclusion matches that of the first supposed sequence.

The next two poems form a pair. They too tell a story of a kind, and are not autobiographical either. The first is addressed to a ghost of 'blighted fame', who was 'vain', 'weak' and 'unlamented'. The second has a twist. Reminded of God's mercy, the speaker realizes that it is the dead reprobate who is fortunate – 'He rests, and I endure the woe,/That left his spirit long ago.'

The next six poems, written before the original work of transcription was completed, also form a sequence. The first considers the apparent incompatibility of heavenly and earthly experience. The next grapples with conventional admonitions about death and conscience. The third depicts Hope heartlessly flying off to Heaven and leaving the speaker desolate. The fourth, 'My Comforter', is a reply to 'Hope'. The poet rejoices in a secret inner light, but is resentfully conscious of the world's misery, until calmed by a comforter. In the next poem, she *chooses* to dream that all the misery in creation is confined to this world, and that the stars are free from evil and death. This note of wilfulness is taken up in the last poem. Unable to integrate her mood with a glorious summer's day, the poet is consoled by voices which assure her that after death the world's vicissitudes are seen differently, and, though the vision fades, she knows that she can at least *deem* her 'fond creation true'. Like the first eight poems, this sequence, which appears to be a structured meditation reaching a definite conclusion, may refer to the poet's own experience, but this cannot be taken for granted.

The remaining poems in the second Notebook were transcribed in the order of their composition (except for two written within days of each other in April 1845). It is much more difficult to read them sequentially. They indicate a more inclusive preoccupation with the themes of survival after death, the continuation or obliteration in death of the distinctions between good and evil, the legitimacy of reverie, the rival powers of nature and the life within, the problem of suffering, the promises of heaven, and the nature of God (immanent and subjective, or transcendental and eternal). All these questions remain open. The second Notebook, too, though never reduced to the status of rough papers, gives the impression of a project abandoned, or overtaken by matters more urgent and significant for the writer.

Before considering what those matters might be we need to consider the significance of the changes which Emily Brontë made to the twenty-one poems from the 1844 Notebooks selected for publication in 1846. Apparently she made three kinds of amendment to the texts – minor verbal changes, considered changes of sense, and the fundamental transformation of one whole poem.

A typical verbal alteration is to be found in 'Sympathy' (129). In the manuscript the first stanza reads:

> There should be no despair for you
> While nightly stars are burning –
> While evening sheds its silent dew
> Or sunshine gilds the morning –

In print the two dashes become a comma and a period, 'sheds' becomes 'pours' and 'Or' becomes 'And'. The change from 'sheds' to 'pours' is explained by a later alteration in the third stanza. In manuscript the third line reads, 'And winter pours its grief in snow', but in print the verb is 'sheds'. This establishes a subtle link between winter's falling snow and autumn's falling leaves, implying perhaps that the outpouring of snow gives the winter relief from sorrow. Another minor change is the retitling of 'Riches I hold in light esteem' (83), the eighth poem in the second Notebook, where it seems to me to be in the poet's own voice. Calling the poem 'The Old Stoic' removes that impression. Finally there are minor name and title changes to the Gondal poems chosen for publication.

In Winifred Gérin's judgement, the second group of emendations soften the religious unorthodoxy of the poems in manuscript 'in favour of more conventional readings' (*Emily Brontë*, p. 185). The clearest case of such deference to orthodoxy seems to be in the fourth and penultimate stanzas of 'Self-Interrogation' (93). In manuscript they read:

'And though I think that Conscience lies
'And Time should Fate condemn –
'still weak Repentance clouds my eyes,
'And makes me yield to them' ...

Look on the grave where thou must sleep
Thy last and strongest foe –
'Twill be endurance not to weep
If that repose be woe

This suggests that Conscience is a liar, that Repentance is either a weakness or a feeble motive, and that damned souls can exhibit Promethean endurance in Hell – all very un-Christian sentiments, apparently. In the printed version, however, the speaker of stanza four admits only to having 'said' that Conscience lies, 'weak' is changed to 'sad', and stanza 11 reads: 'It is endurance not to weep/If that repose be woe' (that is, there is courage in not weeping at the *prospect* of suffering after death). The manuscript version, however, is less overtly unorthodox than Gérin suggests. Its final stanza reads:

The long fight closing in defeat,
Defeat serenely borne –
Thy eventide may still be sweet –
Thy night, a glorious morn –

Even in the Notebook, therefore, the final defeat which is 'serenely borne' takes place, not in Hell, but before death, while the prospect of a glorious morning seems incompatible with damnation. Thus the changes in the 1846 version do no more than correct unintended inconsistency. Unhappily, Emily Brontë also dropped the striking oxymoron in the final line. The printed poem ends 'Thy midnight rest may still be sweet,/ And break in glorious morn' – which is conventional indeed.

A different kind of change is represented by the surgery performed on 'Julian M. and A.G. Rochelle' (81). The first three stanzas of this poem in manuscript represent the Julian of the title waiting secretly for his 'angel'. None of this is printed in 'The Prisoner, A Fragment' (124), which begins with the hero wandering through 'dungeon crypts' and being struck by a young prisoner (a former childhood companion) who defiantly describes to him the consolations of mystical experiences in her prison cell. In 'The Prisoner', the hero (who is not named) is abashed by this declaration, and sees the young woman's exalted experiences and expectation of translation to heaven as proof of her innocence. In the manuscript, however, Julian acts on his feelings: the gaoler leaves him alone with the prisoner; he notices a 'flash of longing' in her eye, calls her by name, helps her escape, and hides her for thirteen weeks; his kindred accuse him of cowardice – a war is in progress – but he endures the shame, and is rewarded with 'equal love' from Rochelle. Thus, unlike some poems in the 1844 Notebooks, the manuscript version of 'The Prisoner' celebrates the choice of love over duty in the case of Julian, and love over 'vision' in the case of Rochelle. Within weeks of its composition, however – it is dated 'August 1845' – Emily Brontë turned it on its head. As calling 'Riches I hold in light esteem' 'The Old Stoic' also suggests, her poems seem not to have had any stable meaning for her at this time, though she still took minute interest in the logical coherence and aesthetic effect of their different versions.

On the evidence so far adduced, then, it seems fairly certain that some time between May 1844 and late 1845 the two projects on which Emily Brontë embarked in February 1844 broke down. There are indications also of a serious instability in the drift, the direction of her poems, and the view of life they suggest. This may be linked to remarkable limitations in her work in terms both of technique and content.

Technically Emily Brontë's vocabulary and repertoire of metrical forms are unimpressive. As Inge-Stina Ewbank points out, 'the word "wild" ... occurs in at least one third of ... the poems'.[8] Her verse can be experimental as in 'Light up thy halls! 'Tis closing day' (37), 'The Death of 'A.G.A.'' (81) and 'Come, the wind may never again' (109), but she rarely departs from the metrical resources of the hymnal and ballad book. Only five poems are wholly in pentameters,[9] and there are no sonnets, elaborate stanza-forms, or blank verse.

Thematically, too, the poems are limited. Emily Brontë never writes about money, work, poverty (except that of aristocratic exiles), painting or literature. Music is rarely more than a simple nostalgic tune.[10] She has no political ideas – 'Royalist' and 'Republican' have no ideological significance and her conceptions of liberty and slavery are notably undeveloped. There is no social life in the poems, no feasts, balls or funerals, nor descriptions of domesticity – just glimpses of a garden or a parlour.[11] They depict a simple cycle of birth, love, ambition, suffering and death. Life is uncertain. Human beings probably come from God.[12] For the young soul earth may be an alien home but childhood is often a time of love, comradeship, and play in the countryside.[13] Elders sometimes oppress the young, and parental sorrow, desertion or death can cause an early introduction to suffering; a child may even be cursed from birth, and though young adulthood is a time of adventure and love, it destroys childhood joy.[14] The incitements to adventure are loyalty, excitement, a broken heart or glory.[15] Love can be pure, loyal and passive, or possessive, unfaithful and restless. Virtuous lovers often die, or are betrayed by vicious partners. When both lovers are passionate and amoral, the results are also tragic.[16] The pursuit of love or glory often leads to betrayal, violence, sorrow, exile, imprisonment or death. Death is either the ultimate test, or a moment of release, but what follows is obscure. Pain in the afterlife may take the form of loneliness or of rage; beatitude may be rest, release from exile, reward for virtue, or absorption into God. On the other hand, heaven may be an exile, and there may be other worlds free of earthly evils.[17] Here, however, the offspring of the dead are destined to repeat the cycle.

The human condition in the poems is thus narrowly conceived and thinly imagined. They focus on joy, sorrow, excitement, love, loss, suffering, death, hell and heaven as hypotheses, anxieties, desires and memories – there is no attempt to represent the world realistically, and the mental states of the characters and of the poet, together with her views of human experience generally in this world and the next seem inconsistent and contradictory. Moreover, some time between 1844 and 1845 even Emily Brontë's attempts to give her poems narrative and meditative order apparently collapsed. Yet this situation, clearly delineated in the manuscript and printed record, generated some of the greatest English poems written in the nineteenth century.

We can begin to see how this was possible by accepting the apparent limitations and inconsistencies in Emily Brontë's poems as the consequences of an effort to 'reduce' experience, in a philosophical sense, to typical instances – joy, sorrow, nature, fantasy, visitation, thinking and willing. Read thus, the poems constitute the poetic equivalent of Husserl's device of the epochē, by which, as an act of intellectual self-discipline, the origins and explanations of mental events are put 'in brackets' and the mind is emptied of its intellectual presuppositions so that it can concentrate on perceiving and expressing what happens within it, on what Husserl was to call 'absolutely ... fixable ... essences ... not only those whose very "content" is of the senses ... but also ... perception, imagination, recollection, judgment, emotion, will, with all their countless particular forms' ('Philosophy as', p. 111).

Of these phenomenologically essential forms in Emily Brontë's poems, joy is crucial, and of the forms of joy only love – and perhaps adventure – has a powerful presence. Childhood play, domestic pleasure and so forth are remembered in times of loss and sorrow, but love is pivotal to the dialectic of joy and sorrow and the experience of nature, time, vicissitude, fantasy, fate and the ultimate acts of seeing and willing which joy and sorrow impose on the mind as necessities. Love is an adult but not an erotic experience. For example, in the songs of Julius to Geraldine (34, 35) and Augusta's words to Lord Alfred (76), the lovers are out of doors, and experience of the beloved is indistinguishable from that of nature, or is intensified by way of contrast with it. The conditions of this love are isolation, exposure to the elements, and shared feeling reinforced by nature. Julius's most powerful experience of Geraldine is of sitting with her under a tree in the snow.

That is why, apart from conventional signs of beauty and colouring, the gender of lovers in the poems is of little importance. The interest is in what Husserl calls 'pairing', by which, when the mind is confronted with another human being, 'two data ... appearing with mutual distinctness ... *found phenomenologically a unity of similarity* ... a living mutual awakening and an overlaying of each with the objective sense of the other' (*Cartesian Meditations*, pp. 112–13). This can include the pairing of one's own body with someone else's. Merleau-Ponty describes this as a process in which the self as well as the other is discovered, and in which the other appears as 'the completion of the system'.

> No sooner has my gaze fallen upon a living body in the process of acting than the objects surrounding it ... are no longer simply what I myself could make of them, they are what this other pattern of behaviour is about to make of them.
>
> my body [discovers in] ... the body of another ... a miraculous prolongation of my own intentions, a familiar way of dealing with the world ... my body and the other's are one whole, two sides of one and the same phenomenon. (*Phenomenology of Perception*, pp. 353, 354)

This is an everyday experience, but isolated and intensified it describes love in Emily Brontë's poems – the discovery of the beloved, of the self in the beloved, of the beloved in the world, and of the self, the beloved and the landscape as constituting a harmonious system in experience.

> And I can tell by thine altered cheek
> And by thy kindled gaze
> And by the words thou scarce dost speak,
> How wildly fancy plays –
>
> Yes I could swear that glorious wind
> Has swept the world aside
> Has dashed its memory from thy mind
> Like foam-bells from the tide. (85)

But even a lover's body carries with it the possibility of absence, if only on the horizon of consciousness –

> At such a time, in such a spot
> The world seems made of light

> Our blissful hearts remember not
> How surely follows night – (76)

Consequently, the distinctive feature of love in Emily Brontë's poetry is the possibility of death, absence, refusal to share the landscape, actual or anticipated infidelity. Awareness of this distinguishes adult from childhood love – adults have the power to say no – so that the most radical expression of love is not passion but coerced presence. Love expresses itself as enslavement, as in the case of Douglas and Angelica in 'The Death of A.G.A.' (81), or it is itself enslaving: '*Life* bows to my control, but, *Love* I cannot kill!' (37). In both cases, actual and possible loss impels the mind towards fantasy.

But loss of childhood, parents, a sovereign, peace, freedom, or homeland, as well as of a lover, are also incitements to fantasy, and fantasy, for Emily Brontë, is the terrain of freedom. Some critics have seen her universe as wholly deterministic, and there *is* a fatalistic character to the Gondal sequence. Lovers and warriors are overwhelmed by arbitrary events and inner compulsions. Mental states from nostalgia to exaltation arise in the mind unbidden.[18] Some are actively unpleasant, yet without them the mind can be reduced to abject longing.[19] But the mind can still choose what it would like to recall, or anticipate, at least in the absence of stronger feelings.[20] 'I could think' (41) is characteristically expressive of its powers. As Husserl puts it: 'Everywhere ... an "I can and do, but I can also do otherwise than I am doing" plays its part – without detriment to the fact that this "freedom" is always open to possible hindrances' (*Cartesian Meditations*, p. 45).

Freedom is circumscribed in two ways. There is the importunity of cruel fact –

> Was I not vexed in those gloomy ways
> To walk unlit so long?
> Around me, wretches uttering praise
> Or howling o'er their hopeless days –
> And each with Frenzy's tongue –
>
> A Brotherhood of misery,
> With smiles as sad as sighs –
> Whose madness daily maddening me,
> Turning into agony
> The Bliss before my eyes – (103)

There is also the reflexiveness of intelligence itself, conscious of its own arbitrary attentiveness –

> No let me linger leave me let me be
> A little longer in this reverie ...
> a vision dear though false for well my mind
> Knows what a bitter waking waits behind (60)

In merely thinking about its own blissful states, the mind risks their destruction. But such reflexiveness is itself free. By scrutinizing its own awareness of ineluctable fact and its own compulsions and instabilities, the meditating mind cannot even provisionally delineate its own future – how it will value this or that feeling, even how, next time, it will value 'I could think'.

Emily Brontë's *epochē* thus 'lays open', in Husserl's words *'an infinite realm of being of a new kind'* in which 'for each kind of actual experience, and for its universal variant modes (perception, retention, recollection, etc.), there is a corresponding pure fantasy, an "as-if experience"' – an apriori poetic, in effect, corresponding to Husserl's 'apriori science ... of pure possibility (pure imaginableness)'. This development is a potential threat to consciousness, by depriving it of support in the everydayness of the world which a more naïve engagement with 'actual experience' automatically provides, operating in particular as a cruel reminder of the insubstantiality of vision. On the other hand, it discloses to the mind the comprehensiveness of its productions – 'subjective processes, abilities and dispositions – possible self-experience that can be perfected, and perhaps enriched, without limit' (*Cartesian Meditations*, pp. 27–8, 29).

The poems of 1844 and 1845 certainly bring self-experience to a high degree of abstraction. They show us a mind grasping the absolute self-sufficiency of its own lyrical utterances and their subservience to the poet's changing will as she writes them and subsequently makes sense of them. Self-expression is thereby released from the constraints of continuity and structure. But according to Husserl, even 'the natural attitude' implicitly acknowledges this kind of sovereign self-awareness (ibid., p. 37). In other words, even the narrative poems in the 1839 and Gondal Notebooks which are predicated on 'the natural attitude', and are elements of a larger, connected structure, carry with them a *hidden* self-sufficiency which later readings or emendations can elucidate. This is why poems like 'Riches I hold in light esteem' (83) and 'Julian M. to A.G. Rochelle' (123) can be changed at will, and why the period of Emily Brontë's greatest creativity coincided with the collapse of the projects begun in 1844. There was no crisis or change in outlook. It was simply that the underlying homogeneity in her work disclosed itself: *all* the poems were grounded in the absolute sufficiency of a mind willing to concentrate on immediate experiences as they arise, and to make its own way across that anomalous and always unstable territory.

But this carries with it the danger of solipsism. Initially Emily Brontë seems to be what Merleau-Ponty identifies as an 'orator', which means that a reader of her poems is a 'listener' – as it were in her presence. 'The orator's thought', Merleau-Ponty suggests, 'is empty while he is speaking' (*Phenomenology of Perception*, p. 180), and if a text is read expressively, the 'listener', too, 'has no thought marginal to the text itself'. The words have a direction – *un sens* – but their specific meaning is only 'coming into being' as they are being uttered, speech providing the *sens* with 'an empirical support for its own non-being', until it is able 'to catch up with itself again', until the sentence is complete. Once spoken, however, Merleau-Ponty believes, even abstract and philosophical language constitutes 'a linguistic and a cultural world', 'an acquired fortune' of 'available significances', which makes possible 'other acts of authentic expression – the writer's, artist's or philosopher's' (ibid., p. 197). But precisely these intertextual opportunities are excluded from Emily Brontë's verse. Her poems may imply a notional reader as listener but they refuse participation in a shared cultural and linguistic world in a way that isolates the reader as thoroughly as it does the poet.

It is true that images of dungeons, imprisoned souls, the skies, darkness descending and dawn breaking evoke 'a substratum of sensational romantic literature',[21] and 'the hymnal and the prayer book'.[22] The strongest influence seems to be Byron, though there are evocations of Coleridge and Shelley, and the melodramatic, sado-masochistic Gondal poems recall Restoration and eighteenth-century tragedy. But even after they have been 'spoken', the poems ignore this literary fortune. There is no felt tension between their Byronic agonizings and their intermittent evangelical piety, nor, in a poem as mixed in quality as 'Julian M. and A.G. Rochelle' (123), between exaltation and banality. No mode of consciousness is constituted in Emily Brontë's verse other than the intense, isolated 'oratorical' experience each poem generates and re-evokes.

This explains the fascination her writing had for Georges Bataille. Bataille distinguishes between the '*feeble communication*' which is concerned with coordination in the present and planning for the future, and 'powerful communication' which underlies 'feeble communication' and is concealed by it. Powerful communication 'abandons the consciousnesses that reflect each other, to that impenetrability which they "ultimately" are'. It is 'based on the emotions of sensuality, festivity, drama, love, separation and death'. Moments of powerful communication 'only have significance in the instance in which they appear ... it is contradictory to plan their repetition', and they presuppose 'the sovereignty of individuals' whose communication rises 'above the laws which ensure the maintenance of life' (*Literature and Evil*, pp. 171–2). They are what literature is while, in Merleau-Ponty's account, it is being spoken.

The communication depicted in Emily Brontë's poems fits this account exactly. Once again 'Aye there it is! It wakes tonight' (85) is a representative instance. At the level of frenzy which it depicts, life ceases to be calculated; the two consciousnesses which reflect each other in the poem surrender 'to that impenetrability that they "ultimately" are'. The experience of the ecstatic is completely open to the observer, just as any reader is deemed to be instantaneously and unproblematically open to the language in which this shared experience is described. This involves not just what Merleau-Ponty calls 'available meanings' in 'a common world', but more radically 'the emotional content of the word', its 'gestural sense', by which 'words, vowels and phonemes are so many ways of "singing" the world', and the human body is empowered to 'live' it (*Phenomenology of Perception*, pp. 186–7). Emily Brontë's best poems have this kind of 'life' – they constitute experiences which enunciate their own completeness and invite us to 'pair' them with no less discrete experiences of our own. Each of the poems, in Jacques Blondel's words, becomes *'un fragment de réalité'*.[23] This is how they overcome their incipient solipsism. They invite us to share an *experience*, not a literary or cultural context.

This is particularly the case with their gestural reproduction of loss. The Gondal poems are all structured around suppressed 'facts' – the graveside laments of Augusta (4) and Rosina (116) conceal all that has happened since the death of the beloved – while the voices that come and go in the second 1844 Notebook are anonymous, the minds to which the words are addressed (except in the dialogue poems) impenetrable. We do not know the sex of the persons in 'Aye, there it is! It wakes tonight' (85), nor whose death is mourned in 'Death, that struck when I was most confiding' (117). Yet the effect is not a distancing one. The opacity of the verse 'pairs' with the helplessness of the persons in the poems. The language glimpses but does not grasp, or grasps and then surrenders; yet its inadequacy in the face of plenitude reproduces the experiences of glimpsing, desiring, grasping and losing of which, for the people in the poems, that plenitude consists.

The poems thus isolate themselves 'irresponsibly' – hence their notorious childishness. Denis Donoghue, following Hélène Tuzot, sees Emily Brontë in terms of the legendary child lost in the forest who invents 'a new world, emanating from the self as centre', and whose response to the loss of the real world is 'wilful disengagement' ('The Other Emily', p. 165). Blondel detects an extraordinary egoism and childish lack of awareness in the Gondal poems (*Emily Brontë Expérience*, p. 184). These are qualities which appeal particularly to Bataille. Isolated in the now of experience, even when experience is a memory, the poems generate intensity at the expense of the future. Emily Brontë even abandons the project of preserving her own work, of coordinating, for the sake of the future, the chaos of the Gondalian 'past'.

But such intensity is necessarily temporary. The check, the shocked return to what Bataille calls 'reduced life' – to rationally connected, future-oriented life – is an inexorable consequence of reaching the furthest point in the quest for intensity (*Literature and Evil*, p. 30). Yet even this 'unsatisfaction' is turned compulsively by the poet – Bataille cites Baudelaire – 'into a permanent object', and here poetry betrays itself, for to make anything permanent is to locate it in the adult, future-oriented world. Precisely this self-defeating structure becomes the theme of one of the most celebrated poems, 'Cold in the earth, and the deep snow piled above thee!' (116). The mind of Rosina and the mind of the reader are taken to the furthest point of intense unease, the excruciating desire to 'indulge in Memory's rapturous pain', and the terror of allowing that rapture to obliterate all other experience; but finally the poem has to stop; 'the empty world', sought or unsought, reasserts itself; the poem 'releases its object' – mere consciousness – yet 'tries to seize the release, to make its own self-defeat into a permanent object' – a text with a future, ultimately a poem by Ellis Bell.

Bataille's account of Emily Brontë is seriously misleading, however, in one respect. He associates powerful communication with cruelty and violence, but in the poems (though not in *Wuthering Heights*) pain and death (actual or in prospect) are experiences of consciousness, not the body. The worst that happens to human bodies is physical restraint, exposure to the elements, and in a few cases wounding by a sword or dagger. No significance attaches to the sex of the body so wounded – the killing of Augusta is not more or less shocking or exciting than the killing of Julius. The poems achieve their abstracted, childish intensity solely through a formal self-sufficiency which isolates each of them from all poetry whatsoever, including other poems by Emily Brontë.

This is why they cannot be used to elucidate her opinions. In spite of poems such as 'Shed no tears o'er that tomb' (58), and the Brussels *devoir*, '*L'Amour Filial*',[24] many critics believe that Emily Brontë rejected the doctrine of Hell. Perhaps she did; but the two most important poems on this topic are ambiguous. In one (72), Fernando de Samara declares,

> A God of *hate* could hardly bear
> To watch through all eternity,
> His own creation's dread despair!

– but he goes on to say that even if he went to Heaven after all, the pain he is now feeling could not be obliterated. He then fantasizes about Augusta enduring eternal suffering to match his own: when it comes to inflicting pain on others, Fernando is more than a match for any 'God of *hate*'. So Hell *can* be contemplated, after all, but only by those capable of desiring to inflict it on (say) a former lover. In the second poem on this theme, 'Far, far away is mirth withdrawn' (73), a woman persuades herself that a dead reprobate will find divine forgiveness, but she is brought up short by the thought that he is resting, that her entire experience has been 'fancy', and that *she* is now undergoing *his* punishment. In both poems, the experience of Hell is both intolerable and a vivid possibility. The issue cannot be closed: the moment between entrancement and return to quotidian consciousness can be 'robed in fires of Hell, or bright with heavenly shine' (123). Death may be sleep 'without identity' (115), an experience of unutterable loneliness (98), or a soothing dream (107). We are nowhere offered anything so limited as an opinion, never mind a doctrine. Instead we confront the possibilities which consciousness must live with once they have been entertained, but to none of which it gives, or seeks to give, assent.

The same applies to the poems' treatment of orthodox belief. In 'O between distress and pleasure' (65), Hope admonishes the poet for dreaming about the past; in 'How beautiful the Earth is still' (121), one of the speakers is taught by a 'thoughtful Spirit' to cast the 'anchor of Desire/Deep in unknown Eternity', and to recognize that 'It is Hope's Spell that glorifies ... All Natures million mysteries'. But elsewhere (99), Hope is a manifestation either of cosmic cruelty or spiritual self-deception, who abandons the poet to 'frenzied pain' and soars heartlessly to Heaven.

Providence is equally problematical, Julius's victory being a type of the inexplicable injustices of history. In the Brussels *devoir*, 'Portrait: Le Roi Harold avant la Bataille de Hastings', (*The Belgian Essays*, pp. 96–103), Harold is destined by Heaven to die, though his soul is divine; but to such a hero death is a gaoler opening prison doors. The *devoir* thus questions the justice of Providence while playing down the importance of historical events in the light of personal moral experience. As John Hewish notes of the *devoirs* generally, 'reflection ... veers between heterodox extremes and near orthodoxy'.[25] But this is not because Emily Brontë is trying 'to reconcile a *mondo cane* with Christian belief' (*Emily Brontë. A Critical*, p. 66), nor, as J. Hillis Miller suggests, because for her Nature's 'insanity lies in the fact that the good of one part is the evil of another's part' (*The Disappearance*, p. 164), but because she could see so many implications in the facts, symbols, dreams and intuitions which commanded her attention. 'Le Papillon' (*The Belgian Essays*, pp. 176–9) clearly specifies the status of both the points of view to which it alludes: its sense of Nature's cruelty is *only* a product of mood (of the imagination in winter), and the emergence of the butterfly is *only* a symbol of hope – neither is *evidence*. The problem is not that religious views are inconsistent but that the mind is the locus of their inconsistency, the centre of its own dislocation. In '"Enough of Thought, Philosopher"' (115), the speaker who has not had the vision knows that he will remain the field in which the three streams continue to oppose each other, until he is released by death.

The nature of such a consciousness is illuminated by 'A Day Dream' (105), when the consolation afforded by vision is undercut by a laconic reminder of the mind's power to 'deem/Her fond creation true – '. The only reality is a consciousness which persists through successive experiences of contradiction, and which can afford to be uncertain about the world because it can intuit a personal Ego which fixes itself and abides, which intermittently thinks, and which, as Husserl puts it, 'can go on continuously' in that 'founding stratum', without which no one can 'have the sense "Objective World"' (Cartesian Meditations, p. 96). In 'A Day Dream', change in objective time (the seasons) and in immanent time (vision) is problematical, but only because there is a self, persisting through both, which intermittently sees itself so persisting, and so can assume the position of '"disinterested onlooker"', above the naively interested Ego' (Cartesian Meditations, p. 35). The poet's 'self' can see experiences in terms of type, and gives us an example of Fancy's 'fond creations'. She knows that Nature includes other consciousnesses, 'distributed one knows not how in infinite space, as objects of possible intercommunion' (ibid., p. 130), but the task of holding everything together falls to her alone, since once the stage of naïve immersion in experience is transcended, a universal synthesis can never be assumed. No longer a gift, the world becomes not a problem but a duty.

The transcendental self in 'A Day Dream' is not, however, an abstract, notional consciousness. The sophisticated, self-wounding twist of the last stanza points to a distinctive combination of personal and moral difficulties, which was the price Emily Brontë had to pay, on 5 March 1844, for ignoring 'all positions taken toward the already-given world', and for acknowledging that, as Husserl put it in a late essay, the relevant 'concepts ... have a proper sense only in the individual personal sphere. Spiritual being is fragmentary'.[26] For Emily Brontë, the 'world, with all its Objects ... derives its whole sense and [the] existential status, which it has for [her] from ... [herself] as the transcendental Ego, the Ego who comes to the fore only with the transcendental–phenomenological epochē' (Cartesian Meditations, p. 26). Reflection, writes Merleau-Ponty, 'is a system of thought no less closed than insanity, with this difference, that it understands itself, and the madman too' (Phenomenology of Perception, p. 23). Hence the anxiety felt by Husserl's meditator: having 'parenthesized' everyone and everything, including himself 'qua human person', he cannot see how he will 'ever attain others and [himself] <as one among others>'. He does not even understand how he will be 'be retained qua ego' (*Cartesian Meditations*, p. 150). For Emily Brontë, *qua* poet, this was a personal anxiety. Her indifference towards others (and sometimes towards Nature) has an aggressive character, but she is uncomfortable at being indefinitely trapped in the role of onlooker reflecting on her own experiences, and not simply – naïvely – experiencing them. It is painful never to be finally absorbed either into Vision or into Nature, to be destined always to end up thinking about thought. Husserl is again relevant: 'No matter what the circumstances ... the transformed attitude can only be a temporary one. It can take on a lasting character ... only in the form of an unconditional determination of will to take up again the selfsame attitudes in a series of periods that are temporary but intimately bound together' ('Phenomenology and the Crisis', p. 167).

And there is an additional problem, over and above that of loss and return. Emily Brontë cannot parenthesize the moral: for her clarity is a test of truthfulness as well as intelligence. The moral challenge with which we are thus confronted is her openness to contradiction. We cannot work through the 'logic of [her] imagery', as Donoghue claims to do. 'The distinction between God and man may persist as an interim rhetoric,' he writes, 'but it cannot remain when the one center becomes All' ('The Other Emily', p. 164). But the one centre does *not* become All in two important late poems, 'A Day Dream' (105) and 'Julian M. to A.G. Rochelle' (123): both poet and prisoner deliberately return to the fragmented world of love and irony. Similarly 'My Comforter' (103) elucidates 'a latent thought' in which consciousness has apparently reconciled contradictory states of being – the Hell of a *mondo cane*, the bliss of Heaven – these being simultaneously states of mind and possible states in the world. The Comforter comes like a gentle wind, and in opposition to the oppositions of Heaven and Hell in which the poet stood previously, we are offered a delicately provisional illumination of self-consciousness *imagining* itself comforted:

> And yet a little longer speak
> Calm this resentful mood
> And while the savage heart grows meek,
> For other token do not seek,
> But let the tear upon my cheek
> Evince my gratitude –

To attempt to guarantee more than this involves a blasphemous refusal to accept temporality and contingency. Augusta recognizes the religious truth that 'our souls are all divine', which Lord Alfred's love revealed to her, but she then makes their love a cult in its own right, an alternative Heaven (76). In the next poem Emily Brontë wrote (77), an anonymous, rejected voice cries out for its 'angel' to 'comfort' it, but the angel is then explicitly identified as an 'idol'. What is at issue in both poems is not the viability or validity of love or vision, but the openness of a consciousness which seeks such experiences to other aspects of the truth.

This problem is given its most intense expression in 'O, thy bright eyes must answer now' (110), a poem at once Christian (there would be no problem if it were not) and agnostic. In it Emily Brontë addresses a person, or power, her 'ever-present' slave, comrade and King, her 'Darling Pain' and 'God of Visions', who is either identical with the God of Religion or a blasphemous figment. But even in the latter case, no other God may exist. Thus the question

> am I wrong, to worship where
> Faith cannot doubt, nor Hope despair,
> Since my own soul can grant my prayer?

is concerned both with motives and with truth. Is it a misreading, wilful or otherwise, to worship such a presence as divine? The question problematizes the Christian virtues of Faith and Hope. If Faith cannot doubt nor Hope despair, can either be said to exist? The transcendent solipsism which is this poet's delight and anxiety thus calls in question those acts by which consciousness identifies itself as Christian, and in focusing on this, and *not* on the existence of God, as the ultimate question, it interrogates the poet's powers of mind, *independently* of whether she is a Christian or an unbeliever. It thereby constitutes conscience as the judge of faith and atheism alike, and the ultimate refinement of the poet's being.

There are therefore no grounds for questioning the authenticity of 'Often rebuked, yet always back returning' (201) – at least on account of its alleged inconsistency with other tendencies in Emily Brontë's poetry.[27] In eliding the poet's nature and the world's, the poem acknowledges the first as the means by which the second is constituted; and in then representing this cosmic and personal nature as waking 'one human heart to feeling', and thereby *constituting* 'both the worlds of heaven and Hell', it affirms the validity, not of the real as against the visionary, but of the intelligent generation of experience as against self-indulgent fantasy (such as Augusta engaged in), which is another form of everydayness. It is another poem about conscience, about consciousness as the supreme judge of its own truthfulness, and therefore of truth.

It is certainly not inconsistent with 'No coward soul is mine' (125), a poem said to be indebted to Epictetus and the vocabulary of Stoicism, but which is also very assured in its use of the language of the Bible. Just as 'My Comforter' (103) relies on two important terms for the

Holy Spirit (the wind – John 3:8) and the Paraclete or Comforter (John 14:26), so 'No coward soul is mine' (125), echoes references to God as 'Being' (Exodus 3:14 and John 8:58), as 'Breath' (John 20:21) and as 'Rock'.[28] The link between the Imagination and God as Being is also made by Coleridge in *Biographia Literaria*, in the passage from that work which appears to have influenced the line 'Changes, sustains, dissolves, creates and rears'.[29] There are two other important biblical references in the poem. The line 'And Faith shines equal guarding me from Fear' recalls Ephesians 6:16 – 'taking up the shield of faith, wherewith ye shall be able to quench all the fiery darts of the evil one' – and the lines 'So surely anchored on/The steadfast rock of Immortality' not only recall two earlier uses of the same image – 'And anchor all thy weary woes/In calm Eternity' (93), and 'There cast my anchor of Desire/ Deep in unknown Eternity' (121) – but all three recall Hebrews 6:18–9: 'that ... we may have strong encouragement, who have fled for refuge to lay hold of the hope set before us; which we have as an anchor to the soul, a hope both sure and steadfast and entering into that which is behind the veil'.

There was certainly nothing heterodox in the belief that God comes to rest in the breast of the believer and imparts His power to her. The following remarks were made in a sermon preached in Oxford on 31 July 1833:

> our friends and relations, whom we are right in loving, these too, after all, are nothing to us here ... we see them, and they act upon us, only (as it were) at a distance, through the medium of sense; they cannot get at our souls; they cannot enter into our thoughts, or really be companions to us ... after all, they vanish before the clear vision we have, first of our own existence, next of the presence of the great God in us, and over us, as our Governor and Judge, who dwells in us by our conscience, which is His representative. (*Parochial and Plain*, I, p. 21)

Five years later the same preacher, John Henry Newman, writing on the topic of 'the literal indwelling of God within us', declared:

> God is everywhere as absolutely and entirely as if He were no-where else; and it seems to be essential to the existence of every creature, rational and irrational, good and evil, in heaven and hell, that in some sense or other He should be present with it and be its life ... If this notion of the literal indwelling of God within us ... be decried as a sort of mysticism, I ask in reply whether it is not a necessary truth that He is with and in us, if he is everywhere?[30]

I am not suggesting that Emily Brontë's notorious reserve on matters of religion concealed Tractarian beliefs from the entrenched Evangelicalism of her family. No one actually knows what it concealed. Indeed I think that Revd Patrick Brontë would have gone along with Newman's views in both the passages I have quoted, as would Charlotte and Anne Brontë. All I am suggesting is that 'No coward soul is mine' is not at all the radical theological declaration it has been taken to be, but an affirmation of commonplace Christian teaching, which calmly answers the question left open at the end of 'O, thy bright eyes must answer now' (110). The God within the poet's breast, who enables her to grant her own prayer, is after all almighty, ever-present, transcendent; for though she, and she alone constitutes Him in experience, it is also true – because the experience is hers and she is therefore its true and uniquely authoritative witness – that He is the ultimate ground of her being and of all actual and possible being in all actual and possible worlds. At a late stage in his philosophizing, Husserl postulated a logic of faith which would be 'a proper and most profound mode of grounding true being' precisely because 'theologically religion invokes faith itself as evidence' ('Phenomenology and the Crisis', p. 177). Emily Brontë appears to have anticipated him.

It would seem, then, that she had a less remarkable inner life than many critics have attributed to her. The dilemmas she examines, particularly in the Gondal poems, are often factitious and tendentious, and even in her greatest poems she is never more then experimentally heterodox. Her achievement is none the less distinctive, because of its rhetorical authority and intellectual absorption. We have to think of her as a great actress or musician, too wrapped up in her performance to pay attention to her audience. Hewish is right to refer to her 'genius and reserve' (*Emily Brontë*, p. 16), and Miller to suggest that the private nature of the experiences recorded in the poems is essential to their validity (*The Disappearance of God*, p. 157). They admit no difference between reader and writer. Emily Brontë – at any rate in the Notebooks – is the sole judge of the clarity and honesty of her writing. Hence, perhaps, her habit of attaching her name or initials to individual poems: the author is an integral component of each of them, and they only make sense, for us, in terms of the person in whom and by whom we feel them to be constituted. They alert us to a will and intelligence capable of giving undivided attention to every experience as it develops, without regard to similar explorations or general notions of consistency. Yet this radical disconnectedness is itself consistency – the coming into being of a completely self-reliant conscience.

All this was made possible by Emily Brontë's fidelity to her *epochē*, which for her was not an intellectual device but a personal action, put into effect in Haworth and elsewhere, and carrying with it what it set aside – the presence of her individuality as a person. We do not find a great visionary in these poems – no Julian of Norwich or Teresa of Avila

– but the tireless energy and intellectual integrity with which they parenthesize the world of commonplace truths, united with their deep and sustaining exploitation of the gestural power of language, are quite sufficient to justify the more responsible claims that have been made about her genius.

CHAPTER ELEVEN

The Rights of Celibacy

'She thinks of the abstraction, man,' Sidney Dobell wrote of Charlotte Brontë in 1850, 'with all the blissful ignorance of a boy's dream of woman.'[1] The implication of immaturity in this judgement must have been particularly offensive to a celebrated author in her early thirties, but it continues to shadow Charlotte Brontë's reputation. She is still the insecure, virginal elder sister, anxiously protecting her younger sisters' writings against charges of impropriety and religious unorthodoxy, an only partially emancipated feminist – even her friend Mary Taylor reached this conclusion – and an ideological conservative, unable to mount the kind of unqualified challenge to the social order implicit in the work of her sister, Emily. In her defence, attention has been drawn to the dilemmas and contradictions she had to face as a woman writer, but the implications of her celibate condition have not been given sufficient attention.

The aspects of Charlotte Brontë's writing which Dobell had in mind when he compared her to an adolescent boy – there are in fact three singularly interesting male adolescents in her work, Henry Sympson and Martin Yorke in *Shirley*, and Victor Crimsworth in *The Professor* – are most embarrassingly on display in the presentation of Louis Moore in Chapters VI and XIII of Volume III of *Shirley* (pp. 589–99 and 694–721). In the earlier chapter, Louis wanders around the house, finds Shirley's untidy desk, soliloquizes, and finally pours out his passion for his former pupil in a journal, relishing Shirley's dependence on his strength, the secret pleasure of writing what he cannot speak concerning his feelings for her, the flattering effect of her shyness, the attraction of her faults, and the way her rebellious manner under instruction loosens his tongue. The fantasy intensifies. He would not want a pretty, flawless wife, like Caroline Helstone, with no faults to correct. His powers need the wild instincts of the '*bête fauve*' to manage. When he sees Shirley with Sir Philip Nunnelly he reverses the fable of Semele and indulges in a fantasy of Sir Philip as priest being burned to a cinder by the Goddess Juno. The carriage returns and he scribbles down his intention to take away Shirley's things. She will have to beg for their return.

In Chapter 13, Louis returns to his journal to describe how he summoned Shirley to the schoolroom. Before being sent away, his present pupil, Henry Sympson, who has a fondness for Shirley, growls like a 'young, lame, half-grown lion' because Louis has 'tamed his lioness and [is] her keeper'. In Shirley's presence, Louis controls his feelings. The Sympsons are departing, Louis will cease to be Henry's tutor. Shirley says she thinks of Louis and his brother, Robert, as 'homeless hunters [in] the loneliest western wilds'. Louis wants to know if she imagined them marrying Indian women – a suggestion she finds sordid. He tells her that he really does intend to go to America where the mountain nymph, Liberty, will fill his arms. He knows that Shirley's heart is near to breaking, but that she will not show her feelings or dishonour her sisterhood in her. He deliberately provokes her. Liberty is too unearthly a mate, he tells her: he will take 'some young, penniless, friendless orphan girl' instead, educate her, and 'reward her with [his] love'. Shirley jeers at him for thinking himself 'lord of creation'. She urges him to accept celibacy. He says that after thirty years he is tired of that condition, so she proposes his marrying a stout widow. Louis stipulates that the widow must not be rich, and Shirley mocks him for not being hero enough to marry for money. They accuse each other of pride. Louis protests he is a dependant who knows his place; Shirley that she is a woman who knows hers. Provocatively, he urges the match with Sir Philip. She says she will not be her husband's tutor – a husband must improve *her*. Louis agrees she needs improving; she retorts that if he changed sex he would make an excellent tutor–wife. She insists on calling him plain – his face looks like her mastiff, Tartar's. In which case, he says, she should treat him as she treats the dog. His orphan-girl will do that, she says. He tries to get her to tell him where the orphan-girl is to be found. 'I *never will*,' she says, and is about to leave. He presents himself not as a tutor, but a man and a gentleman, yet at once addresses her as his pupil; to which her 'low answer' is 'My master'.

> "You shall tell me with your own lips, whether you doom me to exile, or call me to hope."
> "Go. I can bear to be left."
> "Perhaps, I too can bear to leave you: but reply, Shirley, my pupil, my sovereign – reply."
> "Die without me if you will. Live for me if you dare."
> "I am not afraid of you, my leopardess: I *dare* live for and with you, from this hour till my death … "

A bald summary is less exhausting than the extended dialogue in the text. Even so the accuracy of Dobell's verdict is evident in the extravagance of the imagery, the gracelessness of the syntax, and the insecure treatment of male consciousness in soliloquy and journal.

One reason for this awkwardness is implicit in Elizabeth Gaskell's account of Charlotte Brontë's marriage to Revd Arthur Bell Nicholls in June 1854. She quotes from a letter sent from Ireland on their wedding journey, in which Charlotte Brontë thanked God that she had made the right choice, and expressed the hope that she would be able 'to repay as [she] ought the affectionate devotion of a truthful, honourable man'.

> Henceforth [Gaskell continues] the sacred doors of home are closed upon her married life. We, her loving friends, standing outside, caught occasional glimpses of brightness, and pleasant peaceful murmurs of sound, telling of gladness within, and gently said, 'After a hard and long struggle – after many cares and many bitter sorrows – she is tasting happiness now!' We thought of the slight astringencies of her character, and how they would turn to full ripe sweetness in that calm sunshine of domestic peace. We remembered her trials, and were glad in the idea that God had seen fit to wipe away the tears from her eyes. Those who saw her, saw an outward change in her look, telling of inward things.[2]

This is sensitively phrased. The effect of Charlotte Brontë's release from the loneliness of life in Haworth after her sisters' deaths is finely realized, and the quotation from the Book of Revelation discreetly anticipates her own imminent death. But the passage is also informed by two powerful ideas. The first is that marriage is an absolutely private state – its joys may only be implied. The living friends, standing outside, include, presumably, older, married women, capable of forming a true idea of how the slight astringencies of the virgin state are turned to full ripe sweetness in the calm and peace of domesticity. And this of course is the second powerful idea in the passage – that a woman is only complete when she becomes a wife and mother, but to qualify for that condition a young woman must remain in decent ignorance of what it will involve. That Charlotte Brontë herself was thus ignorant until her marriage is clear from a letter to the unmarried Ellen Nussey: 'Dear Nell, During the last 6 weeks – the colour of my thoughts is a good deal changed: I know more of the realities of life than I once did ... Indeed – indeed Nell – it is a solemn and strange and perilous thing for a woman to become a wife. Man's lot is far – far different' (*The Brontës*, p. 761)

Celibate women are therefore subject to a series of exclusions – from knowledge of their own potential, from the language in which their present and future condition might be described, and from equality with men and women less ignorant than themselves. This is why the author of *Jane Eyre*, if a woman, was judged by Elizabeth Rigby to have 'forfeited the society of her sex'.[3] But Rigby was wrong: if Charlotte Brontë had been (licitly or illicitly) an initiate, she would have written the love passages between Jane Eyre and Rochester, and between Shirley and Louis, more 'convincingly' (that is, more discreetly), and would therefore have disqualified herself, not from the society of other women, but from the exclusion signalled in Gaskell's text. It was this exclusion which impelled her to make good the celibate's claim to full and serious utterance and so to achieve distinctiveness and distinction as a writer.

Her teacher in Brussels, Constantin Héger, knew the seriousness and passion of this claim. She wrote to him on her return to Haworth early in 1844 with a lack of inhibition which alarmed him. He rebuked her. She seems to have replied with 'a letter that was less than reasonable, because sorrow was at [her] heart' (*Charlotte Brontë*, p. 269). She tried to keep the correspondence cool. His anxieties were not assuaged, and he eventually refused to reply. She went on writing, trying to limit her letters to six-monthly intervals, and concentrating mainly on neutral, family matters – but she refused to be constrained by notions of correctness which denied her the right even to allude to the pain correctness caused her:

> I have done everything; I have sought occupations; I have denied myself absolutely the pleasure of speaking about you – even to Emily; but I have been able to conquer neither my regrets nor my impatience. That, indeed, is humiliating – to be unable to control one's own thoughts, to be the slave of a regret, of a memory, slave of a fixed and dominant idea which lords it over the spirit.
>
> Did you not visit Cologne or Coblenz? Tell me, in short, *mon maître*, what you will, but tell me something. To write to an ex-assistant-governess (No! I refuse to remember my employment as assistant-governess – I repudiate it) – anyhow, to write to an old pupil cannot be a very interesting occupation for you, I know; but for me it is life. Your last letter was stay and prop to me – nourishment to me for half a year. Now I need another, and you will give it me ... To forbid me to write to you, to refuse to answer me would be to tear me from my only joy on earth, to deprive me of my last privilege. (*Charlotte Brontë*, pp. 291–2)

The language of humiliation, hunger and abject need is the authentic voice, in one of its aspects, however much Mary Taylor and Harriet Martineau might wish it otherwise, of the celibate woman seizing on the resources of the language to express the pain of her condition. But this penetration of culturally imposed barriers, this abandonment of linguistic reserve, was unwomanly. It is so still, if only because it arises from a denial of adult status, something no human being should have to claim by force. But it was because such status would be denied her, even by as wise a friend as Gaskell, that Charlotte Brontë was propelled into her notably astringent appropriation of the English language.

One of the topics on which her language is most uninhibited is in her treatment of persons of her own sex. Here is William Crimsworth's description of Juanna Trista, one of the *pensionnaires* in Mdlle Reuter's establishment.

She had precisely the same shape of skull as Pope Alexander the Sixth; her organs of benevolence, veneration, conscientiousness, adhesiveness, were singularly small, those of self-esteem, firmness, destructiveness, combativeness, preposterously large; her head sloped up in the penthouse shape, was contracted about the forehead, and prominent behind; she had rather good, though large and marked features ...

Juanna was not very thin, but she had a gaunt visage, and her ... brow ... presented space enough for the legible graving of two words, Mutiny and Hate; in some one of her other lineaments – I think the eye – cowardice had also its distinct cipher. Mdlle Trista ... made noises with her mouth like a horse, she ejected her saliva, she uttered brutal expressions; behind her and below her were seated ... two or three examples of that deformity of person and imbecility of intellect whose frequency in the Low Countries would seem to furnish proof that the climate is such as to induce degeneracy of the human mind and body ... and with their aid she got up and sustained a swinish tumult, which I was constrained at last to quell. (*The Professor*, p. 103)

As a record of the psychological politics of the schoolroom, this was unmatched in English fiction until D.H. Lawrence described Ursula Brangwen's pupils in *The Rainbow*.

She knew by now her enemies in the class. The one she hated most was Williams. He was a sort of defective, not bad enough to be so classed. He could read with fluency, and had plenty of cunning intelligence. But he could not keep still. And he had a kind of sickness very repulsive to a sensitive girl, something cunning and etoliated and degenerate.[4]

Both writers reshape their experiences by giving them to a teacher of the opposite sex, thus 'compromising' in the mind of an unsympathetic reader their own gender identity. Both resort to a scientific vocabulary (in Charlotte Brontë's case that of phrenology and dated climatological theories of personality, in Lawrence's that of popular post-Darwinian theorising about race and psychology) for the uninhibited expression of personal feeling. And both are shockingly frank in expressing the fear, disgust and hatred which a teacher can feel towards the manipulative sexual consciousness of adolescent students.

The field of battle for Charlotte Brontë is words: she refuses to be unreal in the language she uses about women. In the 'Old Maids' chapter in *Shirley* – a remarkably proto-Lawrentian excursus in which no effort is made to advance the narrative – the appearance of Miss Mann and Miss Ainley is brutally registered, as Caroline Helstone contemplates her own prospects as a parson's niece unlikely to marry. Miss Mann has 'a formidable eye ... it [is] prominent, and [shows] a great deal of white'; it is like 'a steel ball soldered in her head'; she speaks 'in an indescribably dry monotonous tone – a tone without vibration or inflection'. Her 'goblin-grimness scarcely [goes] deeper then the angel-sweetness of hundreds of beauties' – she is an 'honest, conscientious woman', who has suffered and ministered to the suffering – but she has been paid with ingratitude and left with a 'bloodless pallor of complexion, and deeply worn lines of feature', 'a starved, ghostly longing for appreciation and affection', and a single fault, censoriousness (pp. 199–201). Miss Ainley, though 'poorer ... [and] even plainer', is an even better woman, but her evangelical vocabulary invites mockery, she is 'merely sensible', and, though her 'practical excellence' puts Caroline to shame, Caroline achieves 'neither health of body nor continued peace of mind' in her attempts to emulate Miss Ainley (pp. 203–6). These descriptions acquire additional signifi-cance as a record of Caroline's thoughts and feelings, the Caroline whom even Louis Moore imagines is 'the soul of conscientious punctuality and nice exactitude', but who, even so, has a store of slight asperities secreted behind her 'insular grace and purity' (pp. 595–6).

The thoughts and vocabulary of another prospective old maid, Lucy Snowe, in *Villette,* are even more disruptive of the easy assumptions we, Louis Moore, Gaskell, Rigby and Dobell are inclined to make about the mental horizons of virgins. The description of the Rubenesque picture, 'Cleopatra', may seem aggressive and naïve in a way that 'we' might expect from Lucy Snowe:

> I calculated that this lady, put into a scale of magnitude suitable for the reception of a commodity of bulk, would infallibly turn from fourteen to sixteen stone ... she appeared in hearty health, strong enough to do the work of two plain cooks ... out of abundance of material – seven-and-twenty yards, I should say, of drapery – she managed to make inefficient raiment. (*Villette*, p. 285)

But if Lucy Snowe fails to acknowledge the painting's sexuality, she will have exposed her own ignorance (of art as well as of sex); yet if she does acknowledge it, or seems self-consciously to avoid doing so, she will have convicted herself either of prurience or of prudishness. Her sarcastic, threatened, diction is thus the price she must pay if the inci-dent is to be dealt with in terms which reflect her real situation. (It was the price Charlotte Brontë had already paid in her letters to M. Héger.) Certain words and incidents are destined to be interpreted in specific ways simply because they come from the pen of a chaste unmarried woman. Whatever the writer's intentions – erotically charged or not – the effects of what she writes are bound to seem relatively unintended, properly subject to additional interpretation by the emotionally better circumstanced reader, male or married.

Lucy Snowe regains control, however, in the key chapter, 'Vashti', for which 'Cleopatra' is a preparation. The acting of Vashti, named after the rebellious Queen of Ahasuerus in the Book of Esther, transcends but does not evade the sexuality in the painting. The actress and her performance are evidently inseparable. Lucy Snowe writes:

> Behold! I found upon her something neither of woman nor of man: in each of her eyes sat a devil. These evil forces bore her through the tragedy, kept up her feeble strength ... They wrote HELL on her straight, haughty brow. They tuned her voice to the note of torment. They writhed her regal face to a demoniac mask. Hate and Murder and Madness incarnate, she stood.
> It was a marvellous sight: a mighty revelation.
> It was a spectacle low, horrible, immoral ...
> Place now the Cleopatra, or any other slug, before her as an obstacle, and see her cut through the pulpy mass as the scimitar of Saladin clove the down cushion. (pp. 369–71)

Vashti is a spectacle the virginal Lucy can respond to, but it leaves the sexually self-confident Dr John unimpressed: '*impressionable* he was as dimpling water, but, almost as water, *unimpressible*' (p. 372). As the play reaches its climax, the encounter between Vashti and her fate, between actress and audience, is explicitly sexualized – 'quivering in conflict ... her throes, her gaspings, breathing yet of mutiny ... an inordinate will ... resisted to the latest the rape of every faculty' (pp. 373–4); but it is the virginal Lucy who responds to the encounter, who allows herself to be penetrated by it and to surrender to it, and it is the young doctor who bites his under-lip and knits his brow but keeps his spirit intact for the young Paulina whom he is about to meet after so many years. The virginal consciousness in the theatre, and that of the self-assured old maid recalling it years later (I take it Paul Emmanuel dies at sea) has a familiarity with passion Graham cannot match: we cannot imagine him using the word 'rape' with Lucy Snowe's tough-mindedness.

The ignorance inherent in the virgin state thus seems to offer opportunities for speculative freedom which a celibate woman, or man, can seize if so minded, but which anyone who achieves sexual knowledge by conventional means will probably miss. The conventional is not, of course, identical with the respectable. In *Villette*, Graham and Polly are eminently respectable, while Ginevra and Count de Hamal are the reverse, but all four, though in different ways socially and sexually knowing, are confined by the superficial conventions of the sub-genres (Trollopian love-story, sub-Gothic romance) into which their personal histories are ironically fitted. Sexual success, it seems, is predicated on a willingness to confine one's sexual identity and sexual imaginings within the culturally determined limits disclosed in established literary conventions.

An example of this is the subtly perceived Pelet in *The Professor*, intelligent, 'Parisian' in his 'notions about matrimony and women'

(p. 69), but gentleman-like (once he has tested the waters) in avoiding topics of conversation with William Crimsworth which he might expect to share with a more fraternal, less old-maidish companion. Yet it is Crimsworth whose imagination is emancipated. Attracted first and most strongly by 'Frances' mental points', he still derives 'a pleasure, purely material' from her brown eyes, fine skin, well-set teeth, and delicately proportioned figure, a pleasure which, if more 'temperate' than that of the average 'sensualist', is more 'fastidious' also (pp. 240–41). Moreover, he is capable, as Pelet could never be, of confronting the paradox of plunging into an acute mental disorder as soon as he and Frances have declared their love. This pre-marital 'hypochondria' is seen with diagnostic insight as the resurgence of an adolescent condition following a loveless childhood, in which a boy's disordered dream of woman and devastating depression are explicitly aspects of each other:

> She [hypochondria] had been my acquaintance, nay, my guest, once before in boyhood; I had entertained her at bed and board for a year; for that space of time I had her to myself in secret: she lay with me, she ate with me, she walked out with me ... taking me entirely to her death-cold bosom, and holding me with arms of bone ...
> I repulsed her as one would a dreaded and ghastly concubine coming to embitter a husband's heart toward his young bride; in vain; she kept her sway over me for that night and the next day, and eight succeeding days. Afterwards my spirits began slowly to recover their tone. (pp. 242–3)

A condition (though hardly the guarantee) of such introspective power and prosopopoeic adventurousness would seem to be a degree of deprivation in childhood which blocks conventional maturing and sensitizes while isolating the young adult.

Such a process seems relevant not only to her characters but to Charlotte Brontë herself, and if her appropriation of the male point of view in *The Professor* has embarrassed her critics, it is worth speculating how that embarrassment might be affected were it to be shown, *per impossibile*, that parts of the novel, say the account of Crimsworth's voyeuristic spying on the adjacent girls' school, had been copied from an Angrian fiction of Branwell's. Charlotte Brontë certainly had a capacity for thought experiments in androgyny beyond the powers of most minds whose sexual formation has been conventional. The whole of *The Professor* is such an experiment (though by no means Charlotte Brontë's first, or most urbane, as the later Angrian stories attest). Louis Moore's Journal is another. Moreover, Charlotte Brontë's characters are themselves willing to imagine gender reversals with a remarkable lack of anxiety – Louis Moore fantasies about Sir Philip playing Semele, and Shirley Jove, while Shirley casually imagines Louis as another man's tutor and *wife*.

The most daring of these thought experiments in androgyny is under-taken in public by the self-conscious and apparently deeply inhibited Lucy Snowe, acting the role of a 'fop' in competition with a 'bear' or 'sincere lover', played by Dr John, for the love of a beauty, played by Ginevra Fanshawe, in the fête play at Mme Beck's school (*Villette*, p. 196). But Lucy dresses in male clothes only to the waist: she thus thinks herself into a man's life without sacrificing her identity as a woman. (It is possible, of course, to attribute this to prudishness, but then a virgin's behaviour, speech and writings can always be read in terms of his or her supposed timidities.) As the performance gets under way, she feels 'the right power come' (p. 195). To an unspecified degree she is herself drawn to Dr John, with whom Ginevra is also conducting a flirtation; but as the play proceeds Lucy realises that Ginevra has her eye on the handsome de Hamal in the audience, so she decides to 'become' de Hamal for the purposes of the performance, thus forming an unspoken alliance with her rival for Dr John's attentions in order to 'eclipse' the latter in his role of sincere lover. She thereby avenges the neglect inflicted on her by the young Dr John (or Graham Bretton as he then was), and proleptically her prompt dismissal from his life when he meets Polly again on another theatrical occasion. She also defines Dr John/Graham's role in her narrative. And this freedom and power arise precisely from her situation as a woman who is clever, plain, poor, and so supposedly *hors de combat* in the battle of the sexes.

The theme of androgyny in Charlotte Brontë's work is evident in her proto-Lawrentian readiness to embody sexual and political contradic-tions in her characters. Crimsworth's friend, Hunsden, in *The Professor*, is a case in point:

> I had never observed him closely before; and, as my sight is very short, I had gathered only a vague, general idea of his appearance; I was surprised now, on examination, to perceive how small, and even feminine, were his lineaments; his tall figure, long and dark locks, his voice and general bearing, had impressed me with the notion of something powerful and massive; not at all ... I suspected his soul had more of will and ambition than his body had of fibre and muscle. Perhaps, in these incompatibilities of the 'physique' with the 'morale,' lay the secret of that fitful gloom; he *would* but *could* not, and the athletic mind scowled scorn on its more fragile companion. (p. 32)

Hunsden has extensive European connections and a cosmopolitan out-look unusual in a Yorkshire businessman. In contrast to William's aggressively masculine and narrow-minded elder brother, Edward, he does not hunt with the pack: Edward, significantly, recovers from bank-ruptcy and gets 'richer than Croesus by railway speculations; they call him in the Piece Hall a stag of ten' (p. 284). But Hunsden is also a snob, and dislikes William's decision to marry a lace-maker. Frances takes umbrage at his uncomplimentary remarks about Switzerland, and warns him that if he married a Swiss woman, he might find himself smothered 'even as your own Shakespeare's Othello smothered Desdemona' (p. 257).

But more is under scrutiny here than the boundaries in language, story and feeling between the sexes. The relations between Hunsden and Crimsworth are complex and confusingly defensive. Hunsden addresses Crimsworth on first meeting him after a long separation in 'an indifferent, quiet voice ... whose nonchalance seemed to intimate that it was much the same thing whether I answered or not' (p. 211); Crimsworth refuses to disclose the state of feeling between himself and Zoraide; neither admits the significance for Crimsworth of his mother's portrait, or for their relationship of Hunsden's buying it – 'There is a sort of stupid pleasure in giving a child sweets, a fool his bells, a dog a bone', Hunsden writes in a letter accompanying the picture (p. 222). This mutually aggressive stand-offishness may be read as Charlotte Brontë's account of masculine denial of emotion, but the relationship between Crimsworth and Hunsden has remarkable affinities with other, even more intimate relationships in her fiction, pointing to a grammar of intimacy which includes the erotic and transcends it.

Emily Brontë famously responded to Mary Taylor's declaration that her religious views were a matter between God and herself with the words 'That's right' (*A Chainless Soul*, p. 109). This is usually seen as revealing something about Emily's beliefs, but it may also be a mark of a pervasive reserve in Brontë family culture. In any case, silence in Charlotte Brontë's fiction is consistently represented as a right and a duty, especially in love. Shirley's capacity for reserve in moments of intense erotic disclosure makes Louis Moore love her. In his Journal he recalls deliberately provoking her with a description of connubial intimacy with 'Liberty', his American wife. Shirley is seized by a 'sense of half-painful, half-pleasing shame' (*Shirley*, p. 700) – she has been invited by her tutor and the man she loves to contemplate sexual intercourse – but she quickly recovers her self-command:

> I saw she had felt insurrection, and was waking to empire – she sat down. There was that in her face which I could read: it said, 'I see the line which is my limit – nothing shall make me pass it. I feel – I know how far I may reveal my feelings, and when I must clasp the volume. I have advanced to a certain distance, as far as the true and sovereign and undegraded nature of my kind permits – now here I stand rooted. My heart may break if it is baffled: let it break – it shall never dishonour me – it shall never dishonour my sisterhood in me. Suffering before degradation! death before treachery!' (pp. 700–701)

There are thus affinities, emotional, psychological and political, between oppression and freedom. Each involves vigilant, wilful control over utterance and silence; minute, relentless introspection and observation of others; intense loyalty; and the impassioned defence of self against intrusions from without. These tensions are not suspended by love, but they are transformed by it. That is why the relationships of enemies, Edward and William Crimsworth, William Crimsworth and Zoraide Reuter, Lucy Snowe and Madame Beck, reflect the relationships of friends and lovers, Crimsworth and Hunsden, William and Frances, Lucy Snowe and Paul Emmanuel.

The imperative of secrecy is particularly powerful in Shirley – not surprisingly in a character developed from Charlotte Brontë's recollections of her sister. To demand privacy generates an obligation to grant it to others. Shirley will not intervene in the relations between Caroline and Mrs Pryor, although she knows the latter's identity. Even to tell Caroline about Robert's feelings towards herself would open the question of her own relations with Louis and would violate Caroline's private world. Wounds of the spirit are as private as the possibly poisonous dog-bite which she secretly cauterizes and secretly fears.

The figure of Shirley leads to that of Lucy Snowe, and her relationship not only with the other characters in *Villette*, but also with the readers for whom, white-haired and probably alone, she writes her history. (I read the novel as the work of a mature, middle-aged woman, who from beginning to end controls her writing, not, as Sandra Gilbert and Susan Gubar do, as someone who in 'the process of writing her story ... has become less evasive' – *The Madwoman in the Attic*, p. 434). Like the unspecific, yet finally individuated narrator of *Shirley*, Lucy Snowe arbitrarily keeps the reader in the dark about facts that would clarify the narrative – notably the identity of Dr John – but in her case reserve as narrator is linked to reserve in the young woman whose story she is recalling. (In *Shirley* the narrative technique somewhat awkwardly models but does not participate in the privacy of the central characters.) Lucy resists describing the family disaster which caused her so much suffering as an adolescent, and left her alone as a young woman. We know only that 'the steersman' of the family bark, whether in harbour or not, spent more time 'stretched on the little deck' than at the wheel, and that ultimately there was a terrifying shipwreck (*Villette*, p. 46). This is appropriate both to the character of Lucy Snowe and a culture in which, as Elizabeth Gaskell was to affirm, domesticity is private. Lucy Snowe 'will permit the reader to picture [her]' passing her life as a 'great many women and girls are supposed to', but clearly she demands a more serious construction from us. Yet she will not do the choosing on our behalf. Her integrity, that is, her privacy, and ours, are equally at stake in the apportioning of interpretative responsibilities.

The text does, however, suggest how these responsibilities may be met. We have already examined the poor figure Dr John cuts in the fête play and when Vashti is performing. He cuts a poorer one after sending Lucy the long-awaited reply to her letter. Her attempt to read it is interrupted by the appearance of the nun, which Dr John, of course, Lucy being a frustrated virgin, puts down to 'a highly nervous state' (p. 356). But there was nothing hysterical about the vision, the 'nun' being the flesh-and-blood de Hamal. We collude with Graham if we accept Gilbert and Gubar's view that 'the nun comes out of Lucy's diseased brain', because Lucy 'has already played the role of de Hamal on the stage, and now *he* is playing her role as the nun' (*The Madwoman in the Attic*, p. 425). In the play Lucy deliberately takes on the de Hamal persona to punish Dr John. The whole point of the nun, on the other hand, is that 'she' has *nothing* to do with Lucy's inner state, and everything to do with the love situation Lucy had the wit to diagnose during the fête play. The 'nun' is the proof of Lucy's sanity, not, as Elaine Showalter suggests, 'an externalized representation of Lucy's own primal but now stunted desires'.[5]

In any case Graham's behaviour is even more reprehensible than an easy, sexist misdiagnosis. Seeing Lucy's tension, he uses his personal powers, 'consolations of tone ... caressing kindnesses' (*Villette*, pp. 353–4), to soothe and comfort her. Then he returns the letter, which he had found and had been hiding all the while. We may contrast this vain and trivial secrecy with Lucy's proud refusal to tell him that she had known him at Bretton, which Gilbert and Gubar cite as an example of her withholding 'information from other characters out of sheer perversity' (*The Madwoman in the Attic*, p. 418). It is Graham's economy with the truth that is perverse. Yet Lucy recalls his comforting her in strikingly generous terms:

> I have been told since, that Dr. Bretton was not nearly so perfect as I thought him: that his actual character lacked the depth, height, compass, and endurance it possessed in my creed. I don't know: he was as good to me as well to the parched wayfarer – as the sun to the shivering jail-bird. I remember him heroic. Heroic at this moment will I hold him to be. (p. 354)

Gilbert and Gubar overlook this passage when they claim that 'until the end of the story, [Lucy] persistently disclaims warm feelings for [Graham]' (*The Madwoman in the Attic*, p. 418). 'I have been told': but in her account of his reaction to the Vashti, Lucy will herself insist that she 'never' saw him in the light of 'a serious, impassioned man' (*Villette*, p. 372), and she will then recall how his mother decked him out while asleep in one of her own sky-blue turbans. By the time she comes to tell her story, therefore, the middle-aged Lucy Snowe knows what a light, minor figure Graham Bretton was and continued to be. She brilliantly encapsulates his personality in the opening chapters of the novel. She subsequently shows that his way of keeping secrets is contemptible compared with hers. She depicts him reduced to the figure of a doll when dressed up as a woman, whereas she acquired the skills of a seducer when she dressed as a man. Even so she reserves the right to continue thinking of him as 'heroic'. Just as the reader is free to construct the story of Lucy's adolescence and middle age, so Lucy's own past remains an arena of choice for her. She will indulge the rapturous pain of longing for a shallow handsome man if she wants to, a privilege merited and controlled by reserve.

The significance of such reserve in Charlotte Brontë's system of values is disclosed in Shirley's remarkable reply to Robert Moore's proposal of marriage. What shocks Shirley is that Robert should interpret her 'frank kindness' to him as 'an immodest manoeuvre to ensnare a husband': '"*Loved* you!" she cried. 'Why, I have been as frank with you as a sister – never shunned you – never feared you ... ' (*Shirley*, pp. 608–9). Love greater than that between brother and sister casteth out fear, but only eventually; it begins by requiring it, and the secrecy that fear prompts – something Robert simply fails to understand.

Thus the bond between William Crimsworth and Hunsden is a kind of loving. They are Charlotte Brontë's Rupert Birkin and Gerard Crich – even to the point of wrestling together: 'he swayed to and fro; so I grappled him round the waist. It was dark: the street was lonely and lampless. We had then a tug for it; and ... both rolled on the pavement, and with difficulty picked ourselves up' (p. 24). *The Professor* is in many respects a naïve text, but it is by no means timid in its attempts to explore the inner lives of friends and lovers.

In psycho-analytic theory and practice, secrets are usually regarded as pathogenic, poisons extruded by disclosure from neurotic subjects. This is how the flaunted secrecy in which Charlotte Brontë's protagonists indulge is commonly interpreted. According to Russell Meares, however, there is 'a class of hidden ideas and experience which is fundamentally different from the "pathogenic secret." In this case, that which is concealed is not something alien, of which the bearer wishes to be rid, but something highly valued.'[6] The case-history with which Meares introduces this concept is that of a frail, shy young woman who 'seems to feel that she is composed of a series of ideas, and that should they be lost, she will cease to exist'. This is obviously a case of pathological frailty, but, he suggests,

it does seem that, for most of us, there are threads of thoughts and
images which are [similarly] felt as intensely 'personal' and important. Not all thoughts are given the same value. Those concerned
with things commonly sensed are frequently regarded as peripheral
and passed about in small talk and gossip. Those most valued are
perceived as a kind of inner core. They remain secret except under
unusual circumstances.

Secrets are disclosed with care in a developing dialogue with
others who can be trusted to share and respect them. They become
the coins of intimacy, and the currency of its transactions. ('The
Secret', p. 259)

Meares cites Virginia Woolf's experience of ending and publishing her
books as one of possible or actual loss, and he detects 'a theme of lyric
eroticism' (ibid., p. 260) in a passage from *The Waves* which he thinks
may account for her description of being unable to read her own work
'without blushing – shivering and rushing to take cover' (p. 261). The
sexual implications are clear. Meares quotes H.M. Lynd on the etymo-
logical connection between shame and sexuality, and 'the similarity
between the feelings evoked by bodily and genital exposure and those
engendered through "exposure of particularly sensitive and intimate
and vulnerable aspects of self"'. He notes that neurotic and endangered
subjects can take refuge in extreme silence to protect the secrets with
which they are inwardly identified. Other strategies include the telling
of deliberate lies.

In a discussion of the Brontës the normal is as important as the
neurotic in this structure of feeling. 'It is in the confessional', Meares
maintains – and this is clearly relevant to Lucy Snowe's resort to confession, and Charlotte Brontë's – that 'the "pathogenic secret" is to be
found in its purest form', whereas 'the creative secret' is something the
mind wants to hold on to and not expel by disclosure. Another difference between the two is that the pathogenic secret is 'relatively static',
while the 'creative secret ... invites elaboration. It is exposed in a
relationship so that the other may add to it, modify it, or in other ways
nourish it. It is not exposed in order to be lost' (p. 264).

Meares's paper suggests that if impassioned defensiveness is a condition of love, it is not its fulfilment. In accordance with this principle,
love in Charlotte Brontë's fiction permits the penetration of fear and
weakness, and is consequently always a power relationship; but the
lover has to pass the test of reading, understanding and *identifying with*
the beloved's secret, in effect her 'Angrian' fantasies. Rochester studies
Jane Eyre's paintings, William Crimsworth, Louis Moore and M. Paul
read their pupils' *devoirs*. The most impressive examples of private
writing in Charlotte Brontë's work, myth constructions that were to
remain unrivalled until Olive Schreiner's *The Story of an African Farm*,

are Shirley's depiction to Caroline of 'the first woman' (*Shirley*, p. 360) on the evening when they agree to commune with Nature instead of going to church, and the *devoir* preserved by Louis Moore. Both are clearly modelled on the *devoirs* which Emily wrote for M. Héger, but are much more expansive than their laconic originals. 'The First Blue Stocking', in particular, and within it the quasi-biblical narrative of '*La Première Femme Savante*', are extraordinarily revealing, not just of Shirley's mind, and therefore implicitly of Emily Brontë's, but also – because the entire conception is hers – of Charlotte Brontë's. In a sense all Charlotte Brontë's writing is 'private', but particularly her descriptions of pictures and dreams, and the journals and exercises of her characters. Reading them, we stand in relation to her as Louis Moore (who himself is her fantasy) stands in relation to Shirley. It is hardly surprising that Martineau, Taylor and Rigby all felt there was something indecent in her fiction. Publication was as difficult for Charlotte Brontë as it was to be for Virginia Woolf.

At the heart of the exchanges about writing and painting in *The Professor, Jane Eyre, Shirley* and *Villette* is the recognition that really to understand the fantasies of others, you must share their susceptibilities and vulnerabilities. Louis Moore makes unintelligible marks on Shirley's papers, M. Paul is upset by Lucy Snowe's acting, even Rochester is almost literally struck by Jane's paintings, because they speak to their own condition. This is why Charlotte Brontë's lovers repeatedly return to the condition of master and servant, teacher and pupil. Paradoxically, it is at the moment when the authoritarian male, exercising his 'rights' to inspect the consciousness of the governess he has employed, or the virgin he is instructing, betrays himself by acknowledging his own susceptibility to her secrets, that real equality between lovers is established.

> "And are we equal then, sir? Are we equal at last?"
> "You are younger, frailer, feebler, more ignorant than I."
> "Will you be good to me, and never tyrannize?"
> "Will you let me breathe, and not bewilder me? You must not smile at present. The world swims and changes round me. The sun is a dizzying scarlet blaze; the sky a violet vortex whirling over me" ...
> "You name me leopardess: remember, the leopardess is tameless" ...
> "Tamer or fierce, wild or subdued, you are *mine*."
> "I am glad to know my keeper, and am used to him. Only his voice will I follow: only his hand shall manage me; only at his feet will I repose" ...
> "How much do you love me?" ...
> "Ah! you know: I will not gratify you: I will not flatter" ...
> (*Shirley*, pp. 711–12)

If this almost gives Shirley the role of her dog in her relations to Louis, we should recall that it is to Tartar that she compares *him*. Their consciousness is mutual, the teacher–pupil relationship reciprocal and reversible, and the intercourse negotiated in this extravagant proviso scene is, at the level of the flesh and the spirit, one of equality.

This is deeply disruptive of all that is implied in Gaskell's respect for the privacy of Revd Arthur Bell Nichols and his bride, as was evident to some of Charlotte Brontë's contemporaries. In the review already cited, Dobell wrote of her:

> In the ecclesiastical tendencies of her education and habits – in the youthful ambiguity of her politics, in the certain old-world air, which hangs about her pictures, we see her passport into circles which otherwise she would never reach. Into them she is carrying, unperceived, the elements of infallible disruption and revolution. ('Currer Bell', p. 232)

Had Dobell had the opportunity to read *The Professor* before writing this, he might have been even more alert to the concealed radicalism in Charlotte Brontë's writing. In the twenty-fifth chapter we are given a remarkably circumstantial description of female desire and its gratification:

> She stopped, her voice was cut off, her eyes suddenly suffused. She and I were standing side by side; she threw her arms round me, and strained me to her heart with passionate earnestness: the energy of her whole being glowed in her dark and then dilated eye, and crimsoned her animated cheek; her look and movement were like inspiration; in one there was such a flash, in the other such a power. Half an hour afterwards, when she had become calm, I asked her where all that wild vigour had gone which had transformed her erewhile and made her glance so thrilling and ardent – her action so rapid and strong. She looked down, smiling softly and passively –
> 'I cannot tell where it is gone, monsieur,' said she, 'but I know that, whenever it is wanted, it will come back again.' (p. 272)

And in *Shirley*, the full implications for the entire social order of this virginal vision of sexual love are spelled out by Shirley herself in her memorable encounter with her Uncle Sympson:

> 'Mr. Sympson ... ... I am sick at heart with all this weak trash. I will bear no more. Your thoughts are not my thoughts, your aims are not my aims, your gods are not my gods ...
> ' ... As to your small maxims, your narrow rules, your little prejudices, aversions, dogmas, bundle them off ... I'll none of them ... I walk by another creed, light, faith, and hope than you.'
> 'Another creed! I believe she is an infidel.'
> 'An infidel to *your* religion; an atheist to *your* god.'
> 'An – atheist!!!'

'Your god, sir, is the World ... *Your* god is a masked Death.'
'This language is terrible! My daughters and you must associate
no longer, Miss Keeldar ... '. (pp. 632–4)

This is Charlotte Brontë's reading of her sister's writings, and it is a
reading she endorses. She is evidently exhilarated by the verbal daring
of those writings. She can put God's words into Shirley's mouth ('For
my thoughts are not your thoughts ... saith the LORD – Isaiah, 55:5),
and she does not flinch from the word 'atheist'. But then neither Shirley
nor Emily Brontë were 'God' to themselves, nor were they 'atheists' in
any sense that troubled Charlotte Brontë. In her character's eyes, in her
sister's and in her own, the god of the marriage-market, the god of 'the
World', was a 'fish-tailed Dagon', utterly different from the God they
worshipped, in church or out. And it was the religion of the latter, they
believed – and who is to say they were not right? – which had declared
war on so much that Uncle Sympson, Miss Rigby, Sidney Dobell, and
even the gifted, generous Elizabeth Gaskell took for granted, about
love, about secrecy and about virgins.

PART FOUR

The Management of our Hearts

CHAPTER TWELVE

The Two Eternities:
Race and Soul in *Daniel Deronda*

My title is from Yeats's 'Under Ben Bulben':

> Many times man lives and dies
> Between his two eternities
> That of race and that of soul
> And ancient Ireland knew it all.[1]

We know that Yeats was not sympathetic to George Eliot. Balzac was the only nineteenth-century novelist Yeats liked – 'it is hard', Denis Donoghue suggests, 'to think of Yeats as a reader of *Middlemarch*. When he writes of society, it seems to consist of invisible men ... his imagination is stirred by the theme of race, kindred, blood, consanguinity.'[2] Donoghue has in mind the following passage from 'At Stratford-on-Avon':

> Balzac would have us understand that behind the momentary self which acts and lives in the world, and is subject to the judgement of the world, there is that which cannot be called before any mortal judgement seat, even though a great poet, or novelist, or philosopher, be sitting upon it. Great literature ... is ... the For-giveness of Sin, and when we find it becoming the Accusation of Sin as in George Eliot, who plucks Tito in pieces with as much assurance as if he had been clockwork, literature has begun to change into something else. George Eliot has a fierceness hardly to be found but in a woman turned argumentative ... she grew up in a century of utilitarianism, when nothing about a man seemed im-portant except his utility to the state.[3]

George Eliot and Yeats are thus so apparently at odds that it might seem pointless to mention them together. But if one focuses on *Daniel Deronda* rather than on *Romola* or *Middlemarch*, the passages I have quoted acquire surprising and obvious relevance. Unsympathetic as Yeats was to George Eliot's Positivism – her *submission* to a scientific culture – his involvement in the visionary would have interested her immensely. She might even have used the lines I have quoted from 'Under Ben Bulben' as an epigraph in *Daniel Deronda*. Her imagina-tion, too, was stirred by race, kindred, blood, consanguinity, and her initial impulse was also to treat such matters in verse. And when we turn to the charge that she uses her art to accuse rather than to forgive, the case against her is considerably weakened if we include *Daniel*

Deronda in the account, especially that part of the novel which deals with Gwendolen Harleth. The story of Gwendolen achieves its neutral, compassionate intensity because George Eliot would have us understand that, behind Gwendolen's momentary self which acts and lives in the world, and is subject to the judgement of the world (and of Deronda), there is that which cannot be called before any mortal judgement seat, not even Deronda's.

Nor is Gwendolen's the only such case in the novel. As Daniel hesitates before his second visit to the Cohens, he browses in Mr Ram's shop and finds 'that wonderful bit of autobiography, the life of the Polish Jew, Salmon Maimon',[4] vital elements of which, William Baker suggests, were transferred to the account of Mirah and Mordecai's father, just as there is much in Daniel's mother of the *Hass Liebe* towards the gentile world which Rahel Levin and her husband's friend, Heine, epitomized so vividly.[5] The Princess is the more explicit example of George Eliot's discovering a Balzacian talent for forgiveness, but Lapidoth, whose life and wanderings, according to William Baker, reflect the movement and counter-movement of Jews in the nineteenth century following the break-up of their traditional occupations and settlements, is the more subtle (*George Eliot and Judaism*, p. 118). Though George Eliot's feelings towards him are overtly negative, Lapidoth escapes from what John Bayley calls 'the framework of her studious intentness'. We do not 'as readers feel that our exploration is inhibited or made superfluous by the author's intention: we feel, in fact, our contribution as an allowed aspect of the novel's scope'.[6] The novel, indeed, scrupulously draws us into thinking and feeling about both characters open-endedly. They are historically representative instances of human beings trapped between the Jewish and gentile worlds, who cannot be, and are not, judged either by Jewish or non-Jewish standards. This is an important openness in a novel which chooses to be partisan in the cause of Jewishness.

The more one dwells on *Daniel Deronda*, the more one begins to sense a troublesome continuity between Yeats's mental life and George Eliot's, troublesome because George Eliot's sense of duty and fact disturb our complacency about Yeats's ethical arrogance and wilfully mystical rhetoric, while his philosophically and morally perverse lyricism reminds us of the leaden quality of her high-toned, didactic verse. Nietzsche's contempt for George Eliot seems justified by swathes of *Daniel Deronda*. For all that, there is a continuity between the consciously Nietzschean Yeats and the 'little moralistic' George Eliot.[7] It is startling, for instance, to find Yeats and, of all characters, Mirah, dwelling on the same problem. In 'Easter 1916', Yeats complains that he and the Dublin men who came 'From counter or desk among gray/Eighteenth-century houses' but lived where motley was worn, and Mirah asks, 'Is this world and all life upon it only like a farce or a vaudeville, where you find no great meanings?' (p. 200).

The obvious explanation for this continuity is that George Eliot modified her Positivism. Rationalism, Robert Preyer suggests, led her 'to a careful estimate of how large, impersonal environmental forces determine individual conduct. But alongside this was a "visionary" element which increasingly emphasized the way in which our receptivity (or lack of it) to signs and portents helps us to break free from the tyranny of habitual responses and to find out, in Lawrence's words, "what the heart really wants after all."'[8] In Ulrich Knoepflmacher's judgement, George Eliot crosses the 'boundary of experimental evidence' in *Daniel Deronda*, abandoning 'the analytical manner of *Middlemarch* in order to turn to a more elevated form of presenting higher ethical truths'.[9] And Gillian Beer suggests that in *Daniel Deronda* causal sequence 'is disturbed and pressed upon by resurgence, synchronicity, the miraculous, the hermeneutic, and by unassuageable human need'.[10] More is meant by these claims than that George Eliot indulged in what Daniel Deronda describes as 'a flash of fervour ... an extreme image of what is happening every day' (p. 435). They point to an alleged shift in the content of her beliefs. Baker touches on possible sources for this change, namely Christian David Ginsberg's *The Kaballah, its Doctrines, Development and Literature*, and the writings of Jehuda Halevi, the medieval mystical Jewish poet. *Daniel Deronda*, Baker believes, tries to give credibility to the Kabbalistic doctrine of the transmigration of the soul in its progress towards greater purity, to the possible fusion of one soul with another – also a Kabbalistic teaching – and to Halevi's conviction that in some literal sense Israel really is the heart of mankind (*George Eliot and Judaism*, pp. 143–80). I agree. I suggest, however, that this did not involve any weakening on George Eliot's part of her Positivist principles. On the contrary, *Daniel Deronda* is the most intransigent of Victorian novels because it quite properly wishes to have the best of both worlds.

It opens, admittedly, with a relativist epigraph that puts science in its place as being 'obliged to start with a make-believe unit'; and after a brief flirtation with a facetiously scientific analogy about the proportions of condensed human breath, it moves into a narrative which, after *Middlemarch*, seems thin in its references to science. It is easy to forget, however, how fluently science itself can proceed with a literary reliance on analogy. The following illustrates what I mean:

> control over the approaches to motility ... is like a man on horse-back, who has to hold in check the superior strength of the horse ... Often a rider, if he is not to be parted from his horse, is obliged to guide it where it wants to go ...

> ... Psycho-physiology has fully discussed the manner in which a person's own body obtains its special position among the objects in the world of perception ...
> The ego is first and foremost a bodily ego ... the projection of a surface.[11]

> The ego is a great reservoir from which the libido that is destined for objects flows out and into which it flows back from those objects ... As an illustration of this state of things we may think of an amoeba, whose viscous substance puts out pseudopodia. (Quoted in *The Ego and the Id*, p. 53)

The metaphors are Sigmund Freud's, but the tradition in which he is working was familiar to George Eliot, being precisely that adopted by George Henry Lewes in *Problems of Life and Mind*, and by his friend, Alexander Bain, whose writings on psychology reflect with remarkable consistency of detail, idiom and concept, George Eliot's own procedures for analysing character.[12] This Associationist tradition, which culminates in Freud, frequently relies on metaphors of currents, dams, reservoirs, obstructions, shocks, waves, residues, traces and so forth; and it enables George Eliot to keep *Daniel Deronda* in sustaining contact with the perspectives of science. Similar verbal tactics were adopted by economists; and, not surprisingly, Freud, his Associationist predecessors, and George Eliot herself readily adopt economic metaphors to analyse mental activity. This is why I believe that Freud is a more relevant figure than Charles Darwin if one wishes to define the alternative, non-Yeatsian, relentlessly Positivist tradition, to which George Eliot really adhered while plotting the Jewish part of *Daniel Deronda*, and specifically the views of Mordecai.

Mordecai insists that he is 'a rational Jew'. But, he asks, 'what is it to be rational – what is it to feel the light of the divine reason growing stronger within and without? It is to see more and more of the hidden bonds that bind and consecrate change as a dependent growth – yea, consecrate it with kinship' (p. 490). Freud, too, though he is poised and sad where Mordecai is precipitate and eager, thinks it reasonable to see civilization as grounded in instinct:

> civilization is a process in the service of Eros, whose purpose is to combine single human individuals, and after that families, then races, peoples and nations, into one greater unity, the unity of mankind ... Necessity alone, the advantages of work in common, will not hold them together. But man's natural aggressive instinct, the hostility of each against all and of all against each, opposes this programme of civilization. This aggressive instinct is the derivative and the main representative of the death instinct which we have found alongside of Eros and which shares world-dominion with it. And now, I think, the meaning of the evolution of civilization is no longer obscure to us. It must present the struggle

of Eros and Death, the instinct of life and the instinct of destruction.)[13]

The conclusions are different, but the mode of thought is the same. It involves applying concepts and images from the life of the individual to the development of the species. Given intellectual respectability in the nineteenth century by Auguste Comte and Herbert Spencer, the technique is none the less a venerable one. Halevi had used it in working out a mystical eschatology for the Jews and the whole of humanity; and that is why Mordecai can use Halevi's vision, which is worked out extensively in metaphors drawn from nature, biology, growth and human physiology, to transform the tepid Positivism of his gentile contemporaries without fundamentally destroying its 'scientific' character.

But what content has the word 'soul' in this poetically charged perspective on humanity which none the less tries to anchor itself to the unyielding deliverances of the scientific method? One can begin to get a sense of it from a consideration of Grandcourt as a soulless man. Like all George Eliot's earlier villains, notably the clockwork Tito in *Romola* and Rosamond in *Middlemarch*, Grandcourt's malignity is at least formally represented as a deficiency in feeling, an incapacity for positive human responses, not a real alternative force to virtue and love; it is not Thanatos, just non-Eros. It would be hard to find a single character anywhere in George Eliot's earlier fiction whose evil acts are positively motivated. Memory is a benign force in her work; villains suppress their memories or lack them. That is one reason why her proximity to Freud is troublesome: her character analyses fail to address the power of aggressive impulse, of the death instinct, to register impulse as a buried threat as well as an intimate resource. Grandcourt the sadist is a confirming example. No living man could look less animated than he; among lizards he is unique in not being lively; his false air of demonic strength is based on the erratic quality of his choices, themselves the result of a lack of regulated channels for the soul to move in.

This brings us back to the meaning of the word 'soul'. Its 'medium' (to use a word Lewes and George Eliot constantly resorted to), is a psycho-physiological structure formed out of an inherited physiology enlivened and enriched by accumulating layers of memory, habit, feeling. Of course the distinction between the soul and its well-regulated channels is finally unreal. Daniel's 'fine musical instinct' (p. 153) is at once a medium for his soul to move in – when he hears the Hebrew liturgy, for instance – and a principle of spiritual movement in itself. Even in his long, flexible, firmly grasping hands, there are manifestations of soul, a Titian-like 'combination of refinement with force' (p. 170) – which brings to mind Freud's suggestion that the ego is 'first and foremost a bodily ego ... the projection of a surface'. But the greater emphasis in George Eliot's discussion of the spiritual life falls on the inner conditions, the 'choice organizations' as Herr Klesmer puts it (p. 236), of, for example, the penitent, or artist, or counsellor, or national leader; and the images which repeatedly occur in this connection are those of movement, sensation and struggle.

The experience of body, then, is for George Eliot the vale of soul-making. Klesmer talks of the formation of a singer as a combination of inherited characters – 'a singing throat' and 'a great capacity for receiving discipline' – with training, 'a shaping of the organs towards a finer and finer certainty of effect' (p. 238); later 'the struggle of mind attending a conscious error' wakens 'something like a new soul' in Gwendolen, which has 'better, but also worse, possibilities' (p. 305). This still leaves the meaning of the word obscure, but the only language in which such elusive categories *can* be discussed – as Freud was to discover – is a metaphorical one. But that does not mean that he and George Eliot were not discussing realities. Geneticists now describe genetic codes as 'striving' to reproduce themselves although molecules are incapable of effort or purpose, are only codes by accommodation, and do not have fingerprints – features of the body which are anyway non-hereditary. For all that, DNA is real enough.

DNA provides a useful analogy. Just as we now know that DNA operates *as if it were* a binary encoding of the complete organism, so in *Daniel Deronda* the physique of every human being is an ongoing and inheritable encoding of its life-history, like 'a little flower-seed that absorbs the chance confusion of its surroundings into its own definite mould of beauty' (p. 208). The body is thus the means by which social fact, becoming experience, is written into the text of heredity. Preyer dismisses this Lamarckian superimposition of 'some rather dated speculations concerning the effects of heredity' on the account of Daniel's introspective discovery of his own Jewishness ('Beyond the Liberal Imagination', p. 48), but they are vital to the whole scheme of the novel. Transmission is one of its unifying themes as it is one of the principles of Judaism. The process is both social and biological. Daniel inherits his grandfather's papers, but also a 'yearning – the effect of brooding, passionate thoughts in many ancestors' – thoughts which seem to have been 'intensely present in [his] grandfather', and which, as part of his ancestral life, have lain within Daniel himself 'as a dim longing for unknown objects and sensations'. The 'spell-bound habit' of his inherited frame, during the long years when he was cut off from his Jewish inheritance, was 'like a cunningly wrought musical instrument, never played on, but quivering throughout in uneasy, mysterious moanings of its intricate structure' (pp. 697–8). We, of course, know that such notions are wholly mistaken. But that was not the view taken by the vast majority of scientists of George Eliot's generation. They and George Eliot identified race with soul, and both with the body, or rather they saw each as an encoded form of the other.

This emphasis on race, then, though new in her work, involves no new principle regarding matters of fact. *Daniel Deronda* remains a text which purports to do without miracle. Nearly everything it suggests about vision and art, and their relationship to the intricate structure of bodies – the bodies of mystics, artists or women – can be found in *Romola*. On one important point, however, it is original. Much attention has been paid to the quotation from Aristotle's *Poetics* of Agathon's saying that it 'is part of probability that many improbable things will happen' (p. 473). In *Daniel Deronda*, however, the improbabilities include not only coincidence but also prevision. Here, if anywhere, Positivism comes under pressure, for there is a great difference between generalized anticipations such as Klesmer's 'fervour of created work and theoretic belief which pierces the whole future of a life with congruous, devoted purpose' (p. 222), and 'those quiveringly-poised natures' that not only 'lend themselves to second sight' (p. 438), but are also strikingly accurate in their predictions. How, in short, is Mordecai's remarkably accurate and circumstantial prevision to be explained?

We can begin to understand his case through another example of prevision in the novel, Gwendolen's anticipatory horror of the dead face in the picture. No one, I think, feels that this is a merely literary device. Nor is it a seriously intended instance of supernaturally grounded prevision. What Gwendolen is reacting to is the potentialities within her own intricate structure, her own capacity to kill. But this is remarkable enough. It means that for the first time George Eliot is willing to explore the possibility of evil energy as well as good in the psyche – which is what after all the epigraph of Book One is all about:

Let thy chief terror be of thine own soul:
There ...
Lurks vengeance, footless irresistible ...
And o'er the fairest troops of captured joys
Breathes pallid pestilence.

(p. xxxviii)

The 'captured joys' are familiar enough – they are what have nourished all the noble natures in George Eliot's earlier work, and what nourish the lives of Miss Arrowpoint, for example, and Mirah. But the admission into the soul of a pestilential vengeance is new. The case of Grandcourt is relevant also. I have argued that formally his evil nature is represented as an absence of the positive qualities which energize Daniel and Mordecai: impulse in his life 'is born and dies in a phantasmal world, pausing in rejection even of a shadowy fulfilment'. But his 'strange spiritual chemistry', in addition to its 'lazy stagnation', includes 'a cottony milkiness' necessary for the preparation of 'explosive material' (pp. 291–2). The reference is to the newly discovered chemistry of dynamite. This hesitant but unmistakable recognition of truly malign energies in the lives of Grandcourt and Gwendolen is a braver move in the economy of George Eliot's fiction than a symbolic or literal resort to miracle would have been – it brings her hitherto meliorist and liberal humanism into contact with Freudian sadness, and I shall return to it. It is also important, however, in opening up our understanding of insight and intuition in the novel generally.

Gwendolen's terror is represented, in effect, as a mode of self-knowledge. Like her, Mordecai is deeply sensitive to what is within him, to the 'thoughts of his heart', which, as inherited and racial, are indeed 'too close inwoven with the growth of things not to have a further destiny'. The second important characteristic of his physique is a mind that works 'so constantly in images, that his coherent trains of thought often [resemble] ... dreams', and his hopes take the direct form of images (p. 441). He has already met Daniel before the incident at the bridge, and both, without knowing it, have felt a subtle complementariness of life and mind – just as Gwendolen and Grandcourt do. Thus the actual meeting may be chance, but its character is explicitly understood in terms of antecedent causes.

This does not, however, account for the problem of Mordecai's certainty, before he meets Daniel, that he is going to do so. The important point about this certainty, however, is that it is not *given* to Mordecai in a vision, but is something he *chooses* to believe. That is why it is so important that he is 'sane as well as excitable' (p. 446): Mordecai knows that he might be proved wrong, that he could be proved to be mistaken, as the insane allegedly could not. 'In the hour when you come to me', he tells Daniel, 'and say, "I reject your soul: I know that I am not a Jew: we have no lot in common" – I shall not doubt, I shall be certain – certain that I have been deluded. That hour will never come' (p. 469). The contradiction in this assertion is the key to its character. Mordecai is 'gambling' on 'certitude'. If souls are lost at the gaming-table in this novel, they are also made in movements of the will, and Mordecai's is completed in a sustained decision to *risk* all the life that is in him – and that includes Jewishness itself – on a chance meeting. At The Hand and Banner he confirms this when he declares that 'the strongest principle of growth lies in human choice', that the human soul 'is set in the royalty of discernment and resolve', and that the 'divine principle of our race is action, choice, resolved memory' (p. 499).

But it is not just Lapidoth, Gwendolen and Mordecai who bind the novel together with their gambling. For better or worse, George Eliot inscribes her own resolved and risky choices in the text as well. Mordecai's excitement in the early phases of his relationship with Daniel is compared to 'that of the experimenter, bending over the first stirrings of change that correspond to what in the fervour of concentrated prevision his thought has foreshadowed' (p. 460). The orientation of Mordecai's mental life is thus fundamentally that of the scientist, and so is George Eliot's. Both operate under the principle that a hypothesis only has validity if it can be falsified. Ten years before publishing *Daniel Deronda*, George Eliot noted 'the absence of any profound research into psychological functions or into the mysteries of inheritance'. She was also quite clear about the lack of 'any comprehensive view of man's historical development'.[14] The novel was a gamble therefore about the validity of hypotheses that had yet to be tested experimentally. It was a gamble also about the future of the Jewish people. In 1876 there was little prospect of a Jewish return to Palestine. The novel was written in the full knowledge that later readers might find it encumbered with a whole range of outdated and erroneous speculations.

And there was another kind of risk in writing it as well. I have suggested that it engages with the dark side of the psyche in the characterizations of Gwendolen and Grandcourt; but theirs is not the only 'spiritual chemistry' which it brings to our attention. In *Impressions of Theophrastus Such* (1880), George Eliot was herself to suggest that our sense of a writer's character comes 'not from what he means to convey, but from what he unconsciously enables us to discern'.[15] And, in fusing science and mysticism in the text of *Daniel Deronda* (as Freud would have been the first to recognize), she engages in processes of free association which expose the 'elder forces', and specifically an element of 'cottony milkiness', in her own mental life. There is a haphazard quality to some of the images of cruelty in the novel that Nietzsche would gleefully have diagnosed. The relationship between Gwendolen and Grandcourt is plainly based on the infliction of pain, but sadistic images are not confined to these two characters. Daniel *approves* of Gwendolen's urge 'to some self-punishment – some scourging of the self that disobeyed your better will' (p. 714); Klesmer tells her she must *submit* to musical training 'as a horse, however beautiful, must be trained for the circus' (p. 239) – a terrible reversal of the horse analogy to be used later by Freud; Daniel's mother finds her *duty* as a Jewess like being 'put in a frame and tortured' (p. 617); Mordecai has *righteous* fantasies about his father being flogged (p. 722); and Mirah's *heroic* response to the intimacy between Daniel and Gwendolen is like that of creatures which 'in intense pain bite and make their teeth meet even through their own flesh' (p. 677). These sadistic images are sanctioned by the text: in them

George Eliot allows us to discern her own intimate reactions to Thanatos. The 'need for punishment', Freud wrote, 'is an instinctual manifestation on the part of the ego, which has become masochistic under the influence of a sadistic superego' (*Civilization and its Discontents*, p. 84), a structure of feeling which for George Eliot is virtually a form of self-indulgence. She is a much more ambivalent figure, therefore, than 'a woman turned argumentative'. Her earlier writing contained many images of flesh being flogged, cut, burnt or bitten – but *Daniel Deronda* celebrates them.

George Eliot had always found publication of her fiction embarrassing, and in publishing the histories of Gwendolen Harleth and Daniel Deronda she was, I suggest, wagering much more than her reputation as a wise, learned, modern-minded, earnest sage. Our sense of this self-consciousness, our sense that she knew she might be wrong about the future, and painfully compromised by writing about what her own heart really wanted after all, must fundamentally change our relationship with the 'bad' half of the novel. To reverse Bayley's formulation, the reader's *valid and adverse* judgements become an allowed aspect within the frame of her studious intentness: this is a text which shrinks from, but does not seek to control, the reactions of its readers. This is why, in Preyer's words, '*Daniel Deronda* has something heroic about it' ('Beyond the Liberal Imagination', p. 35). For it is not just the novel that is 'haunted by the future' (*Darwin's Plots*, p. 181); so is its author. We may think of George Eliot, like Gwendolen Harleth at the gaming table, staking her art, her faith and her privacy on nothing more substantial than ardent hypotheses, and accepting the gaze of the future like Gwendolen under the scrutiny of Deronda. I am certain that we should admire the courage this required of her, even if half of what she staked may have been swept away as literature which has turned into something else.

CHAPTER THIRTEEN

Justice and Freedom:
The Portrait of a Lady

I

I propose to examine ways in which Henry James represents choice and freedom in *The Portrait of a Lady*. The character with whose freedom he is most concerned is Isabel Archer, who is unwittingly made the subject of an experiment in freedom when her dying cousin, Ralph Touchett, arranges for her to inherit his father's money so that he may observe the consequence of so fine a person enjoying the opportunities for choosing which great wealth brings. The issues raised by this experiment have preoccupied moral philosophers since Aristotle, but, this being a novel by James, our approach to Ralph's experiment demands considerable caution. James warns us, indeed, that his intentions with respect to his heroine are to 'awaken on the reader's part an impulse more tenderly expectant' than would be consistent with making her a 'victim of scientific criticism'.[1] At the very least this is a warning against reductively rationalizing the text.

One of the questions which the experiment raises is whether human freedom is after all no more than freedom from practical constraints and limitations, something money can buy. At one point Isabel comes near to thinking that it is. Walking alone through the London streets, and thinking of her plans to spend the winter travelling wherever she wants in the company of her friend, Madame Merle, she has a vivid sense of 'the absolute boldness and wantonness of liberty' (II, p. 35). But she is preoccupied also with the question of how she *ought* to act. 'A large fortune', she remarks, 'means freedom and I'm afraid of that. It's such a fine thing, and one should make good use of it' (I, p. 320). Her situation thus highlights some vexed questions. Is it possible to form a rational plan of life and stick to it, and, having done so, how can one rationally identify the appropriate premises for making decisions in the light of such a plan? On the one hand, Isabel feels justified in treating her own wants as the premises of her practical reasoning, since she has 'an unquenchable desire to think well of herself ... a theory ... that one ... should move in a realm of light, of natural wisdom, of happy impulse' (I, p. 68); on the other she has intimations of an objective moral order and a fear of doing 'anything wrong'. At first she thinks she can identify the wrong – it is 'to be mean, to be jealous, to be false, to be cruel' (I, pp. 68–9) – but as her situation develops, everything becomes more problematical.

In particular, the difficulties of her forming and being practically faithful to a plan of life are increased by the fact that she is doubly deceived. In the first place she is not told Ralph's role in securing her fortune, so that almost until his death her relations with him are not on an entirely open footing. More seriously, she is deceived by Madame Merle and Gilbert Osmond about the true parentage of their daughter and her stepdaughter, Pansy. In principle neither of these deceptions affects Isabel's freedom, but they do make it difficult for her to understand the motivations of those closest to her, and therefore to base her own plans and expectations on a realistic appraisal of her world.

The difficulties confronting her, however, are not just external. There are forces within her which complicate her understanding and ours of the decisions she makes. James's reticence in this area adds to our problems. In particular he does not tell us exactly what happens on the three occasions when Isabel receives proposals of marriage. None is directly reported. The first occurs before she leaves America. We are told that Caspar Goodwood is 'quite a splendid young man', and that he inspires her 'with a sentiment of high, of rare respect', but we are not told why she refuses him (I, p. 47). Later, in England, but before coming into her money, she rejects the (in some ways) more eligible Lord Warburton, and again the grounds for her doing so are undisclosed. Her acceptance of Osmond is equally mysterious: we learn about it in the course of a conversation she has with Caspar. The few clues we are given about her feelings on these occasions only add to the mystery. It seems Isabel is afraid of something: 'Deep in her soul – it was the deepest thing there – lay a belief that if a certain light should dawn she could give herself completely, but this image, on the whole, was too formidable to be attractive. Isabel's thoughts hovered about it, but they seldom rested on it long; after a while it ended in alarms' (I, pp. 71–2). Is this fear sexual? A lover, we are told, might have described her reluctance to think about marriage as 'something cold and dry', but it is only at the end of the novel that her most impassioned suitor, Caspar, seems dangerous to her.

A stronger clue is given in her reaction to Osmond's first declaration: she begs him to stop

> with an intensity that expressed the dread of having, in this case too, to choose and decide. What made her dread great was ... the sense of something within herself, deep down, that she supposed to be inspired and trustful passion. It was there like having a large sum stored in a bank – which there was a terror in having to begin to spend. If she touched it, it would all come out. (II, p. 18)

This is sexually suggestive, but indications of a fear of choice itself are also strong. Isabel seems to be afraid of what she and Lord Warburton call her 'remarkable mind' (I, p. 154) – not least because she finds it so difficult to explain her actions. She does not 'know why' (I, p. 160) she rejects Warburton, and she is 'surprised' (II, p. 50) by her acceptance of Osmond, yet years later she says of the latter decision that it was 'perfectly free; it was impossible to do anything more deliberate' (II, p. 284). But can one be said to choose freely and deliberately if one does not know what one is doing?

Isabel's is thus a problematical study of freedom not least because James is initially so careful not to narrate what happens at the moments when she makes up her mind. He begins to do so only after Isabel has married and set up house with Osmond and Pansy in Rome. Her relations with Pansy are complex. At an early stage in Osmond's pursuit of Isabel, the subject of Pansy arises in a conversation between Mrs Touchett (who dislikes Osmond) and Madame Merle. Madame Merle thinks Isabel is fond of the child, to which Mrs Touchett replies, 'Another reason then for Mr Osmond's stopping at home! Otherwise a week hence, we shall have my niece arriving at the conviction that her mission in life's to prove that a stepmother may sacrifice herself – and that, to prove it, she must first become one' (I, p. 398). Isabel's tendency to sacrifice herself on Pansy's behalf becomes a dominant motif in the novel.

Making decisions about Pansy causes Isabel particular difficulties, and the moments when she makes them seem paradigmatic. The first occurs in Rome after Pansy has fallen in love with the apparently feeble Mr Rosier. Pansy has been educated to strict obedience in an Italian convent and is fearful of her father. Rosier's chances are extinguished, therefore, when Lord Warburton, still haunted by his feelings for Isabel, shows an interest in marrying her stepdaughter. Isabel, no longer happy in her marriage, has become Pansy's protector and friend. But she remains committed to 'the idea of assisting her husband to be pleased', and when Warburton calls one evening, she is 'on the point of taking the great step of going out of the room and leaving her companions alone', but finds that she cannot 'rise to it; something held her and made this impossible ... a vague doubt – a sense that she was not quite sure' (II, pp. 177–8).

The occasion is slight but significant. In a series of later incidents Isabel is similarly 'unable' to act on her professed intentions. Having sworn she will 'never make another promise' (II, p. 304), she promptly undertakes to visit Ralph on his deathbed if he summons her. The summons duly comes and she decides to leave for England even though Osmond sees this as 'the most deliberate, the most calculated, opposition' to his wishes, and a violation of their marriage. 'How can you call it calculated?' Isabel protests, 'I received my aunt's telegram but three minutes ago.' 'You calculate rapidly,' Osmond, convincingly, replies (II, p. 354). Her decision to leave Rome is thus explicitly a decision to leave her husband, yet within hours of making it she promises Pansy (immured in her convent for loving Mr Rosier) that she will return. By the time she reaches London, however, she claims to have forgotten her reason for making this considered undertaking. 'Perhaps I shall find another,' she tells her friend, Henrietta Stackpole. 'You'll certainly never find a good one,' Henrietta replies (II, p. 398).

Anyone who finds Isabel's behaviour at these moments convincing will have problems with the notion of intention. Isabel is conscious of deliberation in her decision making – particularly in accepting Osmond and in promising Pansy to return to Rome – yet she continually 'loses' her reasons and finds herself unable rationally to account for her actions. She is also unable to stick by intentions articulated in advance. Both tendencies suggest an inability to develop a medium-term stability in her plan of life, and so to achieve an adult identity. This makes it difficult to account for her choices. Her actions never seem out of character, yet one has little confidence in adducing convincing reasons for them.

Equally problematical is whether Isabel has the power to refrain from acting as she does at the moment when she acts and vice versa. It might be thought that her power to perform or not to perform a particular action could be settled independently of the circumstances obtaining at the moment she performs it. This is obviously true of physical acts, such as walking through a door. But what of speech acts? The words 'I will marry you', for example, are specific to the occasion on which they are uttered and Isabel's capacity to say them (and not just use them in other contexts) is untestable apart from those times when the opportunity to do so occurs. And what applies to speech acts can surely apply also to physical actions which are like speech acts. That she finds it 'impossible' to leave Pansy and Warburton alone together, even though she thinks she wants to do so, has obviously nothing to do with her long-term physical ability to walk through doorways. We may reasonably interpret it as an inability to utter a specific non-verbal signal. In effect, until the contextualizing moment, Isabel (and the reader) cannot know in advance what she (or any one else) is capable of.

This is a radical uncertainty. It compromises the unity of her character. We seem to be confronted with serious personal fragmentation – with speeches and actions that happen independently of statable reasons and yet appear deliberate, with a disturbing independence of action and speech, as if they were in contention. Is it possible that, in James's world and in ours, the processes of decision making are ultimately independent of reasons, whether verbalized or not, that Isabel's understanding, her sensitivities, her imagination and her intellect, are at the mercy of arbitrary and possibly self-destructive processes of willing, that the 'fine'-ness of her moral sense, of which she is so proud, is irrelevant to the crucial decisions in her life? Is that the outcome of Ralph Touchett's experiment?

II

We have identified two obstacles in the way of Isabel's acting with morally significant freedom: the opacity of other people, signified in the deceptions of Madame Merle, Gilbert Osmond and Ralph Touchett; and the opacity of Isabel to others and to herself. A third, characteristically for James, is her position as a young American in Europe. How far is her life merely the outcome of this situation, that is, of social forces? A related problem is whether values are socially determined or derive from an objective moral order to which some 'fine' human beings gain access. Isabel is strongly inclined to the latter view, but that may be her 'American' or 'feminine' naïvety.

If expatriation involves emancipation from powerful social determinations in one's native culture, James's expatriate characters have a freedom denied to native Europeans. Ralph Touchett, for one, came to England from America as a child, and 'became at last English enough. [But his] outward conformity to the manners that surrounded him was ... the mask of a mind that greatly enjoyed its independence, on which nothing long imposed itself, and which, naturally inclined to adventure and irony, indulged in a boundless liberty of appreciation' (I, p. 49). For other characters, however, notably Henrietta Stackpole and Caspar Goodwood, the fact that the American ethos is allegedly highly individualistic complicates the issue; by demonstrating their independence of character in Europe, they may merely be affirming their Americanness, and perhaps illustrating the vulnerability of American values in a stronger, older culture.

Isabel is involved in these ambiguities as soon as she arrives in England. She tells Ralph's father that she is 'sure the English are very conventional' and he agrees that they are; but when she remarks that this cannot leave much room for unexpectedness, Mr Touchett is less sure. 'You can't tell what they'll like,' he says. 'They are inconsistent; that's their principal interest' (I, pp. 78–9). Isabel is delighted with this prospective variety, yet when Warburton proposes, she finds herself instinctively resisting 'his system', partly on the grounds that she has 'a system and an orbit of her own', and partly because Caspar has just arrived from America and he has 'no system at all' (I, p. 144). The word 'system' here is ambiguous. Is the 'system', which Isabel regards as being in some sense hers, American as against European, or is it (either in fact or in her opinion) special to her?

The reference to Caspar further complicates the matter, because we learn later that one reason for Isabel's allegedly not being in love with him is that he is so predictably individualistic. When he is alone with her, he talks 'too much about the same subject' – presumably his love for her – and he always dresses 'in the same manner ... the figure, the stuff [is] so drearily usual' (I, p. 165). He is therefore either an individuated non-conformist – with no system at all – or the nugatory bearer of the unsophisticated individualism of his native country. A complementary ambiguity attaches to Warburton. Is he a sign of a socially determined upper-class English 'system', or an emancipated nobleman, who acts unpredictably in contrast to the unrelieved predictability of his American rival? In any case what does predictability imply – conditioned inflexibility or a mature fidelity to a plan of life?

III

What needs to be shown, therefore, is whether men and women can establish a plan of life for themselves, and not simply in consequence of their cultural inheritance, and freely act on it. I shall focus on three such plans, the first two of which, in modern fashion, seem to be premissed on the wants of those who form them, the third on an old-fashioned notion of objective moral norms.

The two modern plans of life are those of Caspar and Osmond. Caspar premisses his practical reasoning on the traditional urge to love and work – he just wants to run the business he inherited and to win the woman he loves. Osmond, more originally, claims to conduct his life on the pleasures of good form, aesthetic and social. This could be the result of an inability to assimilate the deeper values of Europe as Ralph assimilates them – in which case Osmond becomes a socially marginalized, humanly vacuous victim of a new cosmopolitanism. However, it could arise from the hardness of his heart, or from an intellectually defensible recognition (such as a sympathizer with Pater or Nietzsche might have made) that, in a world without fixed points of reference, there is nothing to hold on to but arbitrary and ultimately meaningless forms.

By way of contrast with her lover and her husband, Isabel is unwilling to develop a plan of life – or at least is uncertain about doing so – on the basis of her own wants, however impressive the wants of someone as finely constituted as herself might be. Her problem is working out the practical consequences of such an intuition. In response to a declaration that she wishes to be treated with justice, Ralph warns her 'that justice to a lovely being is after all a florid sort of sentiment' (I, p. 122). This is a characteristically difficult statement to interpret. Ralph speaks with authority as a man who has won his spiritual independence, but perhaps in this case he is reacting with embarrassment to Isabel's declaration because in the matter of her inheritance he has treated her with some disingenuousness. On the other hand (or perhaps at the same time) he may be gently directing her towards an awareness of the dangers of relying on grand moral categories in the conduct of everyday life.

In spite of this warning, however, Isabel persists in her search for a vision of justice and a plan for its application to her own circumstances. When the manipulative part played by Madame Merle in the making of her marriage becomes clear to her, she prays, in the midst of her uncertainties, 'Whatever happens to me let me not be unjust ... let me bear my burdens myself and not shift them upon others!' (II, p. 159). As we have seen she subsequently makes undertakings to Pansy which take the form, apparently, of absolute obligations. Even more striking is the pressure this 'old passion for justice' exercises on her when she recognizes that Osmond's claims on her are specious, yet feels that his apparent sincerity is 'a merit' towards which something is due (II, p. 356). In the face of everyone else's scepticism, Isabel persists in her pursuit of objective values, even if with doubtful success. The exact nature of her difficulty, however, remains obscure. Is her practical reasoning vitiated by pursuit of a chimerical goal (as Ralph's warning perhaps implies) or is it confused by fear of the demands justice will make on her? – in which case, presumably, she needs to subdue her own wants (or more specifically her fears) so as to act according to an objectively valid logic of goodness.

In either case, Isabel has two problems. First, the world in which she lives is not one in which a self-disclosing system of objective values is unambiguously available; and second, though her pursuit of justice is based on an intuition that justice is what one person owes to another and therefore implies some kind of solidarity between human beings, she seems entirely alone in her commitment to it. She needs, therefore, to belong to society (to avoid an individuality like Caspar's which refuses social adaptation – at least as she sees it), yet at the same time to resist mere social determination of her values and conduct.

Her relations with Madame Merle and Osmond develop out of this dilemma. Isabel is initially drawn to Madame Merle because Madame Merle has no 'tonic wildness', is 'too perfectly the social animal', and exists 'only in her relations, direct or indirect, with her fellow mortals'. But she is also 'deep', 'her nature' speaking 'none the less in her behaviour because it spoke in a conventional tongue' (I, p. 274). Madame Merle has thus apparently achieved the synthesis of convention and individualism which Isabel is seeking – except that she is also a wicked woman whose secret individuality is grounded in an all but flawless willingness to defy the common decencies implicit in the social conventions which she observes in her outward actions.

Osmond, on the other hand, presents himself overtly as the individualist. If Madame Merle's individuality is implicit in her conventionality, Osmond's respect for social form seems to be a consequence of his choice as an individual of a plan of life based on form. This at any rate is what he claims when Isabel confesses to a chaotic inability to stabilize her own plans. 'I make a new one every day,' she says, and regards herself as frivolous in consequence; she thinks one should 'choose something very deliberately, and be faithful to that'. Thus prompted, Osmond confesses his own chosen path. It is 'to be as quiet as possible ... Not to worry – not to strive nor struggle. To resign myself. To be content with little' (I, pp. 380–81)). Osmond is of course being manipulative in this scene, and he is no less so when he tells Isabel that her wandering about as if the world belonged to her is 'beautiful', and that everyone ought to make life 'a work of art' as she does (II, pp. 14–15). But this does not mean that he is not also speaking sincerely and truthfully. There is no reason to doubt that he has indeed 'studied ... wilful renunciation' of all that is positive in life except for 'Correggios and crucifixes' (I, p. 381).

Moreover, in spite of Isabel's imagination supplying 'the human element which she was sure had not been wanting' in this profession (I, p. 383), and in spite also of Ralph's believing her 'deluded' in inventing a theory about Osmond, and then loving him 'for his very poverties dressed out as honours' (II, p. 75), there is a real possibility that she chooses Osmond and what he represents deliberately and clear-sightedly. Perhaps she is afraid of the demands justice might make upon her, and finds in his commitment to form a way of avoiding them with a substitute ideal almost as good. In any case, even after their marriage has degenerated, she still sympathizes with his desire for its continuance as a matter of form, understood as a quality akin both to Correggios and crucifixes and to justice. Recognizing the 'blasphemous sophistry' of Osmond's arguments against her going to the dying Ralph, she acknowledges none the less that he has spoken 'in the name of something sacred and precious – the observance of a magnificent form' – indeed it is the sincerity of his profession that arouses in her once again 'her old passion for justice' (II, p. 356). Their marriage thus seems to have been based on almost identical and certainly compatible wants, and to break down only when Isabel recognizes that wants can no longer serve as the premisses of her practical reasoning, that she must act after all in the light of her old passion.

Isabel's quarrel with her husband is thus a quarrel about choice. For Osmond choosing amounts to no more than forming a plan of life based on his wants, and having the ability and opportunity to opt for the practical steps required to achieve it. Making Pansy obedient to his will is something he wants; there is this way of doing it, and that; he has the capacity to opt for one or the other or to refrain from acting at all; alternatively he can bring other wants into play, to see how satisfactorily his options accord with his plan of life as a whole. Moreover, he would claim that his way of acting on the basis of his wants is truer to the nature of things and of people than Isabel's apparent attempts to act in the name of justice.

'Justice', of course, at least initially, may only be the strongest of Isabel's wants, but her acceptance of its unqualified claims would proclaim her as someone who has seen herself, her choosing, and the world in a certain light, and this perspective in its turn could entail norms and values that have nothing to do either with the wisdom, goodness or rationality of the particular choices that imply them, or with the wants prompting those choices. Thus even if Isabel is wrong to sacrifice her future to the ideal of marriage and fidelity to the promises she has made to Osmond and Pansy, she might still be right, in fact and in principle, about the *kinds* of choices which human beings can and should make, and which her fanciful idealism points to; and such a vision might make its own demands on her – for example, it might require her never to act in a way that diminished her own or other people's capacity to act justly.

James, however, directly in the voice of the narrator, and indirectly through his characters, notably Ralph, focuses on the possibility that Isabel's idealism may after all express only an irrational fear about her own existential status, about the vulnerability of her ego. In the important sixth chapter, for example, he notes her clear-eyed sense of what it is to act wrongly – it is to inflict 'a sensible injury upon another person ... to be mean, to be jealous, to be false, to be cruel' (I, pp. 68–9) – yet this is how some readers may think she acts towards Caspar in their final scene together, inflicting a sensible injury on him in panic at the prospect of losing the starry-eyed conception of her duty out of which she has constructed a dishonest version of herself.

There is space in James's text, however, for a more complex reading. After the description of Isabel's idealism in the sixth chapter, he adds a warning: 'Of course the danger of a high spirit was the danger of inconsistency – the danger of keeping up the flag after the place has surrendered; a sort of behaviour so crooked as to be almost a dishonour to the flag' (I, p. 69). Perhaps this is what happens in the last chapter; perhaps we are meant to see Isabel as crookedly flying the flag of justice (to Pansy, to marriage as a magnificent form) even though she has really surrendered to fear – of passion, of being no one, of having been wrong. James's carefully chosen expressions, however, have to be given proper weight. The flag is not *wholly* dishonoured; Isabel may behave crookedly in her last scene, but she may at least be *acting*, making a real choice. If we read the last chapter pessimistically in the light of the sixth, therefore, we may still think of her as an agent, and not the determined outcome of extra-personal forces. But we may do so only if we see her as a true back-slider. The ultimate test of her notions of herself as an autonomous moral agent acting according to the objective principles of justice would then be whether she is capable of acting freely and knowingly against the noble principles she has chosen for herself, while still passionately believing in them. Freedom would only exist if Isabel were capable of mortal sin.

IV

We need to examine the final scene between Caspar and Isabel with great care if we are even to approach resolving these issues. Ralph has died. Isabel is staying at his home in England, uncertain about her future. One evening in the garden she is unexpectedly confronted by Caspar, whom she has not seen since Ralph's funeral. His effect on her is powerful, 'a new sensation ... he had never produced ... before ... a feeling of danger'. He tells her that he learnt from Ralph about the unhappiness of her marriage, and that Ralph asked him to do everything for her that she would let him do. He cannot bear to see her paying for her error, and begs her to think of him. This forcibly reminds Isabel of the 'idea of which she had caught glimpses a few moments before', and when he asks her why she should 'go through [the] ghastly form' of returning to Osmond, she replies, 'To get away from *you!*' But this expresses 'only a little of what she felt. The rest was that she had never been loved before.' He presses his cause; she has no children – 'nothing to consider'; the world is all before them and it is very big. 'The world's very small,' Isabel replies, 'at random' – she has 'an immense desire to appear to resist'. At this point James intrudes briefly into the narration. 'I know not [he writes], whether she believed everything he said; but she believed just then that to let him take her in his arms would be the next best thing to her dying. This belief, for a moment, was a kind of rapture.' But the next moment Caspar makes a passionate demand on her – 'Ah, be mine as I am yours' – and his voice seems 'to come harsh and terrible'. Isabel realises this is 'but a subjective fact' and pleads with him to go away. In response he kisses her.

> His kiss was like white lightning, a flash that spread, and spread again, and stayed; and it was extraordinarily as if, while she took it, she felt each thing in his hard manhood that had least pleased her, each aggressive fact of his face, his figure, his presence, justified of its intense identity and made one with this act of possession.

The next moment she is free and in flight through the darkness. She reaches the house. 'She had not known where to turn; but she knew now. There was a very straight path' (II, pp. 430–37). She subsequently returns to Rome.

An important feature of this episode is the recurrence in it of the theme of Isabel's fear. Does this fear deprive her of her reason, prevent her from bringing other considerations into play, other wants, or her own high idealism? If so the reader who is moved by the ending of the novel has a problem. If the full potential of Isabel's spirit and the most important act of her life are not significantly related, if her decision is out of character and surd, then her tragedy has no meaning.

But as well as taking account of the hell below Isabel's consciousness, we should acknowledge the possibility of a heaven above it. The scene with Caspar, after all, *reverses* that of the fall in *Paradise Lost*. In it a man in a garden tempts a woman to abandon her duties in a fallen world and fly with him to paradise. It even contains an allusion to the closing lines of the poem, but Isabel's reply to Caspar's suggestion that the world lies all before them is that the world is small. In any case she ends on the straight path that leads back to the helpless Pansy and marriage. Is James really suggesting that it may be possible for someone like Isabel to act in a way that transcends her own wants, and yields to objective moral norms? Would the mortal sin have been surrender to Caspar?

It is my view that this is exactly what James is suggesting, that the Isabel he presents exemplifies a supreme altruism, a transcendence of calculation which is grounded specifically in a capacity to give an unconditional respect for the freedom of others in all that she does – which is the only form her freedom, or anybody else's, can take.

Her role as the giver of freedom in the novel is crucially evident in her relations with Madame Merle and Osmond, both of whom take the opposite attitude, and then find that as coercers they are themselves coerced. Ralph is the first to notice this, 'that under the guise of caring only for intrinsic values Osmond lived exclusively for the world. Far from being its master as he pretended to be, he was its very humble servant, and the degree of its attention was his only measure of success'

(II, p. 144). The contrast between Osmond and Isabel in this respect is subsequently given authorial endorsement:

> Her notion of the aristocratic life was simply the union of great knowledge with great liberty; the knowledge would give one a sense of duty and the liberty a sense of enjoyment. But for Osmond it was altogether a thing of forms, a conscious, calculated attitude ... He had an immense esteem for tradition; he told her once ... that if one was so unfortunate as not to have it one must immediately proceed to make it ... [From] what source he had derived his traditions she never learned. He had a very large collection of them, however, ... and ... [the] great thing was to act in accordance with them; the great thing not only for him but for her. (II, pp. 198–9)

As Isabel herself comes to realize, for Osmond, the 'real offence ... was her having a mind of her own at all' (II, p. 200). It is this which makes Osmond and Ralph enemies, the latter being, as Osmond recognizes, 'an apostle of freedom', and therefore a threat to the project on which Osmond has set his heart, to deny Isabel 'freedom of mind' (II, p. 245).

Such projects, however, extinguish Osmond's own freedom, and Madame Merle's as well – notably in their pursuit of Warburton as a husband for Pansy. 'How much you must want to make sure of him!' Isabel exclaims at one point (II, p. 264), an insight reinforced in a later conversation with Madame Merle, who is convinced that for her own reasons Isabel is putting pressure on Warburton to abandon his pursuit of Pansy. 'Let him off – let us have him!' she cries. The 'us' alarms Isabel. 'Who are you – what are you?' she asks. 'What have you to do with my husband? ... What have you to do with me?' 'Everything!' Madame Merle answers, and Isabel realizes at last 'that Madame Merle had married her' (II, pp. 326–7). The ambiguous syntax is particularly telling. Two important developments in Isabel's thinking occur almost at once – she sees Madame Merle as *wicked*, and she realizes that Osmond must have made her pay cruelly for involving him in a marriage which has become distasteful to him; at which thought she exclaims, characteristically, 'Poor, poor Madame Merle!' (II, p. 331).

Isabel, then, may be defined as someone who leaves other people in their own willing. (So, incidentally, does her aunt, Mrs Touchett.) The response of those others to the freedom thus bestowed upon them is an exact, painful measure of their goodness. It is no exaggeration to say that in the face of Isabel's toleration of their wickedness, Osmond and Madame Merle cast themselves into hell.

We need to look again at Isabel's last scene with Osmond. She interrupts him as he is working meticulously in water colours, copying an antique coin. The telegram has just arrived summoning her to Ralph's deathbed. She tells Osmond of her wish to go; he forbids her to do so, and says any decision on her part contrary to his wishes would be 'the most deliberate, the most calculated, opposition' (II, p. 354). She protests at the injustice of this, and declares that it is his opposition to her that is 'calculated' and 'malignant'. In reply he speaks quietly but eloquently of their union, and almost persuades her that it is 'like the sign of the cross or the flag of one's country ... something sacred and precious – the observance of a magnificent form', thus reviving the image of her country's flag used earlier as a symbol of her own good faith (II, p. 356). But she persists and the following exchange takes place between them:

> 'I suppose that if I go you'll not expect me to come back,' said Isabel.
> He turned quickly round, and she could see this movement at least was not designed. He looked at her a little, and then 'Are you out of your mind?' he inquired.
> 'How can it be anything but a rupture?' she went on; 'especially if all you say is true?' She was unable to see how it could be anything but a rupture; she sincerely wished to know what else it might be.
> He sat down before his table. 'I really can't argue with you on the hypothesis of your defying me,' he said. And he took up one of his little brushes again. (II, pp. 357–8)

The loss of control is slight but exactly matches Osmond's inability to confront the possibilities opened up by Isabel's power to choose. Her freedom is an undiscussable chaos. As he takes up one of his little brushes again, he shrinks from that chaos into impotence like a touched sea-anemone.

Madame Merle's moment of damnation follows quickly. It is less decisive (the prospect of repentance is held out) but more explicit than Osmond's. Having decided to return to England, Isabel goes to see Pansy in her convent. She now knows that Madame Merle is Pansy's mother, and when the two women meet at the convent, Madame Merle realizes that Isabel has discovered the truth, and that her 'only safety' is 'in not betraying herself' (II, p. 378). But she is not so well defended as Osmond, and Isabel senses her insecurity at once.

> That Madame Merle had lost her pluck and saw before her the phantasm of exposure – this in itself was revenge, this in itself was almost the promise of a brighter day. And for a moment ... Isabel enjoyed that knowledge ... [If] she had turned and spoken she would have said something that would hiss like a lash. But she closed her eyes, and then the hideous vision dropped. What remained was the cleverest woman in the world standing there within a few feet of her and knowing as little what to think as the meanest. Isabel's only revenge was to be silent still – to leave Madame Merle in this unprecedented situation. (II, p. 379)

Isabel's freedom is to be silent, *not* to inflict pain – Madame Merle's punishment being an inability to think, to use the freedom Isabel has allowed her.

The contrast between the paralysis which Isabel's refusal to challenge their choices induces in Osmond and Madame Merle, and the play of feeling, thought and action between Isabel and Ralph could not be greater. A passage describing these complexities must be quoted at length.

> Ah yes, if Gilbert were jealous of her there was perhaps some reason ... It was not that they talked of him – it was not that she complained. His name was never uttered between them. It was simply that Ralph was generous and that her husband was not. There was something in Ralph's talk, in his smile, in the mere fact of his being in Rome, that made the blasted circle round which she walked more spacious. He made her feel the good of the world: he made her feel what might have been. He was after all as intelligent as Osmond – quite apart from his being better. And thus it seemed to her an act of devotion to conceal her misery from him ... It lived before her again ... that morning in the garden at Florence when he had warned her against Osmond ... She had told him then that from her at least he would never know if he was right; and this is what she was taking care of now. It gave her plenty to do; there was passion, exaltation, religion in it ... [In] playing a part before her cousin, [she] had an idea that she was doing him a kindness ... [The] kindness consisted in mainly trying to make him believe that he had once wounded her greatly and that the event had put him to shame, but that, as she was very generous and he was so ill, she bore him no grudge, and even considerately forbore to flaunt her happiness in his face. Ralph smiled to himself, as he lay on the sofa, at this extraordinary form of consideration; but her forgave her for having forgiven him. (II, pp. 203–4)

At this stage, the relation between Isabel and Ralph is flawed because there is a withholding of truth on both sides, but its foundation, originating in Ralph, and indirectly reflected back on him from Isabel, is an exchange of freedom which goes far beyond his being the ultimate source of her mere wealth, because it makes possible the unbearable beauty of the openness between them when he is dying. He confesses to having enriched her and so to having probably 'ruined' her; she admits to having 'always tried to keep [him] from understanding; but that's all over'. 'I always understood.' Ralph says. 'I thought you did,' Isabel replies, 'and I did n't like it. But now I like it.' 'You do n't hurt me. You make me happy,' Ralph tells her, and there is 'an extraordinary gladness in his voice'. They have moved into a mutuality which is identical with the autonomy each accords the other. Isabel is thus free to make a remark that is puzzling and troublesome – but that is the price both must pay for freedom. He asks her if it is all over between Osmond and herself. 'Oh no,' she answers; 'I don't think anything's over' (II, pp. 414–15).

This is troublesome because it seems to contradict the implications of her decision to defy Osmond and come to see her cousin. Her last recorded words to Osmond, quoted above, indicate her sense at the time that to leave Rome would be to end her marriage. Overwhelmingly her friends see her decision to do so as an act of self-liberation. 'I don't believe', Ralph tells her, 'that such a generous mistake as yours can hurt you for more than a little' (II, p. 417). For his part, Caspar feels personally liberated by Isabel's action since until her defiance of Osmond he felt obliged to accept her presentation of herself as a loyal and faithful partner in a successful marriage. When he meets her in the garden, however, he can say to her:

> ' ... today I know on good authority. Everything's clear to me today. It was a good thing when you made me come away [from Rome] with your cousin. He was a good man, a fine man, one of the best; he told me how the case stands for you. He explained everything; he guessed my sentiments. He was a member of your family and he left you – so long as you should be in England – to my care ... Do you know what he said to me the last time I saw him – as he lay there where he died? He said: "Do everything you can for her; do everything she'll let you".' (II, p. 588)

Even in death, Ralph respects Isabel's freedom, and in repeating the words, 'everything she'll let you' Caspar shows that he does so too. They accept that their shared longing to liberate Isabel from Osmond does not license their attempting to control her, even though Isabel's desire to be free of her husband is hardly to be doubted. But unlike them, she cannot see that anything is 'over'. Why not? What flag is she continuing to fly, and with what justification?

Having listened to Osmond's objections to her going to see Ralph, Isabel concludes that 'going when Osmond wished her to remain' would be an act of 'violence'. 'What he thought of her she knew, what he was capable of saying to her she felt; yet they were married, for all that, and marriage meant that a woman should cleave to the man with whom, uttering tremendous vows, she had stood at the altar' (II, p. 361). She has apparently identified here a principle of interpersonal truthfulness and fidelity, an ideal or maxim which she has thought out and accepted for herself, not because she finds it appealing, not because it has become one of her wants, and certainly not because it is a magnificent form, but because it is logically entailed in the very notion of unconditional respect for the freedom of the other people to whom she is committed, and is in that sense an objective norm of justice. To have made faithfulness to the tremendous vows she exchanged with Osmond conditional on his conducting himself humanely would have been to limit and qualify *his* capacity to do so, and any attempt to control his freedom would have been logically incompatible with her own.

But she then acts against the maxim of obedience which she has thus identified: she defies Osmond and goes to the dying Ralph. This decision cannot, however, be described as back-sliding, because in leaving Rome she is acting in the light of other obligations equally entailed in the free interpersonal exchanges of her life. The point that she makes in her final exchange with Ralph, however, is that even if one does from time to time have to act in defiance of a moral norm, one does not stop being bound by it subsequently: that is the sense in which nothing is ever 'over'. She has overridden the demand of one obligation in deference to the demands of another, but the first obligation remains in place – the generosity motivating a mistaken promise cannot of itself justify setting it aside. In any case she has given fresh undertakings to Pansy, so that even if Osmond has lost his own capacity for freedom and thereby unwittingly released Isabel from obligations towards it, obligations to his daughter remain. But the real issue is not whether Isabel is bound by particular obligations to specific individuals but whether she is bound by obligations to herself as the person who instantiates the principle of justice to which she adheres, as the woman who now *is* her own values. May she, in the interests of the joy of union with Caspar, cease to be that woman? She decides (apparently) that she may not.

For many readers a conscience as demanding as this would be better described as a sado-masochistic super-ego, and James himself may have thought so too. But even that would not be inconsistent with the kinds of insight into the workings of freedom which I believe the novel makes available to us. James allows *us*, after all, to make up our own minds – he refuses control over his own text, and thereby constitutes our freedom and his own within it. But such gestures of freedom, in an author or in a character, are necessarily elusive and fragile: they can easily be concealed behind explicit meanings which seem to deny them. Freedom so conceived and so dedicated is a principle of knowledge in ignorance, of intimacy in isolation, of vision in blindness. We do not after all *really* know each other. The certainties of freedom are those of the wise heart, its confidence faith. It cannot be directly represented in logical or scientific language. It is violated to the extent that arguments are adduced which purport to determine assent to it. Nevertheless *The Portrait of a Lady* seems to me to illustrate with terrible clarity three major principles: that freedom consists in willing the freedom of others; that willing the freedom of others imposes on those who undertake it obligations which are absolute, specific, open-ended and irreversible; and that a conscience informed by such a logic can indeed act according to objective norms, independently of personal wants, or can decline to do so. The possibility of acting according to conscience is the one hope that Isabel Osmond holds out to us – and it leaves the young Caspar Goodwood with a broken heart.

Notes

Introduction: Nothing New

1. David Hume, *A Treatise of Human Nature*, edited, with an Annotated Index by L.A. Selby-Bigge. Second edition with text revised and variant readings by P.H. Nidditch, Oxford: The Clarendon Press, 1978, pp. 252–3; hereafter *A Treatise*.
2. Derek Roper (ed.) with Edward Chitham, *The Poems of Emily Brontë*, Oxford: The Clarendon Press, 1995, no. 126; spelling of l. 24 emended; all later quotations from Emily Brontë's poems are from this edition, and are indicated by number; minor emendations of spelling are not noted.
3. J. Hillis Miller, 'But are things what we really think they are?', *TLS*, 9–15 October 1987, p. 1104.
4. See pp. 50, 59–60, 84, 87–8.
5. John Henry Cardinal Newman, *An Essay in Aid of A Grammar of Assent*, with an Introduction by Nicholas Lash, Notre Dame [and] London: University of Notre Dame Press, 1979, p. 96; hereafter *A Grammar of Assent*.
6. 'If the cause be known only by the effect, we never ought to ascribe to it any qualities, beyond what are precisely requisite to produce the effect ... Allowing, therefore, the gods to be the authors of the existence or order of the universe; it follows, that they possess that precise degree of power, intelligence, and benevolence, which appears in their workmanship.' David Hume, *Enquiries Concerning Human Understanding and Concerning the Principles of Morals*, edited with Introduction etc. by L.A. Selby. Third edition with text revised and Notes by P.H. Nidditch, Oxford: The Clarendon Press, 1975, pp. 136–7; hereafter *Enquiries*. Newman refers to this argument in *The Idea of a University Defined and Illustrated*, edited with a Preface and Introduction by Charles Frederick Harrold, New York: Longmans, Green and Co., 1957 edn, p. 36; hereafter *Idea of a University*. See also ibid., p. 52.
7. John Stuart Mill, *An Examination of Sir William Hamilton's Philosophy and of the principal philosophical questions discussed in his writings*, London: Longmans, Green, Reader and Dyer, 1867 edn, p. 551; hereafter *An Examination*.
8. See Richard Dawkins, *The Blind Watchmaker*, London: Penguin Books, 1991 edn, p. 4.
9. John Henry Cardinal Newman, *Discussions and Arguments on various subjects*, London: Longmans, Green and Co., 1899 edn, p. 303; hereafter *Discussions and Arguments*.
10. *The Collected Letters of Thomas and Jane Welsh Carlyle Volume 12 1840*, edited by Charles Richard Sanders et al., Durham, North Carolina: Duke University Press, 1985, p. 106; hereafter *Collected Letters*.
11. See pp. 59–60.
12. John Henry Newman, B.D., *Parochial and Plain Sermons*, London, Oxford and Cambridge: Rivingtons, 1869 edn, IV, pp. 808–81; hereafter *Parochial and Plain*.

13. John Henry Cardinal Newman, *The Arians of the Fourth Century*, London: Pickering and Co., 1883 edn, p. 155; hereafter *The Arians*.

14. See Daniel C. Dennett, *Brainstorms. Philosophical Essays on Mind and Psychology*, Brighton: Harvester Press, 1985, pp. 267–85.

15. George Berkeley, *Philosophical Commentaries, Philosophical Works*, edited by M.R. Ayers, London: Dent, 1975, p. 198.

16. See Daniel C. Dennett, *Consciousness Explained*, London: Allen Lane The Penguin Press, 1991, pp. 259–62.

17. *Newman's University Sermons Fifteen Sermons Preached before the University of Oxford 1826–43*. By John Henry Newman, with introductory essays by D.M. MacKinnon and J.D. Holmes, reprinted from the third edition 1871, London: SPCK, 1970, pp. 229–30; hereafter *University Sermons*.

18. John Henry Newman, *Essays Critical and Historical*, London: Basil Montague Pickering, 1871, I, p. 192; hereafter *Essays Critical*.

19. John Henry Newman, B.D., *Sermons Bearing on the Subject of the Day*, London, Oxford and Cambridge, Rivingtons, 1869, pp. 185–6; hereafter *Sermons Bearing*.

20. John Henry Newman, *Apologia Pro Vita Sua*, edited, with an Introduction and Notes, by William Oddie, London: J.M. Dent, 1993, p. 83; hereafter *Apologia*.

21. See pp. 63–5 for further discussion of 'the culture of the copy'.

22. Quoted in Alan Sheridan, *Michel Foucault, The Will to Truth*, London and New York: Tavistock Publications, 1890, p. 125.

23. Walter Pater, 'Coleridge's Writings', *Essays on Literature and Art*, edited by Jennifer Uglow, London: Dent, 1973, p. 1; hereafter 'Coleridge's Writings'.

24. Sir Leslie Stephen, 'Newman's Theory of Belief', *An Agnostic's Apology and Other Essays*, London: Smith, Elder & Co., 1893, p. 170.

25. Walter Pater, *The Renaissance. Studies in Art and Poetry*, with an Introduction and Notes by Kenneth Clark, London and Glasgow: Fontana/Collins, 1961 edn, p. 218.

26. *The Philosophical Notebook of John Henry Newman*, edited by Edward Sillem, Louvain (Belgium): Nauwelaerts Publishing House, 1969, II, p. 158.

27. Richard Dawkins, *The Selfish Gene*, Oxford: Oxford University Press, new edn, 1989, p. 192.

28. John Henry Cardinal Newman, *An Essay on the Development of Christian Doctrine*, London: Longmans, Green and Co., 1909 edn, p. 36; hereafter *Development of Christian*.

29. See *University Sermons*, p. 200 and *Development of Christian*, p. 62 as examples of Newman's deeply considered and sustained attachment to this idea.

30. J. Hillis Miller, *Versions of Pygmalion*, Cambridge, Massachusetts, and London: Harvard University Press, 1990, p. 18.

31. Ludwig Wittgenstein, *Tractatus Logico-Philosophicus*, translated by D.F. Pears and B.F. McGuinness, London: Routledge, 1992 edn, pp. 57, 74; hereafter *Tractatus*.

32. Michael Polanyi, *Personal Knowledge. Towards a Post-Critical Philosophy*, London: Routledge & Kegan Paul, 1958, *passim*.

33. Maurice Merleau-Ponty, *Phenomenology of Perception*, translated from

the French by Colin Smith, London and Henley: Routledge & Kegan Paul, 1981 edn, p. xvii.

34. For Merleau-Ponty's comments on this topic see pp. 166–7.
35. K. Marx, 'Theses on Feuerbach', K. Marx and F. Engels, *On Religion*, London: Lawrence and Wishart, second impression, n.d., p. 70.
36. John Henry Cardinal Newman, *Certain Difficulties Felt by Anglicans in Catholic Teaching Considered*, London: Longmans, Green and Co., 1891 edn, II, pp. 248–9.
37. William Myers, *Milton and Free Will: An essay in criticism and philosophy*, London: Croom Helm, 1987, p. 162.

Chapter 1: Where are Nathaniel Hawthorne, Emily Dickinson and Daniel C. Dennett?

1. Daniel C. Dennett, 'Why everyone is a novelist', *TLS*, 16 September 1988, p. 1029; hereafter 'Why everyone is'. See also Douglas R. Hofstadter and Daniel C. Dennett (eds), *The Mind's I. Fanatasies and Reflections on Self and Soul*, Brighton: Harvester Press, 1981, pp. 350ff.
2. Daniel C. Dennett, *Brainstorms. Philosophical Essays on Minds and Psychology*, Brighton: Harvester Press edn, 1981, reprinted 1986, p. 184.
3. Daniel C. Dennett, *Elbow Room. The Varieties of Free Will Worth Wanting*, Oxford: The Clarendon Press, 1984, p. 3.
4. Stanislaw Lem, 'Non Serviam', *The Mind's I*, p. 305.
5. Nathaniel Hawthorne, 'My Kinsman, Major Molineux', *The Snow-Image And Uncollected Tales*, Ohio: Ohio State University Press, 1974 edn, pp. 229–31. The moral economy of this tale is implicitly and brilliantly delineated in Slovoj Žižek, *The Metatases of Enjoyment. Six Essays on Woman and Causality*, London, New York: Verso, 1994, pp. 57–70.
6. This is Dennett's version of Spencer's 'law of multiple effect. "*Every active force produces more than one change – every cause produces more than one effect.*" See p. 37.
7. 'Letters', *TLS*, 7–13 October 1988, p. 1109.
8. Emily Dickinson, *The Poems*, edited by Thomas H. Johnson, Cambridge, Massachusetts: The Belknap Press of Harvard University, 1963, 3 vols, II, pp. 773–4.
9. Charles Taylor, 'Responsibility for Self', in A. Rorty, *The Identities of Persons*, Berkeley: University of California Press, 1976, pp. 28–9.
10. This argument is directly opposed to the views of John Stuart Mill, who insisted that behaviour is *determined* by conscious 'spiritual' motives. See pp. 34, 59, 62.

Chapter 2: Evolution and Progress: Herbert Spencer, Thomas Hardy and Amartya Sen

1. Amartya Sen, 'On the Darwinian View of Progress', *London Review of Books*, vol. 14 no. 12 (5 November 1992), pp. 15–16, 18–19; hereafter 'On the Darwinian View'.

2. See Herbert Spencer, *The Principles of Psychology*, London and Edinburgh: Williams and Norgate, third edn, 1881, 2 vols, I, pp. 291–504 for a full account of Spencer's speculations about evolution.

3. Daniel C. Dennett, *Kinds of Minds. Towards an Understanding of Consciousness*, London: Weidenfeld and Nicolson, 1996, pp. 92–3.

4. Herbert Spencer, 'Progress: Its Law and Cause', *Essays on Education etc.*, London: J.M. Dent, Everyman's Library edn, 1911, p. 176; hereafter 'Progress'.

5. Gottlob Frege, *The Foundations of Arithmetic: A logico-mathematical inquiry into the concept of number*, translated by J.L. Austin, Oxford: Blackwell, 1980 edn, p. vi.

6. Alfred Tennyson, *In Memoriam*, edited by Susan Shatto and Marion Shaw, Oxford: The Clarendon Press, 1982, p. 80.

7. Thomas Hardy, *Tess of the d'Urbervilles: A Pure Woman*, London: Macmillan, 1974 (The New Wessex edn), p. 174.

8. Jacques Monod, *Chance and Necessity. An Essay on the Natural Philosophy of Modern Biology*, translated by Austryn Wainhouse, London: Collins, 1972, p. 96.

9. Herbert Spencer, 'Moral Education', *Essays on Education*, p. 108.

10. Galen Strawson, *Mental Reality*, Cambridge, Massachusetts and London, England: The MIT Press, 1994, p. 3.

11. This thought experiment will be readily recognized as deriving from one of Dennett's favourites. See *Elbow Room*, pp. 38–43 and 'Why everyone is', p. 1028.

12. Another idea of Dennett's; see pp. 18–19, 32 and *Elbow Room*, p. 305.

13. See pp. 53, 87–8 and *Consciousness Explained*, pp. 111–43.

14. See *Kinds of Minds*, p. 156.

Chapter 3: Why John Stuart Mill chose to go to the Devil

1. [Sir W. Hamilton], 'M. Cousin's *Course of Philosophy*', *The Edinburgh Review*, October 1829, p. 215; hereafter 'M. Cousin's *Course*'.

2. [Sir W. Hamilton], 'Philosophy of Perception', *The Edinburgh Review*, October 1830, p. 165.

3. According to Frege, any 'argument' (number) can be substituted for x in the algebraic expression '$2.x^3 + x$', the function in this expression being 'what is present in

$$\text{``}2.x^3 + x\text{''}$$

over and above the letter "x"; we could write this somewhat as follows:

$$\text{``}2.(\ )^3 + (\ )\text{'''}.$$

Gottlob Frege, 'Function and Concept', *Collected Papers on Mathematics, Logic, and Philosophy*, edited by Brian McGuinness, Oxford: Basil Blackwell, 1984, p. 140. (It may help the non-mathematical reader to be reminded that . is a sign of multiplication.)

4. The concept horse (or class of horses) does not include itself, since a concept (or class) is not a horse. The concept (or the class) of horse-

related things does include itself, because the concept (or the class) of a horse-related thing *is* a horse-related thing. But if the concept of concepts (or class of classes) that do not include themselves is excluded from itself, it thereby becomes included in itself, and in consequence should no longer be included ... The vicious regress is unanswerable, and makes a complete alignment of correctly formed sentences with the world in principle impossible.

5. J. Veitch, *Hamilton*, Edinburgh: William Blackwood, 1882, p. 90.

6. Dennett blames Descartes for this misleading image, but it was proposed by Hume (see p. 1), and is unavoidable in an Associationist theory such as Mill's. An exclusively empiricist philosophy would in any case seem to imply something like it.

7. This most basic of all arguments against free will is addressed in the essays on Amartya Sen (Chapter 2), George Eliot (Chapter 12) and Henry James (Chapter 13).

8. H.L. Mansel, *The Limits of Religious Thought*, Oxford: for John Murray, London, 1858, p. 28.

9. Gottlob Frege, 'Thoughts', *Collected Papers*, p. 368.

10. A. Ambrose (ed.), *Wittgenstein's Lectures, Cambridge, 1932–35*, Oxford: Blackwell, 1979, p. 22. Anthony Kenny holds that Frege's essay is infused with 'Cartesian poison', and that Frege's later work was targeted by Wittgenstein. (See Anthony Kenny, *Frege*, London: Penguin Books, 1995, p. 212). Perhaps it was, but if so Wittgenstein was mistaken. Actually I think the error is Kenny's. There is nothing in Wittgenstein's 'celebrated arguments against private languages' which denies the reality of private experience. Suppose, for example, that in the whole of human history, only Oscar Wilde has been able to detect a difference in the fragrance of white and purple lilac. It is true that he would have been unable to put this experience into words, and could not therefore have been perfectly confident of its ongoing consistency and reliability. He *would*, however, have been able to share 'thoughts' on the subject with others, including Frege and Wittgenstein.

11. Bertrand Russell, *History of Western Philosophy and its Connection with Political and Social Circumstances from the Earliest Times to the Present Day*, London: Routledge, 1991 edn, p. 740.

Chapter 4: Walter Pater and the Higher Decadence

1. Walter Pater, *Marius the Epicurean. His Sensations and Ideas*, London: Macmillan and Co., Ltd, 1921 edn, 2 vols, I, p. 129; hereafter *Marius*.

2. Terence Hawkes, 'Making = Taking', *London Review of Books*, vol. 19, no. 15 (31 July 1997), p. 16.

3. Walter Pater, 'Style', *Essays on Literature and Art*, pp. 77–8; hereafter 'Style'.

4. I am grateful to Gowan Dawson for bringing this to my attention.

5. John Henry Cardinal Newman, *Loss and Gain: A Tale of the Third Century*, London: Burns and Oates Ltd, 1887, p. 370.

6. H.L. Mansel, *Prolegomena Logica. An Inquiry into the Psychological Character of Logical Processes*, second edition, corrected and enlarged, London: Rivingtons, n.d., p. 138.

Chapter 5: Arnold and Newman: The Phenomenological Option

1. *The Poems of Matthew Arnold*, edited by Kenneth Allott. Second edition edited by Miriam Allott, 1979, no. 68; all quotations from Arnold's poems are from this edition, and are indicated by number.
2. Terry Eagleton, *Criticism and Ideology. A Study in Marxist Literary Theory*, London: NLB, 1976, p. 107.
3. *The Letters of Matthew Arnold to Arthur Hugh Clough*, edited with an introductory study by Howard Foster Lowry, Oxford: The Clarendon Press, 1932, p. 41; hereafter *Letters to Clough*.
4. A. Dwight Culler, *Imaginative Reason. The Poetry of Matthew Arnold*, New Haven: Yale University Press, 1966, p. 256.
5. 'The Study of Poetry', *The Complete Prose Works of Matthew Arnold*, edited by R.H. Super, Ann Arbor: The University of Michigan Press, 1960–77, XI, p. 170; hereafter *Complete Prose*.
6. 'Preface to Poems (1853)' (hereafter 'Preface'), *Complete Prose*, I, p. 4.
7. John P. Farrell, 'Matthew Arnold's Tragic Vision', *PMLA* (January 1970), p. 110; hereafter 'Tragic Vision'.
8. J. Hillis Miller, *The Disappearance of God. Five Nineteenth-Century Writers*, Cambridge, Massachusetts: Harvard University Press, 1963, p. 259; hereafter *The Disappearence*.
9. Matthew Arnold, *God and the Bible. A sequel to 'Literature and Dogma'*, *Complete Prose*, VII, p. 160.
10. See Edmund Husserl, 'Philosophy as Rigorous Science', *Phenomenology and the Crisis of Philosophy*, translated with notes and an Introduction by Quentin Lauer, New York: Harper Torchbooks, 1965, p. 124; hereafter 'Philosophy as'.
11. Matthew Arnold, *Literature and Dogma. An Essay Towards A Better Apprehension of the Bible*, *Complete Prose*, VI, p. 222.
12. Jacques Derrida, *Writing and Difference*, translated, with an Introduction and Additional Notes by Alan Bass, London and Henley: Routledge & Kegan Paul, 1981 edn, p. 10.
13. See A.O.J. Cockshut, *The Unbelievers: English Agnostic Thought 1840–1890*, London and Glasgow: Collins, 1964, p. 63.
14. Matthew Arnold, *St Paul and Protestantism*, *Complete Prose*, VI, p. 51.
15. Park Honan, *Matthew Arnold: A Life*, London: Weidenfeld and Nicolson, 1981, p. 161.
16. Edmund Husserl, *Cartesian Meditations. An Introduction to Phenomonology*, translated by Dorion Cairns, The Hague: Martinus Nijhoff, 1977, p. 155.
17. Charles Stephen Dessain, *John Henry Newman*, third edn, Oxford etc.: Oxford University Press, 1980 edn, p. 22; hereafter *Newman*.
18. Cardinal Karol Wojtyła, *The Acting Person*, translated from the Polish by Andrzej Polocki, Dordrecht, Holland/Boston, USA/London, England: D. Reidel Publishing Company, 1979, p. 168.

Chapter 6: Autobiography and the Illative Sense

1. '["When they (my elders) named some object, and accordingly moved towards something, I saw this and I grasped that the thing was called by the sound they uttered when they meant to point it out. Their intention was shewn in their bodily movements, as it were the natural language of all peoples: the expression of the face, the play of the eyes, the movement of other parts of the body, and the tone of voice which expresses our state of mind in seeking, having, rejecting, or avoiding something. Thus, as I heard words repeatedly used in their proper places in various sentences, I gradually learnt to understand what objects they signified; and after I had trained my mouth to form these signs, I used them to express my own desires."] These words, it seems to me, give us a particular picture of the essence of human language. It is this: the individual words in language name objects – sentences are combinations of such names. – In this picture of language we find the roots of the following idea: Every word has a meaning. The meaning is correlated with the word. It is the object for which the word stands.
    Augustine does not speak of there being any difference between kinds of word. If you describe the learning of language in this way you are, I believe, thinking primarily of nouns like "table", "chair", "bread", and of people's names, and only secondarily of the names of certain actions and properties; and of the remaining kinds of word as something that will take care of itself.' Ludwig Wittgenstein, *Philosophical Investigations*, translated by G.E.M. Anscombe, Oxford: Blackwell, 1986 edn, p. 2.
    'Augustine, we might say, does describe a system of communication; only not everything that we call language is this system. And one has to say this in many cases where the question arises "Is this an appropriate description or not?" The answer is: "Yes, it is appropriate, but only for this narrowly circumscribed region, not for the whole of what you are claiming to describe."
    It is as if someone were to say: "A game consists in moving objects about on a surface according to certain rules ... " – and we replied: "You seem to be thinking of board games, but there are others. You can make your definition correct by expressly restricting it to those games"' (ibid., p. 3).
2. Charles Kingsley, 'What, Then, Does Dr. Newman Mean?' in *Apologia*, p. 32; hereafter 'What, Then'.
3. John Henry Cardinal Newman, *The Via Media of the Anglican Church. Illustrated in Lectures, Letters, and Tracts Written Between 1830 and 1841. In Two Volumes, with a Preface and Notes*, London: Longmans, Green and Co., 1885 edn, vol. I, pp. v–vi; hereafter, *Via Media*.
4. Thomas Carlyle, *Sartor Resartus. The Life and Opinions of Herr Teufelsdröckh in Three Books*, New York: Charles Scribner's Sons, 1896, p. 87.
5. Quoted by K.J. Fielding, 'Carlyle and Cromwell: The Writing of History and "DRYASDUST"', in Fred Kaplan, Michael Goldberg and K.J. Fielding, *Lectures on Carlyle & His Era*, Santa Cruz: The University Library, University of California, 1985, p. 57.
6. Saint Augustine, Bishop of Hippo, *The Trinity*, Introduction, translation, and notes [by] Edmund Hill, O.P. , New York: New City Press, 1991,

Book X, Chapter 4 (pp. 298–9); Book XIV, Chapters 3 and 4 (pp. 378–87).

7. 'The human body is the best picture of the human soul'. *Philosophical Investigations*, p. 178.

8. Leslie Stephen, 'Newman's Theory of Belief', *An Agnostic's Apology and other essays*, London: Smith, Elder & Co., 1893, p. 170; hereafter 'Newman's Theory'.

9. Luce Irigaray, *The Sex which is Not One*, translated by Catherine Porter, Ithaca: Cornell University Press, 1985, p. 29.

10. 'Scripture and the Creed', *Discussions and Arguments*, p. 133.

11. 'The "subject" of writing does not exist if we mean by that some sovereign solitude of the author. The subject of writing is a *system* of relations between strata: the Mystic Pad, the psyche, society, the world. Within that scene, on that stage, the punctual simplicity of the classical subject is not to be found. In order to describe the structure, it is not enough to recall that one always writes for someone; and the oppositions sender–receiver, code–message, etc., remain extremely coarse instruments. We would search the "public" in vain for the first reader: i.e., the first author of a work. And the "sociology of literature" is blind to the war and the ruses perpetrated by the author who reads and by the first reader who dictates, for at stake here is the origin of the work itself. The *sociality* of writing as drama requires an entirely different discipline.' Jacques Derrida, *Writing and Difference*, pp. 226–7. (This gnomic utterance is interestingly consistent with Dennett, the Mystic Pad in particular being remarkably close to the multiple drafts model of consciousness.)

Chapter 7: Celibate Men and Angelic Women in *Oliver Twist*

1. John Carey, *The Violent Effigy. A Study of Dickens' Imagery*, London: Faber and Faber, 1973, p. 149.

2. John Bayley, 'Oliver Twist: "Things as They Really Are"' (hereafter 'Things as They Really Are'), *Dickens and the Twentieth Century*, edited by J. Gross and G. Pearson, London: Routledge and Kegan Paul, 1962, p. 58; hereafter *Dickens and the Twentieth*.

3. Graham Greene, 'The Young Dickens', *The Lost Childhood and Other Essays*, Harmondsworth: Penguin Books edn, 1962, p. 61.

4. Humphry House, *The Dickens World*, London, New York and Toronto: Oxford University Press, 1942 edn, p. 44.

5. A.O.J. Cockshut, *The Imagination of Charles Dickens*, New York: New York University Press, 1962, pp. 30–31.

6. Q.D. Leavis, 'Oliver Twist, Jane Eyre and David Copperfield', in F.R. and Q.D. Leavis, *Dickens the Novelist*, Harmondsworth: Pelican Books edn, 1972, pp. 152–3.

7. A. Kettle, *An Introduction to the English Novel*, London: Hutchinson and Co., 1967 edn, 2 vols, I, p. 117.

8. C.B. Cox, 'In Defence of Dickens', *Essays and Studies*, 11, London: John Murray, 1958, p. 95.

9. Walter Bagehot, *Literary Studies*, London: Longmans, Green and Co., 3 vols, II, pp. 150–51.

10. G.H. Lewes, 'Dickens in Relation to Criticism', *Charles Dickens*, edited by Stephen Wall, Penguin Critical Anthologies, Harmondsworth: Penguin Books, 1970, pp. 197–202; hereafter *Charles Dickens*.

11. Henry James, 'Our Mutual Friend', in *The House of Fiction*, London: Mercury Books, 1962 edn, pp. 253–8; hereafter *House of Fiction*.

12. W.M. Thackeray, 'Catherine', *Fraser's Magazine*, XXI (February 1840), p. 211.

13. J.R. Kincaid, *Dickens and the Rhetoric of Laughter*, Oxford: The Clarendon Press, 1971, pp. 50–75.

14. Colin Williamson, 'Two Missing Links in Oliver Twist', *Nineteenth-Century Fiction*, XXII (December 1967), pp. 211–23.

15. Charles Dickens, *Oliver Twist*, edited by Kathleen Tillotson, Oxford: The Clarendon Press, 1966, p. 344.

Chapter 8: The Radicalism of *Little Dorrit*

1. J. Wain, '*Little Dorrit*', *Dickens and the Twentieth Century*, p. 175.

2. R. Williams, 'Social Criticism in Dickens. Some problems of method and approach', *Critical Quarterly*, VI, iii, 1964, p. 219; hereafter 'Social Criticism'.

3. J. Forster, *The Life of Charles Dickens*, edited and annotated with an Introduction by J.W.T. Ley, London: Cecil Palmer, 1928, p. 246; hereafter *The Life*.

4. J. Butt and K. Tillotson, *Dickens at Work*, London: Methuen, 1982 edn, p. 225.

5. G. Orwell, 'Charles Dickens', *Collected Essays*, London: Mercury Books, 1961, pp. 40, 68.

6. Charles Dickens, *Little Dorrit*, edited by Harvey Peter Sucksmith, *The Clarendon Dickens*, Oxford: The Clarendon Press, 1979, p. 371.

7. *Household Words*, XIV, no. 336, 30 August 1856, pp. 145–7.

8. E. Johnson, *Charles Dickens His Tragedy and Triumph*, London: Victor Gollancz, 1952, 2 vols, II, pp. 604–5.

9. E. Wilson, 'Dickens: The Two Scrooges', *The Wound and the Bow, Seven Studies in Literature*, Cambridge, Massachusetts: Houghton Mifflin Company, 1941, p. 26.

10. J. Holloway, 'Introduction', *Little Dorrit*, Harmondsworth: Penguin Books, 1967, pp. 24–5.

11. L. Trilling, 'Little Dorrit', *The Dickens Critics*, p. 293.

12. J. Butt, 'The Topicality of *Little Dorrit*', *University of Toronto Quarterly*, xxix, 1959/60, p. 4.

13. T.A. Jackson, *Charles Dickens: The Progress of a Radical*, New York: International Publishers, 1938, p. 169.

14. K. Marx, 'Towards a Critique of Hegel's Philosophy of Right: Introduction', *Selected Writings*, edited by David McLellan, Oxford: Oxford University Press, 1988, p. 83; hereafter 'Towards a Critique'.

15. Karl Marx and Frederick Engels, *The Holy Family, or Critique of Critical Criticism*, *Collected Works*, vol. 4, London: Lawrence & Wishart, 1975, p. 36.

16. Karl Marx, *The Communist Manifesto*, edited by Frederic L. Bender,

New York, London: W. W. Norton & Company, 1988, pp. 57–8; the word 'patriarchal' is not used here in the sense now commonly given to it. See pp. 134–5.

Chapter 9: The Feral Children of Haworth: Charlotte and Emily Brontë

1. Terry Eagleton, *Myths of Power. A Marxist Study of the Brontës*, London and Basingstoke: The Macmillan Press, 1975, p. 3.
2. Q.D. Leavis, 'A Fresh Approach to "Wuthering Heights"', in F.R. and Q.D. Leavis, *Lectures in America*, London: Chatto & Windus, 1969, p. 98.
3. Sandra M. Gilbert and Susan Gubar, *The Madwoman in the Attic: The Woman Writer and the Nineteenth-Century Literary Imagination*, New Haven and London: Yale University Press, 1984 edn, p. 293.
4. James H. Kavanagh, *Emily Brontë*, Oxford and New York: Basil Blackwell, 1985, p. ix.
5. *Heathcliff and the Great Hunger. Studies in Irish Culture*, London and New York: Verso, 1995.
6. Winifred Gérin, *Charlotte Brontë, The Evolution of Genius*, London, Oxford and New York: Oxford University Press, 1971 edn, p. 567.
7. Edmund Gosse, 'The Challenge of the Brontës', *Some Diversions of a Man of Letters*, London: William Heinemann, 1919, p. 145.
8. Emily Brontë, *Wuthering Heights*, New York and London: W. W. Norton & Company, 1990 edn, p. 37.
9. Charlotte Brontë, *Jane Eyre*, Oxford and New York: Oxford University Press, 1989 edn, p. 14.
10. Currer Bell (Charlotte Brontë), *The Professor*, London: Smith, Elder & Co., 1885 edn, p. 150.
11. Charlotte Brontë, *Shirley*, edited by Herbert Rosengarten and Margaret Smith, Oxford: The Clarendon Press, 1979, p. 109.
12. *The Complete Poems of Emily Jane Brontë*, ed. C.W. Hatfield, New York: Columbia Press, 1967 edn, p. 19.
13. Denis Donoghue, 'The Other Emily', *The Brontës: A Collection of Critical Essays*, edited by Ian Gregor, Englewood Cliffs, NJ: Prentice Hall, 1970, pp. 157–72.
14. J.F. Goodridge, *Emily Brontë: Wuthering Heights*, London: Edward Arnold, 1964, p. 60.
15. Georges Bataille, *Literature and Evil*, translated by Alistair Hamilton, London: Calder and Boyar, 1973, p. 9.
16. Cleanth Brookes, *The Well-Wrought Urn: Studies in The Structure of Poetry*, London: Methuen (University Paperbacks), 1971 edn, p. 137.
17. Tom Winnifrith, *The Brontës*, London and Basingstoke: Macmillan Press, 1977, p. 128.
18. See Brian Wilks, 'Schools and Schooling in the Life and Literature of the Brontë Family', *Brontë Society Transactions*, 18, Part 95, 1985, pp. 355–62.

Chapter 10: Fragments of Consciousness: The Poems of Emily Brontë

1. Emily Jane Brontë, *The Complete Poems*, edited by Janet Gezari, London: Penguin Books, 1992; *The Poems of Emily Brontë*, edited by Barbara Lloyd-Evans, London: B.T. Batsford, 1992; *The Poems*, edited by Derek Roper (see p. 224[n]).
2. '[T]he only God Emily ever recognized was her "God of Visions" ... Emily ... remained immune to conventional religious doctrine along with so much else in her environment'. Katherine Frank, *Emily Brontë: A Chainless Soul*, London: Penguin Books, 1992 edn, pp. 107, 109; hereafter *A Chainless Soul*.
3. Lynn Pykett, *Emily Brontë*, London: Macmillan (*Women Writers*), 1989.
4. Winifred Gérin, *Emily Brontë: A Biography*, Oxford: The Clarendon Press, 1972 edn, p. 159.
5. Mary Visick, *The Genesis of Wuthering Heights*, Hong Kong: Hong Kong University Press, 1958.
6. The Notebook poems are transcribed in order by Lloyd-Evans in *The Poems of Emily Brontë*; Gezari lists them in their order of appearance in *The Complete Poems*, Appendix 1, pp. 200–202, Roper in *The Poems*, Appendix 2, pp. 280–86.
7. Juliet Barker, *The Brontës*, London: Weidenfeld and Nicolson, 1994, pp. 453–4.
8. Inge-Stina Ewbank, *Their Proper Sphere: A Study of the Brontë Sisters as Victorian Female Novelists*, London: Edward Arnold, 1966, p. 108.
9. 20, 28, 60, 116, 117.
10. 32, 39, 57, 159, 199.
11. 40, 79.
12. 25, 87, 111.
13. 39, 53, 62, 81.
14. 6, 49, 111, 112, 120a, 120b, 132.
15. 46, 53, 65, 94, 100, 109.
16. 37, 51, 72, 88, 116.
17. 25, 73, 75, 76, 79, 83, 86, 90, 93, 95, 96, 98, 99, 111, 115, 117, 121.
18. 32, 36, 39, 123, 199.
19. 5, 7, 11, 15, 118, 140.
20. 17, 51, 141, 187.
21. F.B. Pinion, *A Brontë Companion. Literary Assessment, Background, and Reference*, London and Basingstoke: Macmillan Press, 1975, p. 197.
22. Tom Winnifrith, *The Brontës and their Background, Romance and Reality*, London and Basingstoke: Macmillan Press, 1973, p. 32.
23. Jacques Blondel, *Emily Brontë. Expérience Spirituelle et Création Poetique*, Paris: Presses Universitaires de France, 1956, p. 255.
24. Charlotte Brontë and Emily Brontë, *The Belgian Essays*, New Haven and London: Yale University Press, 1996, pp. 156–9.
25. John Hewish, *Emily Brontë. A Critical and Biographical Study*, London: Macmillan, 1969, p. 67; hereafter *Emily Brontë: A critical*.
26. Edmund Husserl, 'Philosophy and the Crisis of European Man', *Phenomenology and the Crisis of Philosophy*, p. 184; hereafter 'Philosophy and the Crisis'.
27. Gilbert and Gubar rightly see the poem as characteristically evincing Emily Brontë's unliterariness. See *The Madwoman in the Attic*, p. 258.

28. There are at least twenty references to God as Rock in the King James Bible.
29. 'The IMAGINATION then, I consider either as primary, or secondary. The primary IMAGINATION I hold to be the living Power and prime Agent of all human Perception, and as a repetition in the finite mind of the eternal act of creation in the infinite I AM. The secondary Imagination I consider as an echo of the former, co-existing with the conscious will yet still as identical with the primary in the *kind* of its agency, and differing only in *degree*, and in the *mode* of its operation. It dissolves, diffuses, dissipates, in order to recreate; or where this process is rendered impossible, yet still it struggles to idealize and to unify. It is essentially *vital*, even as all objects (*as* objects) are essentially fixed and dead.' S.T. Coleridge, *Biographia Literaria with his Aesthetical Essays*, edited by J. Shawcross, London: Oxford University Press, 1962 edn, 2 vols, I, p. 202.
30. John Henry Newman, *Lectures on the Doctrine of Justification*, London, New York and Bombay: Longmans, Green and Co., 1900 edn, pp. 144–5.

Chapter 11: The Rights of Celibacy

1. [Sidney Dobell], 'Sidney Dobell's Article on Currer Bell, contributed to *The Palladium* in 1850', *Transactions of the Brontë Society*, 1965, V, p. 214.
2. Elizabeth Cleghorn Gaskell, *The Life of Charlotte Brontë*, London: Dent (Everyman's Library edn), 1970, pp. 395–6.
3. [Elizabeth Rigby], '*Vanity Fair* and *Jane Eyre*', *Quarterly Review*, lxxx (December 1848), p. 60.
4. D.H. Lawrence, *The Rainbow*, edited by Mark Kinkead-Weekes, London: Penguin Books, 1995, p. 368.
5. Elaine Showalter, *The Female Malady. Women, Madness, and English Culture 1830–1980*, London: Virago Press, 1987, p. 71.
6. Russell Meares, 'The Secret', *Psychiatry*, vol. 39, August 1976, p. 258.

Chapter 12: The Two Eternities: Race and Soul in *Daniel Deronda*

1. W.B. Yeats, 'Under Ben Bulben', *Collected Poems*, London: Macmillan & Co., 1963, p. 398.
2. Denis Donoghue, *Yeats*, Glasgow: William Collins, Sons & Co. (Fontana Paperbacks), 1982 edn, p. 29.
3. W.B. Yeats, 'At Stratford-on-Avon', *Essays and Introductions*, London: Macmillan & Co., 1961, p. 102.
4. George Eliot, *Daniel Deronda*, edited by Graham Handley, Oxford: The Clarendon Press, 1984, p. 356.
5. William Baker, *George Eliot and Judaism*, Salzburg, Austria: Institut für Englishe Sprache und Literatur, Universität Salzburg, 1975, pp. 120, 34–9.
6. John Bayley, 'The Pastoral of Intellect', *Critical Essays on George Eliot*,

edited by Barbara Hardy, London, Boston and Henley: Routledge & Kegan Paul, 1970, pp. 207–8.

7. Friedrich Nietzsche, *Twilight of the Idols*, *The Portable Nietzsche*, selected and translated by Walter Kaufmann, New York: The Viking Press, 1968 edn, p. 515.

8. Robert Preyer, 'Beyond the Liberal Imagination: Vision and Unreality in *Daniel Deronda*', *Victorian Studies*, IV, September 1960, p. 48.

9. Ulrich Knoepflmacher, *Religious Humanism and the Victorian Novel: George Eliot, Walter Pater, and Samuel Butler*, Princeton, New Jersey: Princeton University Press, 1965, pp. 41–3.

10. Gillian Beer, *Darwin's Plots. Evolutionary Narrative in Darwin, George Eliot and Nineteenth-Century Fiction*, London, Boston, Melbourne and Henley: Routledge & Kegan Paul, 1983, p. 188.

11. Sigmund Freud, *The Ego and the Id*, translated by Joan Rivière and James Strachey, New York: W. W. Norton & Company, 1962, pp. 15–16.

12. See William Myers, *The Teaching of George Eliot*, Leicester: Leicester University Press, 1984, *passim*.

13. Sigmund Freud, *Civilization and its Discontents*, newly translated from the German and edited by James Strachey, New York: W.W. Norton & Company Inc., 1962 edn, p. 69.

14. George Eliot, 'The Influence of Rationalism' (1865), *Essays of George Eliot*, edited by Thomas Pinney, London: Routledge and Kegan Paul, 1963, p. 409.

15. George Eliot, *Impressions of Theophrastus Such*, Edinburgh and London: William Blackwood and Sons (*The Works of George Eliot*, Standard edn), n.d., p. 7.

Chapter 13: Justice and Freedom: *The Portrait of a Lady*

1. Henry James, *The Portrait of a Lady*, London: Macmillan and Co., 1909, 2 vols, I, p. 69. The discussion of freedom in this essay depends upon, and responds to, Anthony Kenny's *Will, Freedom and Power*, Oxford: Basil Blackwell, 1975.

Index